The Struggle for South Africa

Robert Davies, Dan O'Meara and Sipho Dlamini

Dedication

At 4.30 p.m. on Tuesday 17 August 1982, Ruth First was killed in a parcel bomb explosion in her office at the Centre of African Studies, Eduardo Mondlane University, Maputo. She was murdered by the South African apartheid regime.

Ruth had been a militant in the South African liberation struggle for almost 40 years. Her contribution to the theory and practice of the ANC and South African Communist Party was immense.

And in the four years in which she was Director of Research at the Centre of African Studies, Ruth worked tirelessly to create a research and teaching institution which would directly serve the process of socialist transformation in Mozambique. For Ruth, Marxism was the theoretical and practical political tool of this transformation. Hers was a Marxism not of texts and quotations, but of deep analysis of Mozambican reality — what Lenin called 'the living soul' of Marxism, the 'concrete analysis of concrete conditions'.

Ruth was always determined to relate Mozambican research to the wider regional context, for she believed profoundly that the struggle for socialism in Mozambique is a central part of the struggle for liberation in Southern Africa.

This book is dedicated to her memory and the ideas she fought and died for.

A luta continua!
Amandla Ngawethu!

The Struggle for South Africa

A Reference Guide to Movements, Organizations and Institutions

Volume Two

Robert Davies, Dan O'Meara
and Sipho Dlamini,
Centre of African Studies,
Eduardo Mondlane University

Zed Books Ltd., 57 Caledonian Road, London N1 9BU.

The Struggle for South Africa was first published in two
volumes by Zed Books Ltd., 57 Caledonian Road, London
N1 9BU, in 1984.

Copyright © Centre of African Studies, Eduardo Mondlane
University, 1984

Copyedited by Mark Gourlay
Typeset by Jo Marsh
Proofread by Louise Hoskins
Cover design by Simon Acuah
Printed in Great Britain at The Bath Press, Avon

British Library Cataloguing in Publication Data

Davies, Robert H.
    The struggle for South Africa.
    Vol. 2
    1. Pressure groups—South Africa
    I. Title   II. O'Meara, Dan
    III. Dlamini, Sipho
    322.43'0968   JQ1969.P7

    ISBN 0-86232-256-1
    ISBN 0-86232-257-X Pbk

US Distributor
Biblio Distribution Center, 81 Adams Drive, Totowa,
New Jersey, 07512

First reprint, 1985

Contents

Volume One

Volume Two

Tables, Figures and Map

List of Abbreviations

AAC	Anglo American Corporation of South Africa Limited
AB	*Afrikaner Broederbond* (Afrikaner Brotherhood)
AECI	African Explosives and Chemical Industries Limited
AET	*Aksie Eie Toekoms* (Action Own Future)
AFCWU	African Food and Canning Workers' Union
AFL-CIO	American Federation of Labor-Congress of Industrial Organizations
Amaprop	Anglo American Properties Limited
Amcoal	Anglo American Coal Corporation Limited
Amgold	Anglo American Gold Investment Company Limited
Amic	Anglo American Industrial Corporation Limited
Anamint	Anglo American Investment Trust Limited
ANC	African National Congress (of South Africa)
ANS	*Afrikaans-Nasionaal Studentebond* (Afrikaner National Students' League)
Anti-CAD	Anti-Coloured Affairs Department
APDUSA	African People's Democratic Union of South Africa
APRP	Azanian People's Revolutionary Party
ARM	African Resistance Movement
ARMSCOR	Armaments Corporation of South Africa
ASB	*Afrikaner Studentebond* (Afrikaner Students' League)
ASSOCOM	Associated Chambers of Commerce
ATI	Anglo Transvaal Industries Limited
AWB	*Afrikaner Weerstand Beweging* (Afrikaner Resistance Movement)
AYRC	Azanian Youth Revolutionary Council
AZAPO	Azanian People's Organisation
AZASO	Azanian Students' Organisation
Bankorp	Bank Corporation of South Africa
BAWU	Black Allied Workers' Union
BC	Black Consciousness
BCC	Black Consultative Council of Trade Unions
BCM	Black Consciousness Movement

BCMA	Black Consciousness Movement of Azania
BENSO	*Buro vir Ekonomiese Navorsing en Staatsontwikkeling* (Bureau for Economic Research and State Development)
BIC	Bantu Investment Corporation
BLS	Botswana, Lesotho and Swaziland
BMWU	Black Municipal Workers' Union
BOSS	Bureau for State Security
BPA	Black Parents' Association
BPC	Black Peoples' Convention
BUF	Black Unity Front
CAHAC	Cape Areas Housing Action Committee
CCAWUSA	Commercial, Catering and Allied Workers' Union of South Africa
CED	Corporation for Economic Development
CIA	Central Intelligence Agency
CIWW	Council of Industrial Workers of the Witwatersrand
CNA	Central News Agency
CNETU	Council of Non-European Trade Unions
COD	Congress of Democrats
COM	Chamber of Mines
COMPRA	Combined Mitchells Plain Residents' Association
CONSAS	Constellation of Southern African States
COPE	Congress of the People
COSAS	Congress of South African Students
COSAWR	Committee of South African War Resisters
CRC	Coloured Representative Council
CP	Communist Party
CPSA	Communist Party of South Africa
CUSA	Council of Unions of South Africa
CYL	Congress Youth League (of the ANC)
D & H	Darling and Hodgson Limited
DMI	Directorate of Military Intelligence
DNP	*Dikwankwetla* (Strong men) National Party
DONS	Department of National Security
DP	Democratic Party
DPP	Democratic Peoples' Party
DRCs	Dutch Reformed Churches
DSAG	*Deutch-sud Afrikanische Gesellschaft* (German-South African Association)
DTA	Democratic Turnhalle Alliance
ESCOM	Electricity Supply Commission
FAK	*Federasie van Afrikaanse Kultuurverenigings* (Federation of

	Afrikaans Cultural Associations)
FCI	Federated Chambers of Industry
FCWU	Food and Canning Workers' Union
Fedfoods	*Federale Voedsel Beperk* (Federal Foods Limited)
Fofatusa	Federation of Free African Trade Unions of South Africa
FOSATU	Federation of South African Trade Unions
FP	Freedom Party
FRELIMO	*Frente da Libertacão de Moçambique* (Mozambican Liberation Front)
FSAW	Federation of South African Women
FVB	*Federale Volksbeleggings Korporasie Beperk* (Peoples' Federal Investment Corporation Limited)
GAWU	General and Allied Workers' Union
GDP	Gross domestic product
GK	*Gereformeerde Kerk* (Reformed Church)
GWU	General Workers' Union
GWUSA	General Workers' Union of South Africa
HNP	*Herstigte Nasionale Party* (reconstituted Nationalist Party*)
HNP/V	*Herenigde Nasionale of Volksparty* (Reunited Nationalist or Peoples' Party*)
IAS	Industrial Aid Society
IC	Industrial Council
IC Act	Industrial Conciliation Act
ICFTU	International Confederation of Free Trade Unions
ICS	The Imperial Cold Storage and Supply Company Limited
ICU	Industrial and Commercial Workers' Union of Africa
IDAF	International Defence and Aid Fund
IDC	Industrial Development Corporation
IIE	Institute for Industrial Education
I & J	Irving and Johnson Limited
ILO	International Labour Organization
INM	*Inyandza* (United) National Movement
ISCOR	Iron and Steel Corporation
ISL	International Socialist League
IUEF	International University Exchange Fund
JCI	Johannesburg Consolidated Investment Company Limited

*A strictly correct translation of *Nasionale Party* should be rendered as 'National Party'. However common English South African usage refers to the 'Nationalist Party' which rendering we have retained.

KDC	KwaZulu Development Corporation
KP	*Konsewatiewe Party* (Conservative Party of South Africa)
LLA	Lesotho Liberation Army
LPP	Lebowa Peoples' Party
MACWUSA	Motor Assembly and Component Workers' Union of South Africa
MAGWU	Municipal and General Workers' Union of South Africa
MAWU	Metal and Allied Workers' Union
MINORCO	Minerals and Resources Corporation Limited
MK	*uMkhonto we Sizwe* (the Spear of the Nation)
MNR	Mozambique National Resistance Movement
MPLA	*Movimento Popular da Libertacão de Angola* (Popular Movement for the Liberation of Angola)
M-Plan	Mandela Plan
MP	Member of Parliament
MWASA	Media Workers' Association of South Africa
MWU	Mine Workers' Union
Nacoc	National African Chambers of Commerce
Nafcoc	National African Federated Chambers of Commerce
NCP	National Conservative Party
NEUM	Non-European Unity Movement
NFBW	National Federation of Black Workers
NGK	*Nededuitse Gereformeerde Kerk* (Dutch Reformed Church)
NHK	*Nederduitsche Hervormde Kerk* (Dutch Reconstituted Church)
NIC	Natal Indian Congress
NIS	National Intelligence Service
NP	Nationalist Party
NPU	Newspaper Press Union
NRC	Natives' Representative Council
NRP	New Republic Party
NUMARWOSA	National Union of Motor and Rubber Workers of South Africa
NUTW	National Union of Textile Workers
OAU	Organization of African Unity
OB	*Ossewa Brandwag* (Oxwagon Sentinels)
OFS	Orange Free State
PAC	Pan Africanist Congress of Azania
PAIGC	*Partido Africano de Independencia de Guiné e Cabo Verde* (African Party for the Independence of Guiné and Cape Verde)

PC	President's Council
PEBCO	Port Elizabeth Black Civic Association
PFP	Progressive Federal Party
POLSTU	Political Students' Organisation
PRP	Progressive Reform Party
PWV	Pretoria-Witwatersrand-Vereniging
Recces	Reconnaissance Commandos
RI	Republican Intelligence
RP	Republican Party
RTZ	Rio-Tinto Zinc Corporation
SAAF	South African Air Force
SAAN	South African Associated Newspapers Limited
SAAWU	South African Allied Workers' Union
SAB	South African Breweries Limited
SABA	South African Black Alliance
SABC	South African Broadcasting Corporation
SABCTV	South Africa, Bophuthatswana, Ciskei, Transkei and Venda
SABRA	South African Bureau for Racial Affairs
SACC	South African Council of Churches
SACLA	South African Confederation of Labour
SACP	South African Communist Party
SACTU	South African Congress of Trade Unions
SADCC	Southern African Development Coordination Conference
SADF	South African Defence Force
SAFEMA	South African Federation of Engineering and Metallurgic Associations
Safmarine	South African Marine Corporation Limited
SAFTU	South African Federation of Trade Unions
SAIC	South African Indian Council
SAIF	South African Industrial Federation
SAIRR	South African Institute of Race Relations
SANLAM	South African National Life Assurance Company
SANTAM	South African National Trust and Insurance Company
SAP	South African Police
SAPPI	South African Paper and Pulp Industries Limited
SAR & H	South African Railways and Harbours Administration
SASM	South African Students' Movement
SASO	South African Students' Organization
SASOL	*Suid Afrikaanse Steenkool, Olie en Gaskorporasie* (South African Coal, Oil and Gas Corporation)
SASPU	South African Students' Press Union
SATLC	South African Trades and Labour Council
SATS	South African Transport Services

SAYRC	South African Youth Revolutionary Council
SBDC	Small Business Development Corporation
SCA	Soweto Civic Association
SEIFSA	Steel and Engineering Industries Federation of South Africa
Soweto	South Western Townships
SP	Security Police
SSC	State Security Council
SWAPO	South West African People's Organization
TC Lands	Transvaal Consolidated Land and Exploration Company Limited
TDC	Transkei Development Corporation
TEBA	The Employment Bureau of Africa
TLC	Trades and Labour Council
TNIP	Transkei National Independence Party
TUACC	Trade Union Advisory Coordinating Council
TUCSA	Trade Union Council of South Africa
UAW	United Automobile and Rubber Workers' Union
UBJ	Union of Black Journalists
UF	Urban Foundation
UK	United Kingdom
UKSATA	United Kingdom South Africa Trade Association
UMSA	Unity Movement of South Africa
UNITA	*União para a Independencia Total de Angola* (Union for the Total Independence of Angola)
UP	United Party
URC	Umbrella Rentals Committee
USA	United States of America
UTP	Urban Training Project
UWO	United Women's Organisation
VIPP	Venda Independence Peoples' Party
VNP	Venda National Party
WASA	Writers' Association of South Africa
Wenela	Witwatersrand Native Labour Association
WFTU	World Federation of Trades Unions
WPF	Western Province Federation (of trade unions)
WPGWU	Western Province General Workers' Union
WPWAB	Western Province Workers' Advice Bureau
ZAPU	Zimbabwe African Peoples' Union

Preface

For us in Mozambique the struggle for South Africa is much more than an academic question.

Along with the South African masses, the people of Mozambique and indeed all of Southern Africa have been victims of the vicious system of exploitation and oppression which the world knows as apartheid. For decades, thousands of our people were compelled to work as low paid migrant labourers in the mines, farms and industries of apartheid South Africa. Our ports and transport system were geared to the needs of South African capitalism, and we served as a market for the commodities of South African industry. Today, with the apartheid system in deep crisis, the states of Southern Africa are subjected to repeated acts of aggression and an ongoing process of destabilisation by Pretória. Both our struggle to build socialism in Mozambique and the collective efforts of the independent states in the region to forge peaceful cooperation between them, represent a profound threat to South African hegemony over Southern Africa. Apartheid South Africa is a fundamental part of the daily reality of our region. All the people of Southern Africa therefore have a direct interest in the outcome of the struggle for South Africa.

The Centro de Estudos Africanos is to be congratulated on producing this clear and comprehensive guide to that struggle. We are proud that despite our limited resources and our difficulties in obtaining the reference material which most universities take for granted, our Eduardo Mondlane University has been able to produce a work of this calibre. This book is free from academic jargon yet firmly based on scientific analytical method.

To my knowledge, no equivalent reference work exists, and I believe that this book will be of use to a wide audience. It is a reflection of the creativity unleashed by our revolution that such a work was produced in the People's Republic of Mozambique.

Jose Luis Cabaço
Minister of Information

Acknowledgements

These two books grew out of the ongoing engagement of the Centre of African Studies with issues relating to South Africa and its place in the struggle for liberation in the region. The first full-scale research project carried out by the Centre dealt with the flow of Mozambican labour to South Africa. Over the years a body of material on South and Southern Africa has been produced. It was felt, however, that within Mozambique there was a pressing need for a more structured and coherent guide to the various organisations involved at all levels of the struggle in South Africa. This guide was originally intended for use by party and state officials, as well as journalists within Mozambique. It was later realised that it might also be of use to solidarity organisations, students, academics and all of those outside Mozambique concerned with South Africa. Both volumes will thus appear in both the Portuguese and English languages.

The idea of a reference manual was first proposed by the Director of the Centre, Aquino de Bragança; the planning of its structure was carried out by a collective of specialists in South African Studies within the Centre, in consultation with the then Director of Research, Ruth First. The actual writing of all material was done by Robert H. Davies, Dan O'Meara and Sipho Dlamini.

The final draft was read and commented upon by the Centre's academic staff. We also wish to thank John Saul, Harold Wolpe and Thozamile Botha for their useful comments and criticisms.

Various drafts of a lengthy manuscript were typed by Vibeke Giagheddu, Luz Klingler, Adelina Lucas, Adelaide Tojais, Luisa Cipriano and Christine Littlejohn.

Introduction:
How to Use this Book

OBJECTIVES

This book is intended to be used as a reference guide to the organisations, movements and institutions involved in the struggle for South Africa in the 1980s. It consists of a collection of analytical essays and entries on various individual organisations. Together, these seek to provide, from a Marxist perspective, both an overview of the issues and processes of this struggle, and more detailed information on the myriad organisations involved. As such, the book is fundamentally concerned with the interlinked processes of, and contradictions around, capital accumulation, class struggle and national liberation in South Africa.

STRUCTURE

The book is structured in such a way as to attempt to cater for the needs of a number of different types of reader.

It contains ten chapters. The first of these comprises four essays. These are intended to provide an overview of the historical development and current functioning of the apartheid system, the trajectory of struggles in contemporary South Africa, and the policies of the South African state in the Southern African region. These essays situate in general terms the more specific chapters which follow.

The remaining nine chapters cover the spectrum of the major organisations involved in the struggle for South Africa. Most chapters contain both an introductory essay and a number of individual entries. The introductory essays provide the historical background and general overview to the theme of the chapter. They link the entries to the wider historical and contemporary context. Thus, for example, Chapter 2 deals with the major forces and economic organisations of the ruling capitalist class. The introductory essays analyse firstly the current structure of the South African economy, and secondly the historical development and current extent of monopoly capitalism in South Africa. The individual entries which follow deal with the various enterprises and organisations which collectively make up the major economic organisations of the capitalist class.

Most of the individual entries within each chapter begin with a portion in a boxed border, followed by a longer text. The boxed portion of the entry provides a resumé of the organisation in question, summarises its class nature and position and role in the current phase of the struggle. These boxed portions are intended for use by those readers who require only the broadest outline of each organisation. For those interested in a more detailed perspective, the complete entry provides a more extensive analysis of the history and current position of the organisation.

Each chapter concludes with a bibliographical note. This indicates the major sources used and includes a brief guide to further reading; it is not an exhaustive bibliography.

Throughout the text, whenever reference is made to events or an organisation discussed elsewhere in the book, this is indicated by a bracketed reference '(see pp.0-00)'. This method of cross referencing has been used in an attempt to reduce to the minimum the repetition unavoidable in a book of this sort.

PROBLEMS OF CLASSIFICATION

Overall, this book is concerned with the question of *power*. It deals with the numerous organisations and forms through which the struggle for and maintenance of power in South Africa takes place; this has been our fundamental perspective and all entries are written around it. This means that, for instance, the entries on individual capitalist organisations are concerned primarily with the power they represent and their place in the struggle for that power. The reader who is looking for more conventional economic information on these organisations — such as earnings ratio per share — will not find it here.

At the outset, because we wished to analyse the struggle for power in South Africa, it was decided that the book should be more than a simple alphabetical catalogue of organisations. Instead we have sought to identify a number of crucial themes and areas of struggle. These are broadly grouped around the capitalist class, its allies, policies and state structures on the one hand, and the forces making up and supporting the national liberation struggle and organised opposition to the regime on the other. These themes provide the basis for individual chapters. The entries in each chapter then examine the principal organisations in these groupings.

An overview of the major divisions of the book and its organisation can be found in the breakdown of the entries within each chapter provided in the Detailed Table of Contents.

Clearly, the actual process of struggle in South Africa is not as cut and dried as our classification suggests. Inevitably there are omissions in the book and we have had to make choices. Certain organisations have been excluded because it was felt that they were not overtly concerned with the immediate issues of struggle and did not therefore justify extensive research.

This is the case, for example, with some churches and sporting bodies which nevertheless play an important role in the cultural life and political organisation of the oppressed population in South Africa. This is also the case with organisations such as the Rotary Club and the Jewish Board of Deputies, both of which are a significant medium for the organisation of specific interests of the capitalist class.

Other organisations were difficult to classify. Where an organisation did not fit easily into the groupings identified in the chapters, either because it crossed our thematic boundaries, or because of its contradictory character and demands, it has been included in Chapter 10, under 'Other Political and Miscellaneous Organisations'. Examples of such organisations are the South African Institute of Race Relations, the Labour Party, the media etc.

A book which deals with current struggles in South Africa is bound to date rather rapidly. This reference manual has been more than two years in preparation. During that time a number of important changes and shifts have occurred. While we have tried to include such changes in the text, it was impossible to remain constantly up to date and complete the book at the same time. The final editing of the manuscript was made in April-May 1983. While in some cases developments of early 1983 are referred to, in general the book covers the period up to mid-1982 — except for the entries in Chapter 2, where we have only been able to include data from the 1981 reports of these undertakings.

HOW TO READ THIS BOOK

The book can be used in two ways. Firstly, it can be used as a reference manual to provide information on specific organisations. For example: if a reader wants information on an organisation called the Port Elizabeth Black Civic Organisation (PEBCO), he or she should refer first to the alphabetical index of organisations at the back of the book. The first reference to the organisation in this index appears in bold type and indicates the page on which the specific entry on the organisation is to be found. Additional references indicate other places in the book where reference is made to PEBCO. In cases such as PEBCO, where an organisation is also commonly known by its abbreviation, the abbreviation also appears in the index and the reader is referred to the full title of the organisation. A list of abbreviations is also provided on p.xiii.

Secondly, the book is intended to provide a coherent analysis of the current struggle in South Africa. The reader interested in a more general analysis of the situation, rather than the detailed account of its component parts, is advised to consult the essays in Chapter 1. These provide an overall view of the historical development and current operation of the system and forms of struggle in South Africa. He or she should then read the introductory essays at the beginning of the subsequent chapters. This type of reading will, however, necessarily involve some repetition.

5. Organisations of Classes Allied to the Capitalist Ruling Class

COLLABORATIONIST LABOUR ORGANISATIONS[1]

Historical Introduction

There are few cases in history where a capitalist ruling class has been able to consolidate its rule without drawing a measure of active support from other classes in society. South Africa is certainly no such case. Under conditions of capital accumulation dependent on the imposition of highly exploitative and coercive measures against black workers and oppression of all blacks, capitalist rule was possible only with support from other classes. Historically these were the white petty bourgeoisie and white labour. However, this alliance between capital and other white classes did not develop automatically, nor even as an inevitable result of racist ideology. Rather it was formed historically, in and through processes of class struggle.

One critical aspect of this process was the incorporation of the major organisations of the 'white labour movement', into a bureaucratic and regulated relationship with the state and capital. Over the course of this century, through complex processes of class struggle and a series of particular state interventions, the major trade unions of white wage earners were transformed. From once militant organisations which constituted a certain threat to capitalist rule, they became bureaucratic organisations acting in a number of ways to support the rule of capital and thwart the challenge of the oppressed masses. More recently, as a result of the Botha regime's attempt to modify aspects of the apartheid system (see p.37), some strain has been placed on relationships between capital and white wage earners. This has not yet, however, resulted in any major section of the 'white labour movement' withdrawing its overall support for the apartheid system of capitalism based on racial oppression. More noticeable at this stage is an ultra reactionary response on the part of certain union groupings to all attempts to partially relax certain forms of job reservation and negotiate with unions of black workers.

As a result of these historical processes the South African trade union movement is currently divided into two distinct sections. On the one side are the sectionalist, and in some cases openly racist, unions dealt with in this chapter. These are based mainly on white wage earners, but also to a lesser extent on a minority of more skilled coloured and Asian workers. Characteristically, these unions have fought for sectional privileges for a minority of wage earners within the system.

Often this has included fighting for job colour bars at the expense of black workers. In addition, since the 1920s they have generally acted in support of the racially exclusive form of state.

On the other side, there are the non-racial unions, based mainly on African workers, but which are generally open to, and in many cases include, members of other racial groups (see Chapter 7).

The Origins of a Racially Divided Trade Union Movement

The origins of today's racially divided trade union movement must be traced back to two major factors: 1) the racial division of labour of South Africa capitalism and; 2) the response of the state to the militant struggles waged by white labour during the early part of this century.

The particular conditions of accumulation in the gold-mining industry 1886-1920, gave rise to a racial division of labour. This was analysed p.8ff, and the analysis will not be restated here. However, three consequences of the racial division of labour need to be stressed. First, skilled and supervisory jobs were predominantly performed by whites, while less skilled work was done by blacks. Second, the dependence of mining capital on ultra-cheap black labour excluded newly proletarianised whites from unskilled jobs. This resulted in large-scale white unemployment and exacerbated the so-called 'poor white problem'. Third, there developed a series of struggles in which capital progressively tried to reduce the role of skilled whites in production, mainly in order to reduce wage costs by substituting black workers for whites. Such struggles were particularly intense in the mining industry during the first quarter of the century, and in manufacturing with the development of monopoly capitalist production after the Second World War. Taken together, these three factors crucially influenced the emerging forms of trade unionism.

The first trade unions were formed in Cape Town by white printers and carpenters in 1881. More important, however, were unions formed by skilled white workers in the Witwatersrand mining industry after 1890. These early unions were characteristically craft unions, that is to say unions only open to workers in certain skilled trades and which acted principally to defend their members' monopoly right to perform certain tasks.

The specific context of the racial division of labour in South Africa led craft unions in the Transvaal to adopt racially discriminatory membership rules and to demand that certain tasks be reserved exclusively for whites.

During the first quarter of the 20th Century, conflicts between capital and white wage earners over the racial allocation of particular tasks dominated the white trade union scene. Mining capital took the offensive and attempted to reorganise a number of labour processes previously performed by white skilled craftsmen into processes performed by a gang of black workers super-vised by a white. Although this preserved the basic hierarchy of whites over blacks, it threatened the interests of white employees in two main ways: first, such reorganisation laid off numbers of white labourers; second, the 'deskilling' inherent in the process threatened to undermine one of the most important levers which white labour possessed in wage bargaining — the dependence of mining capital on their skills. At each stage, therefore, they resisted mining capital's attempts to reorganise labour processes along these lines. On three occasions — in 1907, 1913 and 1922 — conflicts over this question led to large-scale strikes, the most important strikes involving white wage earners during this period.

The basic demand of white wage earners in 1907 and 1922, at least, was for the imposition or restoration of job colour bars. In 1922, for example, strikers marched behind the bizarre slogan 'Workers of the World Fight and Unite for a White South Africa'. But the conflicts which were bitterly fought by a militant white trade union movement also had a definite anti-capitalist/socialist or at least social-democratic content. Gradually, there emerged within the white labour movement, a current which identified the basic problems of white wage earners as deriving from the particular exploitative measures directed against black workers. Such a current was evident as a minority tendency within both the South African Industrial Federation (SAIF), the Transvaal trade union co-ordinating body formed in 1907, and the South African Labour Party until 1915 and thereafter in the International Socialist League and Communist Party (see p.290). It never emerged as the majority tendency within the white labour movement and links between white and black labour in struggle were always fraught with problems. However, it was by no means inevitable that it should have been eclipsed by the more reformist racist tendency in the movement. To understand why this occurred it is necessary to consider the second major factor — the response of the state to the struggles of white labour.

The State and White Labour 1900–1922: the 'Poor White Problem'
One of the earliest forms of state intervention was in respect of the 'poor white problem'. The numbers of 'poor whites' reached 106,518 (8% of the white population) by 1916 and over 300,000 (17.5%) by 1932. However, more important than the numbers affected were the effects which the 'poor white problem' was seen to be having on the capitalist class's political interests.

Firstly, the existence of unemployed whites living in conditions of poverty and frequently in close proximity to blacks was seen as undermining attempts to inculcate the ideology of 'white supremacy' among the black population. Secondly, the poor whites as a marginalised stratum frequently engaged in activities which induced blacks to infringe coercive regulations. Most important was the large number of 'poor whites' illegally selling liquor to blacks. Such sales were banned under laws intended to increase the productivity of African workers and facilitate the maintenance of control over them. Thirdly, 'poor whites' sometimes supported militant struggles by other whites against the capitalist class and the state. Finally, given the weak numerical position of the capitalist class and the relative weakness of the repressive apparatuses in this period, the ruling class needed some degree of support from all other white classes in society. The existence of poor whites weakened the capacity of the ideology of racism to rally that support both among the poor whites themselves and among the white wage earning classes in general.

The capitalist class thus considered the 'poor white problem' a definite threat. As the 1913 Select Committee on European Employment and Labour Conditions put it:

> The magnitude of unemployment among Europeans in South Africa is possibly not greater than in other countries, but the danger posed is much greater because of the presence of the preponderating native population, and constitutes a real social threat . . . [Among the white unemployed there] is a depressing residue of incompetent and apathetic indigents: whose condition constitutes a real danger for society. These are persons who have entered into a corrupting and demoralising intercourse with non-Europeans, with harmful effects on both sections of the population.

The state accordingly intervened to ensure the assignment of whites rather than blacks to specific jobs. Various state departments reserved particular unskilled positions in their departments exclusively for whites. Various attempts were made to persuade or coerce private employers (outside the mining industry) to do the same, and schemes to resettle 'poor whites' in the land as small capitalist farmers were implemented.

The State and Trade Union Struggles by White Labour to 1922

The initial response of the capitalist state to strikes and trade union organisation by white wage earners had been directly repressive. Major strikes were met with the intervention of armed forces to break up pickets, defend strike breakers and disperse strike meetings and demonstrations. In addition, although trade unions were not prohibited, they were not recognised, and every effort was made to encourage or persuade white wage earners not to join unions.

In the course of this period, however, it became apparent that such direct and blatant interventions by the state on the side of capital threatened some of the broader political interests of the capitalist class. In the first place, such interventions did not actually succeed in preventing trade union combination or strikes by white wage earners. On the contrary, they often served to make unions and strikers more militant and anti-capitalist. Secondly, strikes by white wage earners were seen as encouraging African workers also to strike and, thirdly, the large scale deployment of armed force to control striking whites was seen as rendering the state vulnerable to an 'uprising' by blacks.

Accordingly, during this period, the capitalist class began to seek an alternative response to the struggles of white wage earners. This involved attempting to incorporate the white labour movement into a racially discriminatory 'industrial relations system' — racially discriminatory at the insistence of capital so as not to serve as a stimulus to trade union organisation by black workers. The role of the industrial relations apparatuses would be to limit the struggles of white wage earners to forms which did not threaten the fundamental interests of the state or capitalist class. This would be achieved in part by making available certain concessions through institutional-ised bargaining in bureaucratic structures and in part by prohibiting other forms of organisation or struggle.

In the period up to 1922 however, attempts to institutionalise the struggles of white trade unions were only partially successful. In the Transvaal a 1909 act suspended the right to strike and provided for the establishment of 'conciliation boards' to settle disputes involving non-African employees. In 1914, a bill was introduced in parliament, but not enacted, which would have provided for the registration of unions and the establishment of permanently existing 'conciliation boards'. More important during this period were the establishment in particular sectors of non-statutory apparatuses such as 'Conciliation Boards' and 'Boards of Reference' in the mining industry, and an 'Industrial Council' in the printing industry.

While a number of these bodies were functioning by 1920 and were seen as having a significant effect in reducing strikes, the institutionalisation of the 'white labour movement' remained incomplete. The contradictions between mining capital and white labour during this period as well as the growing white unemployment, limited the degree of acceptance on the part of white wage earners of bourgeois ideological apparatuses. This meant, in particular, that their effects on unions remained limited and white labour remained an organised and militant social force. This situation only changed after the 1922 general strike and armed uprising on the Rand.

The 1922 Strike and the 1924 Industrial Conciliation Act
The strike of 1922 was the largest and most militant action ever taken by white labour in South Africa. It erupted after mining capital broke a job colour bar agreement in an attempt to reduce its wage costs in the face of sharply falling gold prices. The strike affected the whole of the mining industry of the Witwatersrand. After it became apparent that the situation was deadlocked, armed strike commandos, incorporating a number of unemployed 'poor whites' as well as striking miners, occupied the Witwaters-rand. The government declared martial law and despatched troops to the area and a five day armed struggle ensued. Several people were killed and hundreds injured; several hundred strikers were subsequently arrested and subjected to penalties ranging from fines and imprisonment to (in four cases) death.

The 1922 strike and 'Rand Revolt' were both major defeats for the militant wing of the white labour movement. They also indicated to the capitalist class the need to intensify its efforts to contain 'white labour unrest' and in particular to incorporate the white trade unions into an effective industrial bargaining system. The strike's defeat led to the dissolution of the SAIF which had been taken over in the course of the strike by its more militant wing.

In 1923, the Smuts government introduced an Industrial Conciliation Bill. This provided for the suspension of the right to strike and the establishment of a highly bureaucratic system (the Industrial Council system) for employers and unions excluding 'pass bearing natives'. The Bill was passed into law in 1924 in a revised form and has served as the statutory basis of the 'industrial relations' system for non-African employees ever since.

The period following the passage of the Act saw an intense effort by the Nationalist-Labour Pact government elected in 1924, as well as the state in general, to persuade or cajole unions into the system. The Pact regime simultaneously attempted to reinforce its credentials among white labour by extending and restructuring attempts to promote the employment of 'poor whites' (under its so-called 'civilised labour' policy). It further amended the Mines and Works Act to grant statutory protection to white miners in their existing places in the industry's division of labour. With a strong tradition of racist, reformist trade unionism already well established in the white labour movement and the left wing soundly defeated after 1922, the late 1920s and the 1930s saw institutionalisation proceeding apace.

This immediately manifested itself in a sharp fall in the number of strikes by white wage earners and a steady rise in the numbers covered by the industrial conciliation machinery. By 1932 there were 41 Industrial Councils covering a total of 46,252 employees, while the annual average number of whites on strike declined to 2,000 compared with an average of nearly 15,000 per year in the period 1910–21 and 26,000 in 1922. But the institutionalisation of the white trade union movement had effects more profound than the mere reduction of strikes: the incorporation of white trade unions into the industrial conciliation system significantly affected the internal organisation of unions. The Industrial Council procedures were centralised, complex and bureaucratised. They thus favoured the formation within unions of a corps of professional negotiators distanced from rank and file members. Over this period, power within unions passed decisively to bureaucratic leaderships, with the effect that rank and file union members became in effect isolated and disorganised.

For a short period, this disorganisation manifested itself in reduction of union membership from 67,200 in 1926 to 58,400 in 1927. Such extreme disorganisation, however, did not last long. By 1929, the union membership had risen again to 69,900. This occurred partly because capitalists began to see advantages in bureaucratised unions and began to assist in union recruitment through check-off facilities and closed shop agreements. As the 1935 Industrial Legislation Commission explained:

> In these days when the employees in a single workshop often number many hundreds, the arrangement of individual contracts of service would present many administrative difficulties and for this reason alone many employers have adopted the policy of encouraging their

employees to link up with unions . . . The better type of employer
also appreciates the fact that well organised and disciplined trade
unions can do much to reduce evasion of industrial legislation by . . .
less reputable [competitors].

Hereafter, disorganisation and isolation manifested themselves not in reduced
union membership but in widespread apathy on the part of rank and file
members.

This was the real and lasting impact of the Industrial Conciliation Act
and the system it established. It made available to white wage earners certain
significant economic concessions, including job colour bars. At the same
time, however, it extracted from the white labour movement a fundamental
political concession for the benefit of the capitalist class — its disorganisation
as a militant social force potentially capable of threatening the rule of capital.
The 'historic compromise' between capital and white labour enshrined in
this Act ensured the decisive dominance within white labour organisations
from then onwards of forces broadly supportive of the capitalist state. It
effectively transformed white trade unions from organisations which had
posed certain problems for capitalist rule, into supportive apparatuses of the
bourgeois state.

At the formal organisational level, the period following the 1922 strike
saw the Department of Labour taking the initiative in forming a new federation
to replace the disbanded SAIF. In 1925 the South African Association of
Employees' Organisations was formed, later called the South African Trades
Union Council. In 1931 it reconstituted itself as the South African Trades
and Labour Council (SATLC), which remained the most important
co-ordinating body until 1954 (see chart p.262).

The Penetration by Afrikaner Nationalism 1934–1948

The other major development giving the present day 'white labour movement'
its specific character was its penetration during the period 1934–48 by front
organisations of the *Afrikaner Broederbond*, particularly the *Nasionale Raad
van Trustees* (National Council of Trustees).

This was initiated in 1934 for two related major reasons. The extreme
political isolation of the Afrikaner petty bourgeoisie in the Transvaal after
1934 necessitated the development of a mass base; in the words of the key
Broederbond trade union organiser, until the petty bourgeois *Broederbond*
began to organise Afrikaner labour, 'Afrikaner nationalism stared death in
the face'. Secondly, the attempt of this Afrikaner petty bourgeoisie
organised in the *Broederbond* to transform itself into a capitalist class
through the 'Afrikaner economic movement', depended heavily on its ability
to mobilise the savings of Afrikaner wage earners to finance their various
projects (see p.268).

The *Broederbond* penetration of the white labour movement sought to
win Afrikaner wage earners away from existing trade unions and into
'Christian national' trade unions organised and controlled by itself. In 1934

it set up the first 'Christian national' union in the railways, *Spoorbond*. In 1937 the *Broederbond* began a protracted struggle with the leaderships of other unions, particularly the Mine Workers' Union and the Garment Workers' Union, for control over these organisations with largely Afrikaner memberships.

During and after the Second World War, the 'Christian national' trade union movement achieved a number of successes. It forced the railways administration to recognise *Spoorbond* in 1942, and captured control of the Mine Workers' Union in 1948, whilst its *Blankewerkersbeskermingbond* (White Workers' Protection Society), formed in 1944, succeeded in recruiting white workers in various other sectors.

A number of factors underlay this success: first was the failure of existing bureaucratic union leaderships to represent the interests of their members and the increasingly visible corruption of officials in some unions. This was particularly important in the take over of the Mine Workers' Union. Second, the existing unions failed to organise large numbers of semi-skilled white industrial workers (mainly Afrikaners) who entered employment during the period of industrial expansion after 1933. Third, the employment for the first time on a significant scale of black workers as industrial operatives created a number of conflicts between industrial capital and less skilled white workers over the racial allocation of jobs. These intensified with the development of monopoly capitalist relations of productions in manufacturing (which implied the 'deskilling' of many jobs) in the post-war period, and provided a particularly fertile ground for the Nationalists to build up support by promising a comprehensive system of 'job reservation'.

The support built up by Afrikaner Nationalists among white wage earners was of decisive importance in enabling the Nationalist Party to come to power in 1948. In the 1948 elections the party won eight 'traditionally labour' seats in the Witwatersrand and five more in Pretoria. It came to power with an overall parliamentary majority of only five seats (see NP entry p.138).

The Nationalist Party penetration of the white labour movement also had important effects on the organisational structure of the latter. In 1947, five right wing unions withdrew from the Trades and Labour Council in protest at the support given by the TLC leadership to the Smuts government's Bill to recognise African trade unions under a tightly controlled industrial relations system. To the TLC right wing, support for this Bill (which fell far short of previous TLC policy that all unions should be able to register under the Industrial Conciliation Act), implied supporting African trade unionism at the expense of white workers.

The TLC right wing now joined 'Christian national' unions which had never affiliated, to form a new federation, the Coordinating Council of Trades Unions — the third registered trade union federation then in existence and the only one explicitly supporting the NP. (see chart p.264).

Developments 1948–1979

This period saw the penetration of monopoly capitalist relations of production in all sectors (with the partial exception of agriculture) and the interpenetration of monopoly capitals between sectors (see p.56). It produced a greater concentration of production and a reorganisation of labour processes which created an increased demand for technical, supervisory and clerical labour. The period after the Second World War saw a rapid 'promotion' of whites from semi-skilled manual employment to fill these positions. This was supported and encouraged by government policy. Moreover, until the crisis of the mid-1970s, this was a period of rising wage levels for white wage earners. Equally important, it saw a sharp widening of the gap between white and black wages.

These changes from the general context within which organisational developments within the registered trade union movement in the apartheid period have to be seen. The major events, briefly, were as follows:

In 1950, the Nationalist Party government enacted the Suppression of Communism Act. Within three years, 33 left wing trade unionists were removed from office under its provisions. This finally broke the vestigial left opposition within the SATLC, allowing the leadership to abandon all commitment to the demands of the black majority of the working class.

In 1954 a Bill was published providing for statutory job reservation. The opposition to the Bill led to the merger of the Western Province Federation of Trade Unions and the TLC in 1954. The new body was originally known as the SA Trade Union Congress, later changing its name to the Trade Union Council of South Africa (TUCSA — see entry p.250). For many years TUCSA was only open to unions 'registerable under the I.C. Act', that is to say it specifically excluded Africans.

When the Industrial Conciliation Amendment Act was eventually passed in 1956, a group of 12 TUCSA unions to the right of the leadership split to form the South African Federation of Trade Unions (SAFTU). At this point, three federations existed in addition to SAFTU, formed in 1955 and based mainly on African workers excluded by all other federations (see p.329). These were:

TUCSA	34 unions	144,000 white, coloured and Asian members;
SA Federation of Trade Unions	12 unions	60,000 white members;
Coordinating Council of SA Trade Unions	13 unions	18,000 white members.

In 1957, with the encouragement of the Department of Labour, these three bodies joined together with the Federal Consultative Council of SA Railways and Harbours Staff Associations to form one body, the South African Confederation of Labour. However, disputes between TUCSA and the by now firmly NP-oriented leaders of the rest of the Confederation led to TUCSA's withdrawal in 1958.

Increasingly thereafter, the Confederation came to be dominated by the leadership of the old Coordinating Council which still retained a separate organisational existence.

By the 1970s the relative positions of the two federations were:

TUCSA	68 unions	166,881 white, coloured and Asian members;
Confederation*	22 unions	179,000 white members;
*(including Coordi-nating Council)	12 unions	28,000 white members.

Post-Wiehahn Developments 1979
The publication of the first report of the Wiehahn Commission of Enquiry into labour legislation, which recommended the modification of job reservation and a policy geared to incorporating open trade unions into the existing bureaucratic industrial relations system (see p.325), posed major questions for each of these registered union groupings. TUCSA has attempted to assert hegemony over the burgeoning African trade union movement and in the process turn unions of African workers into tame replicas of itself (see p.253). The Confederation (or SACLA) was thrown into something of a crisis by the post-Wiehahn legislation. Unable to satisfy either its more 'moderate' wing (which wanted at all costs to avoid a clash with the Nationalist regime) or its more extreme racist wing (which sought an all out struggle to prevent the end of statutory job reservation), SACLA has experienced a number of disaffiliations (see p.257). In the early 1980s the balance within the white trade unions remains fluid, but in general they remain firmly allied to the capitalist class.

Trade Union Council of South Africa (TUCSA)[2]

Federation of bureaucratic registered trades unions, strongly anti-communist and committed to the maintenance of capitalism in South Africa, but never aligned with any of the organisations of Afrikaner nationalism. In the post-Wiehahn period, the 'multi-racial' TUCSA has come to play an important role in support of South African capitalism, functioning as a force attempting to reduce class antagonisms. Its 'parallel union' policy, aims to recruit African workers into separate subsidiary organisations of non-African registered unions. It attempts to make its appeal by offering a 'non-political' form of trade unionism which does not risk hostility from the state. After 1979, TUCSA 'parallels' entered into direct competition for membership with democratic unions, but in the prevailing climate of worker militancy, have generally not grown as fast as the latter. More recently, the

TUCSA leadership refused to condemn the wave of detentions of
trade unionists or the death in detention of Neil Aggett. This
open collaborationist line created certain contradictions within
the organisation resulting in some defections.

Formation and Role
TUCSA was formed in October 1954 by the merger of the SA Trades and
Labour Council and the Western Province Federation of Trades Unions
(WPF). They were drawn together by the publication of the Industrial
Conciliation Amendment Bill providing for: 1) the prohibition of 'mixed'
unions, i.e. unions with white, coloured and Asian memberships and; 2) for
the implementation of statutory job reservation determinations after
investigation by an industrial tribunal. These provisions were opposed not
because the dominant forces within these organisations had any real intention
of engaging in joint struggle with black workers, but because it was feared
that the prohibition on 'mixed' unions might lead to the 'undermining' of
closed shop agreements to the detriment of white workers. Statutory job
reservation was opposed because the TUCSA leadership, like many capitalist
employers, felt it might 'damage industry'. However, this was a far less
serious concern for the TUCSA leadership as evidenced by the fact that it
offered at one point to withdraw its opposition to statutory job reservation
in return for the removal of clauses prohibiting 'mixed unions'.

The dominant forces within both the TLC and the WPF which combined
to form TUCSA in 1954 were 'old guard' trade union bureaucrats nurtured
by the post-1924 industrial conciliation system (see p.246). The extreme
right wing forces within the registered trade union movement had split away
in 1948 to form the Coordinating Council of Trades Unions (see p.248).
The left wing was badly weakened by the assault launched by the Nationalist
regime under the Suppression of Communism Act and eventually left to
join SACTU, formed in 1955 (see p.329).

The basic character of TUCSA's main aims and policy directions emerges
from its constitution which commits the organisation '. . . to oppose communism in all its forms, to resist actively all attempts by any political party
to exploit the Trade Union movement for political ends, and to actively
promote a free trade union movement for the benefit of the South African
economy'. TUCSA has always actively opposed workers' organisations linked
to the national liberation struggle, notably SACTU. Through its 'parallel
unions' it is now attempting to poach members from the more independent
and militant open trade unions. Its leaders have also frequently expressed
their support for the maintenance of capitalism and white political domination
in South Africa and have actively opposed calls for sanctions against the
apartheid regime.

Unlike the other union groupings listed in this chapter, TUCSA affiliated
unions include over 170,000 coloured and Asian workers (who have always
been allowed to join registered unions and in fact, under the 1956 Industrial

251

Conciliation Act, could join 'mixed' unions if these had been formed before 1956). Persons of coloured and Asian origin constituted the majority of TUCSA's 252,734 members in 1980. TUCSA's large coloured and Asian membership is frequently cited in claims that it is a progressive organisation. In reality, however, the position and particular interests of its minority white membership has always been dominant within TUCSA. Indeed, coloured and Asian members were admitted in the first place precisely to prevent them 'undercutting' white workers. This was stated with remarkable frankness by TUCSA's long term President, Tom Rutherford, who in the 1960s argued in favour of admitting coloured and Asian workers in the following terms:

> Up until 1927 we refused to have Indians in the typographical union. They then commenced negotiations separately and practically eliminated the European printer from Natal. We then took them into our union to stop that. The result is that I suppose one could count the number of skilled Indian printers in Natal on the fingers of one hand. They have been almost eliminated. That happened because we took them into the union.

Or, as another former TUCSA leader, Tom Murray, put it:

> TUCSA demands equal pay for equal work but does not support the major demands of all non-white workers, that they should have equal opportunities as well.

Internally, TUCSA maintains a highly bureaucratic form of organisation dominated by white officials despite its majority black membership. Negotiations are carried out by full time officials in statutory bodies with no direct involvement of the workers themselves. TUCSA unions characteristically have little shop floor organisation, the role of members being more or less confined to the payment of dues.

TUCSA and African Workers

TUCSA's position on the question of African trade unionism has passed through several phases. In 1954, when TUCSA was formed, it limited its membership to unions registerable under the Industrial Conciliation Act, i.e. if specifically excluded unions which had African members.

This represented a change from the position of the former Trades and Labour Council. The TLC had formally permitted unions including African members to affiliate, but often only accepted them in practice on the basis of less than full membership, so as not to challenge the hegemony of racist unions within the Council. TUCSA argued that its position on the question of African membership was purely tactical, intended to avoid an onslaught on it by the state, then vigorously pursuing its policy of 'bleeding' African trade unions. TUCSA, however, did nothing to assist unions with African members resisting that onslaught. That was left as the sole task of SACTU, which TUCSA opposed from the outset.

Only in 1959, under pressure from the International Confederation of Free Trade Unions (ICFTU), which feared that 'moderate' trade unionism would lose ground among African workers, did TUCSA modify this position. It agreed to establish a *separate* African federation under its tutelage — the Federation of Free African Trades Unions (FOFATUSA). However, few steps were taken actually to organise and recruit. FOFATUSA's total membership remained derisory throughout its existence.

In 1962, in the face of growing hostility from the International Labour Organization, TUCSA attempted to improve its image by permitting 'properly constituted' African unions to affiliate to it. By 1965, eight former FOFATUSA unions with a total membership of 2,000 (0.004% of the African industrial work-force) had joined.

At its 1968 conference, however, TUCSA reversed this position and excluded its handful of African associates. This was intended to ward off threats of disaffiliation from certain racist unions in the railways (which disaffiliated anyway). Again in 1970, faced with threatened disaffiliations from racist unions of mine officials, TUCSA declared its firm opposition to proposals to modify job colour bar regulations in the Bantustans.

Current attempts by TUCSA to organise 'parallel' unions date back to 1972 when the first signs of increased black worker militancy became apparent. There were strong differences at the 1972 TUCSA conference over the organisation of black workers. A delegate from the Boilermakers' Society asked: 'Has anybody spoken to an African about trade unionism? He does not know what you're talking about. If you take those in Zululand, where they still walk about only with the bottom covered, they don't know what a trade union means'. However, at the 1972 conference TUCSA urged its individual affiliates to take steps to 'establish parallel union organisations for African workers' (which were, however, not permitted to affiliate to TUCSA itself until 1974). In a public speech delivered in 1974, General Secretary Arthur Grobbelaar declared that if African unions were not placed under the 'responsible' control of registered unions 'not only will the Government be brought to its knees, but our present way of life will be destroyed'. Independent black unions, he went on, were 'a wonderful tailor-made device for the enemies of our way of life'. As open trade unions have expanded, TUCSA 'parallels', with the aid and encouragement of some employers, have redoubled their efforts. This has particularly been the case since 1979 when TUCSA resolved to enter into direct competition with democratic unions for membership.

Typically, TUCSA 'parallels' appeal to African workers by offering a 'non-political' form of trade unionism which does not risk hostility from the state. They supported the Wiehahn Legislation of 1979 and rapidly applied for registration, regarding this as providing them with an opportunity to win membership away from democratic unions which remained unregistered. Internally, TUCSA 'parallels' like their 'parent' unions, tend to be run from the top and have weak shop floor organisation. Many of the general secretaries are direct appointees of the 'parent' union. In some cases, the general secretary of the 'parent' union even doubles as general secretary of the 'parallel'.

In short, TUCSA 'parallels' are not genuine independent organisations of the African working class but subsidiaries of organisations supportive of the capitalist system and racially exclusive form of state. Their role in the class struggle is to attempt to reduce class antagonisms and win support for the institutions of the official industrial conciliation system, and through this for South African capitalism. In fact, even the pro-monopoly capitalist *Financial Mail* ironically remarked in 1977, 'When is a union not a union? — When it's a TUCSA parallel'.

In the prevailing climate of worker militancy, TUCSA 'parallels' have not fared particularly well in open battles to poach membership from other unions. For example, the General Workers' Union staved off an attempt to recruit its membership in the Cape Town docks (see p.341). This has led TUCSA to resort to other tactics to maintain its position. One of these has involved entering into closed shop agreements with certain employers in effect compelling its African employees to join the TUCSA 'parallel'.

On these and other key questions, a definite rightward drift has been noticeable within TUCSA in recent years. This is partly due to the influence of a number of former SACLA affiliates which have joined TUCSA following the crisis in SACLA (see p.257). One indication emerged at TUCSA's 1982 conference when a number of delegates called for all unions to be *forced* to register — an even harder position than that currently taken by the Department of Manpower Utilisation.

The wave of detentions of trade unionists and death in detention of Dr Neil Aggett in February 1982, provided another clear indication of TUCSA position. The TUCSA leadership declined to condemn either, refusing even to describe Aggett as a trade unionist. General Secretary, Grobbelaar, reportedly issued a circular stating that 'the council could not support the campaign against detention without trial . . . TUCSA could not subscribe to any attempts which seek the abolition of all laws in respect of detention, since this would imply that TUCSA sought the abolition of the rule of just law'. Later attempts to get TUCSA to condemn the continued detention of Thozamile Gqweta and Sam Kikine of SAAWU (see p.337) brought forth the comment from TUCSA President, Ana Scheepers, that TUCSA would not speak out on behalf of people 'we hardly know or do not know at all'. Widely condemned by other unionists, such positions have opened up certain contradictions within TUCSA itself. One prominent organiser of Lucy Mvubel National Union of Clothing Workers immediately resigned in protest over the position taken over Neil Aggett, and later in the year two affiliates — the National Union of Commercial, Catering and Allied Workers and the National Union of Distributive Workers — with a combined membership of 11,000 — left the Council.

Leadership:
  President: Ana Scheepers
  General Secretary: Arthur Grobbelaar
Other leading personalities:
  R. Kraft
  R. Scheepers
  Lucy Mvubelo, General Secretary of National Union of Clothing Workers
  and leading spokesman for 'parallel unionism'.
In July 1982 Grobbelaar and Mvubelo became patrons of the Free Market
Foundation (see p.125).

TUCSA 'parallel' unions (membership: approximately 32,000):
  MIWUSA — Motor Industry Workers' Union of South Africa
  ALWU — African Leather Workers' Union — Transvaal
  ATEBWU — African Trunk and Box Workers' Union
  GWU — Glass Workers' Union
  SABEU — South African Bank Employees' Union
  ATOBWU — African Tobacco Workers' Union
  NUCW — National Union of Clothing Workers
  TWU — Textile Workers' Union — Transvaal
  EEAWUA — Electrical and Allied Workers' Union of South Africa
  ATWU — African Transport Workers' Union
  NUEI and AW — National Union of Engineering, Industrial and Allied
    Workers.

South African Confederation of Labour (SACLA)[3]

Confederation of exclusively white unions which seeks to 'guard'
the sectional interests of white labour. The Confederation (or
SACLA as it now prefers to style itself) has traditionally taken a
strong pro-apartheid stance, favouring job colour bars and opposing
any form of trade union organisation among blacks. The
introduction of the Wiehahn legislation has thrown SACLA into
a crisis. As a result of disaffiliations, membership fell from 22
unions with 179,700 members in 1980 to 14 unions with about
100,000 members in 1982. SACLA unions are based mainly on
non-salaried employees of central, provincial and local government,
employees of state corporations (such as SATS, SASOL, ISCOR),
and employees in the mining industry.

SACLA was formed in September 1957, in an attempt to merge the three then existing federations which excluded African workers, namely TUCSA, the South African Federation of Trade Unions and the Coordinating Council of South African Trade Unions — as well as the Federal Consultative Council of SA Railways and Harbours Staff Associations. TUCSA, however, withdrew a year later (see TUCSA entry p.250).

The leading force within the Confederation has undoubtedly been the Coordinating Council of SA Trade Unions which maintains its separate organisational existence within the Confederation. The Coordinating Council was formed in June 1948 with the objective of uniting the 'Christian national' trade unions formed by the *Broederbond* in the 1930s and the 1940s, together with a number of right wing unions which broke away from the Trades and Labour Council in 1947 (see p.248). From 1948 to the early 1970s, relations between the Coordinating Council and SACLA on the one hand, and the Nationalist Party leadership and the Department of Labour on the other, were extremely cordial. The Confederation's views were widely canvassed by state and NP officials. There were numerous instances of state intervention to secure concessions over wages, job colour bars, etc. In return, SACLA loyally supported the struggles of other class forces represented in the Nationalist Party.

More recently, this cosy relationship has been placed under strain as a result of the capitalist ruling class's need to respond to the challenge of the popular masses, and in particular the growing militancy of the black working class. The state's eventual response as recommended by the Wiehahn Commission is summarised p.325. SACLA's position on Wiehahn was that it opposed all proposals to modify job reservation legislation and to admit unions including African members to statutory bodies.

Former SACLA President, Attie Niewoudt, was a member of the Wiehahn Commission and issued an extreme reactionary minority report. He argued, among other things, that: 'Black workers be prohibited from joining any trade union in South Africa, whether such a union is registered or not'. This he justified on the grounds that 'The racial composition of the labour force in many undertakings, industries, trades and occupations in South Africa is such that the workers who at present enjoy trade union rights would be swamped by force of numbers, should blacks be admitted to the trade union movement'. On job reservation he argued in favour of the maintenance of the status quo and 'dissent[ed] from the view [of other commissioners] that Blacks be indentured as apprentices in designated trades in white areas'.

Since the passage of the Wiehahn legislation, SACLA has been thrown into something of a crisis. Its former leadership under Niewoudt remained opposed to the Wiehahn measures but backed away from any campaign against them. This led to dissent from both its 'far right' and 'more moderate' sections.

In May 1979, SACLA held a series of meetings with the Minister of Labour over the Wiehahn Report, totally rejecting at the first meeting the majority recommendations. At the second meeting, however, the executive voted by 13 votes to 11 to accept the proposals with reservations. This led to a walk-out from the negotiations by the Mine Workers' Union (MWU), the White Building Workers' Union and the Transvaal Transport Workers' Union. The MWU subsequently resigned from SACLA and called on other disaffected unions to join it in a new organisation. When this appeal failed to attract sufficient support, however, the MWU later rejoined and continued its campaign within SACLA.

In 1980 the far right, led by the MWU, produced a report recommending that the Confederation reject the training of Africans as apprentices and demand the prohibition of all forms of trade union activity by blacks. In a set-back for the far right, however, the SACLA Congress postponed a decision on the report referring it to individual unions for discussion. The MWU's inability to advance its far right positions within the Confederation has led it to recruit members outside the mining industry in an attempt to set itself up as an effective force to resist what it sees as the 'undermining' of the white worker (see MWU entry p.258).

On the other side, several 'more moderate' unions have disaffiliated in recent years. Among these was the 42,000 strong SA Association of Municipal Employees, which resigned in 1980, unhappy at the Confederation's 'increasing conflict with the government'. A number of smaller unions resigned or were expelled in the same year because they had ceased to include clauses in their constitutions restricting membership to whites. In 1981 and 1982, several more unions left for similar reasons, including the Railways Artisans' Staff Association and the Boilermakers' Union, both of which subsequently joined TUCSA. According to the *Financial Mail*, over the two year period to April 1982, SACLA lost eight unions with a combined membership of at least 60,000.

During the course of this crisis a new leadership emerged which seems to be trying to adjust the organisation to the 'new labour dispensation' and 'modernise' its image. The 1982 President, Brian Currie, for example, declared that SACLA would from now on 'react positively to the well intended and increasingly more urgent legislation which the worsening race relations of our country necessitates' whilst at the same time continuing to 'guard the interests of white workers'. The current General Secretary, Wessel Borman, of the SA Iron Steel and Allied Workers' Union is also seen as a 'moderate', his union being one of the key targets from which the MWU sought to poach members. The far right, however, still remains a powerful force as evidenced by the fact that the MWU General Secretary was elected Vice-chairman at the 1982 Congress.

Leadership:
  President 1982: Brian Currie (Attie Niewoudt to 1981)
  General Secretary: Wessel Borman
  Vice-chairman: Arrie Paulus.

Mine Workers' Union (MWU)[4]

One of the most extreme racist unions, militantly opposed to any relaxation of job reservation and to any form of trade union organisation by black workers. Following the Wiehahn legislation, the MWU has tried to assume a vanguard role in the organisation of resistance to changes which it sees as undermining the position of white labour.

It is currently a member of SACLA (having rejoined in 1980 after disaffiliating in 1979) but is trying to recruit members in the iron and steel and other industries at the expense of other SACLA affiliates. This is explained by its General Secretary, Arrie Paulus, as follows: 'We feel that there are so few unions remaining in SA which are prepared to fight for the white workers that the time has arrived for a union to come to the fore and form a white force to care for the interests of whites. Most unions are now going multiracial and we feel there must be a home for the whites'. At the end of 1981 the MWU had about 18,000 exclusively white, and predominantly Afrikaans-speaking, members.

The Mine Workers' Union was formed early in this century as an industrial union open to all white employees in the mining industry. It differed from other existing mining unions (which together with the MWU constituted the Mining Unions' Joint Committee) in that the others were craft unions restricted to white employees in specific crafts or trades. Over the years, as a result of the process of 'de-skilling' and transforming white craft jobs into supervisory jobs (see p.243), the MWU emerged as the largest mining union. Its membership was drawn from the relatively large number of white supervisors with few formal skills but who possessed 'certificates of competency' or 'blasting certificates' (available only to whites, and the key to the operation of the system of job colour bars in the mining industry). After the 1907 strike, which saw the first large influx of Afrikaners into the mining industry, the MWU acquired an increasingly large Afrikaner membership. By the 1930s Afrikaners constituted the majority of its members.

During the first quarter of the century the MWU was an important (though not always leading) force in the struggles between mining capital and white labour which culminated in the strikes of 1907 and 1913 and the 'Rand Revolt' of 1922 (see p.243). After the 1922 strike, the MWU, like the other

mining unions, came to be incorporated into a highly centralised and
bureaucratic industrial relations system, one even more bureaucratic than
those established in other industries under the 1924 Industrial Conciliation
Act (see p.244). Following a recommendation of the 1922 Mining Industry
Board, all forms of recognition of local representatives (shaft stewards) were
withdrawn. Negotiations were restricted to bargaining between union officials
and representatives of the Chambers of Mines over defined questions –
wages, job colour bars and mining regulations. This, plus the granting of an
important concession over job colour bars – statutory protection for the then
existing positions of whites in the industry's division of labour – had the
effect over time of demobilising the rank and file membership and bringing
about a high degree of separation between union officials and the membership.

During the 1930s and 1940s the 'Christian national' trade unionists of the
Afrikaner Broederbond launched a powerful attempt to capture control of
the MWU (see p.247). As the largest single union of white wage earners, and
a crucial prop in the structure of the South African Labour Party, the MWU
was the central strategic target of the *Broederbond*. A number of factors
made it vulnerable to such attacks. Most central was the contradictory class
position of MWU members as both supervisory but also to some extent
productive workers. In the words of the official *Broederbond* history of this
struggle, MWU members 'are not only workers – they are also bosses'.
Nevertheless, MWU members occupied the least privileged and lowest paid
places open to whites in the mining industry. Its membership was predominantly
Afrikaans-speaking and as such was discriminated against by the highly
exclusivist craft mining unions.

The other critical factor was the highly bureaucratic and unrepresentative
character of the union by the 1930s, which was further consolidated in
response to the *Broederbond* assault. The *Broederbond* formed an 'Afrikaner
Union of Mineworkers' in 1935 and the MWU finally persuaded the Chamber
of Mines to conclude a closed shop agreement with it. This agreement bound
the MWU to enforce industrial docility on its members and thereafter the
union became in effect the policeman of the Chamber of Mines. The major
function of its increasingly corrupt leadership was to restrict wage demands
and maintain industrial discipline. Following this closed shop agreement the
'Christian nationalists' fought to wrest control of the MWU from its existing
leadership. Labelling themselves 'reformers' they took maximum advantage
of the increasingly bureaucratic, authoritarian and corrupt character of the
MWU leadership, and, in effect, began to pursue the economic functions of
the union – by fighting for pension entitlements, workmen's compensation
payments etc. In the 1940s the 'reformers' gradually built up support among
the membership. For a number of years, however, they were blocked by a
combination of bureaucratic manoeuvres and interventions in support of the
existing leadership from the Chamber of Mines and the United Party
government. After the leadership's clear capitulation to the Chamber of Mines
over a wage claim in 1944 and a related scandal over misappropriation of funds,
the 'reformers' campaign gathered momentum. By the end of the war it had

become clear that they had won majority support among the MWU rank and file. The predominant feeling was summed up in the following quotation from the evidence of rank and file union members to a government commission of inquiry in 1946, which says as much about their position in the division of labour as it does about their alienation from the union's bureaucratic leadership: 'Broderick [the then General Secretary] has no time for the members and treats them like kaffirs'. The power of the 'reformers' was proved in the widely supported, though short lived, strikes demanding elections in the union in 1946 and 1947. In 1948 after the Nationalist Party election victory, the 'reformers' finally took over control of the union.

Under its new leadership, the MWU generally acted as a loyalist organisation within the Afrikaner nationalist class alliance until the mid-1960s. It joined both the Coordinating Council and the Confederation of Labour (see SACLA entry p.255). In return, it secured a number of concessions, including regular wage increases (though significantly the first of these was not received until after the rise in the gold price following the devaluation of sterling in 1949). Moreover, under the 1956 Mines and Works Act, the restriction of a number of tasks to 'scheduled persons' only (i.e. whites with a blasting certificate) was entrenched.

Despite the 'reformers' campaign against corruption, however, this did not disappear from the union's leadership under the 'reformers'. Dean Ellis, leader of the 'reformers' and General Secretary of the union from 1948, was tried, convicted and sentenced to 18 months imprisonment for corruption in the early 1950s. The sentence was overturned on a technicality on appeal, and Ellis remained General Secretary until his death in 1963.

By the mid-1960s class contradictions had begun to surface within the Afrikaner nationalist alliance and after 1965 the MWU became a major site of struggle between contending forces. The union's present leadership came to power in these struggles.

In 1964, with the support of the Departments of Mines and of Labour, the Chamber of Mines proposed a series of 'experiments' in which African mine workers would be allowed to perform certain tasks previously performed exclusively by 'scheduled' whites. Whites were to be compensated by being placed on a fixed monthly salary and by an offer of improved working conditions. Although it was stated that there was no intention of appointing Africans to higher grades, it was clearly envisaged that the changes, if implemented in the industry generally, would involve a decrease in the number of 'scheduled' persons, i.e. whites, employed.

By June 1965, these 'experiments' were in effect in 12 mines and they divided the MWU. The then executive, led by General Secretary Eddie Grundling, were staunch 'experimentalists': as Grundling put it: 'I would rather have 9,000 persons with a reasonable wage than 16,000 persons dying from starvation'. Yet a growing number of union 'rebels' took the position that higher wages for some would not compensate for lay offs of others, and firmly opposed any change in job colour bar regulations.

The 'rebels' turned for support and advice to Dr 'Ras' Beyers, an extreme right wing lawyer and cattle rancher associated with the pro-Nazi *Ossewa Brandwag* during the Second World War (see p.269) and, by the mid-1960s, with the far right Republican Party. As it became clear that the 'experimentalists' had the support of the Nationalist Party hierarchy, the 'rebels' became more and more openly critical of government ministers whom they saw as allying with employers. In a notorious speech, Beyers asked rhetorically: 'How would the cabinet like it if we appointed a big fat semi-savage as a minister merely because it would cost the country less?'

After a number of manoeuvres by the 'experimentalist' leadership reminiscent of those of the 'Broderick clique' in the period before 1948, the 'rebels' eventually captured control of the union in 1967. Fred Short became General Secretary, and the present General Secretary, P.J. (Arrie) Paulus, was elected to the executive. On taking office, Short vowed to resist with all his might 'the onslaught of kaffir, moor and Indian on the white working community'. From then on the MWU refused to countenance any further changes in job colour bars.

With the onset of the mid-1970s crisis, and in particular the resurgence of trade union organisation among black workers and attempts by the capitalist ruling class to restructure the industrial relations system (see p.325), the MWU has attempted to lead organised resistance to these changes.

In 1979, shortly before the publication of the first Wiehahn Report, the union became involved in an industry-wide strike after an attempt by the O'Kiep Copper Mine to employ three coloureds in vacant 'white' posts. However, despite much rhetoric about 'another 1922', the strike was rapidly defeated. Indeed, the union failed even to secure the return of accumulated benefits withdrawn by management during the strike. Significantly, the hierarchy of the Nationalist Party backed the employers.

With the publication of the Wiehahn Reports, the MWU took the lead in organising a campaign within SACLA to resist all proposed modifications to job colour bars and the industrial relations system. When this failed to generate a sufficiently 'strong' response from the SACLA leadership, the MWU resigned from the Confederation, calling on other like-minded unions to join it in a new co-ordinating body. When this failed to attract sufficient support, the MWU reaffiliated to SACLA in 1980. However, in the same year it sought and obtained permission from the registrar of trade unions to recruit members outside the mining industry. It is currently concentrating its efforts on the iron and steel industries where it is in direct competition with another SACLA affiliate, the SA Iron and Steel and Allied Industries Union.

Within the mining industry itself, where Wiehahn recommended that job colour bars should only be abolished by consensus, the MWU continues to take a hard line. Its congresses have repeatedly pledged the union to '. . . do everything to prevent a black obtaining a blasting certificate in white SA'. On broader political questions, although the MWU and its officers have studiously refrained from making any open affiliations, they have clearly shown their sympathies for parties of the far right, particularly the HNP (see p.153). Paulus, for example, spoke at a number of HNP rallies during the 1981

White Labour Union Organisations		Legislation	
1880s/1890s	Formation of first unions. Based mainly on white wage earners and generally of a 'craft' type dedicated to preserving the interests of skilled workers against 'undercutting' by unskilled workers. Often had racist membership rules and called for job colour bars.		
1907	Formation of South African Industrial Federation (SAIF)		
		1909	Passage of Transvaal Industrial Dispute Prevention Act. Set up negotiating machinery for disputes between employers and 'employees' — the latter defined in the Act so as to exclude 'pass bearing natives'.
1913	Formation of Cape Federation of Labour		
		1914	Introduction, after 1913 and 1914 strikes, of Industrial Disputes Prevention Bill. Passes through House of Assembly but is abandoned in Senate.
1922	Dissolution of SAIF following general strike and armed revolt on the Rand.		

1924		Western Province Federation stays out of SATUC.	Passage of Industrial Conciliation Act, which set up permanent negotiating machinery (Industrial Councils). Employers' organisations and trade unions, not including 'pass bearing natives' as members, given representative status on Industrial Councils.
1925	Formation under tutelage of Dept. of Labour of SA Association of Employees' Organisations, later known as SA Trade Union Council		Industrial Conciliation Act in force. Strikes by white wage earners decline. Industrial Council system established.
1931	SATUC reconstituted as SA Trades and Labour Council	Western Province Federation stays out of SATLC	
1934-36			Formation by members of *Broederbond* and Nationalist Party of 'Christian national' trade union movement. Set up *Nasionale Raad van Trustees*, *Spoorbond* on the railways and began protracted struggle to gain control of Mine Workers' Union and Garment Workers' Union. Industrial Conciliation Act in force

1944		Formation of *Blankewerkersbeskermingsbond* (white workers protection society).
1947	Right wing of SATLC splits away in opposition to Smuts Bill on African trade unions	
1948	'Christian national' faction gains control of Mine Workers' Union which leaves SATLC to join Coordinating Council	Formation of Coordinating Council of Trade Unions
1954	SATLC and W.P. Federation unite to form Trade Union Council of South Africa (TUCSA). Move prompted by fears that prohibition of 'mixed unions' would allow 'undercutting' of whites by coloureds. Left wing forms SACTU on anti-capitalist plaform (see p.329).	Nationalist regime introduces Bill to amend IC Act to allow for statutory job reservation and prohibit 'mixed' i.e. white/coloured unions.
1956	Some TUCSA right wing unions split over TUCSA's stand on ICA 1956. Forms SA Federation of Unions.	Passage of IC Amendment Act incorporating above provisions.

1957	Formation of SA Confederation of Labour (SACLA) attempt to unite all existing non-African union federations. (Pro-apartheid body.) TUCSA leaves in 1958.	
1958	TUCSA SACLA	
1979	Mineworkers' Union leaves SACLA accusing latter of 'selling out the white worker' by not opposing Wiehahn more vigorously. Begins recruiting in iron and steel as well as mining industries.	Publication of Wiehahn Report and introduction of amending legislation (see p.325).
1980	MWU rejoins SACLA after failing to attract other far right unions into a new federation. Continues to try to recruit outside the mining industry.	

election campaign.

Leadership:
    President: Cor de Jager
    General Secretary: P.J. (Arrie) Paulus.

OTHER CLASS ORGANISATIONS

The Afrikaner Broederbond (Afrikaner Brotherhood)[5]

A clandestine and highly exclusive Afrikaner nationalist organisation, the *Broederbond* seeks to act as the 'war council' for the
entire Afrikaner nationalist movement, and co-ordinate and direct
the policies and activities of all Afrikaner political, cultural,
ideological, economic and religious organisations.

The Afrikaner Broederbond (AB) was for many years the central
organising body of Afrikaner nationalism. Its activities were vital
in laying the basis for the coming to power of the Nationalist
Party (NP) in the 1948 election. It was the *Broderbond* which,
in the mid 1940s and through the 'Afrikaner Economic Movement',
first organised the alliance of class forces which the NP was only
able to mobilise politically in 1948.

For much of its history however, the *Broederbond* was a
predominantly petty bourgeois organisation, which fought for
this class's conception of Afrikaner nationalism, the Afrikaner
'*volk*' and 'its' interests. It also always had far stronger roots and
influence in the two northern provinces of the Transvaal and
Orange Free State, than in the Cape Province to the south. This
reflects the different class basis of 'northern' and 'southern'
Afrikaner nationalism. Until recently, the former remained
dominated by the petty bourgeoisie, largely through the *Broederbond* itself, while the latter was largely led by capitalist forces,
mainly through the Cape Nationalist Party (see NP entry, p.139),

The AB played, and continues to play a central role in the
conflicts between the various class forces organised in the Afrikaner
nationalist alliance. These have often tended to take the form of
struggles between the northern-based, petty bourgeois *Broederbond*
and the Cape NP. In the struggles between 'conservative' and
'reformist' factions in the NP after 1978, a new *Broederbond*
leadership under Professor Carel Boshoff reversed its longstanding
policy of exclusive support for the NP in 1981. It was reported
that the formation of a far right opposition party known as

Aksie Eie Toekoms (Action Own Future) took place within the
AB itself (see p.155). The 1982 split in the NP and formation
of the Conservative Party by former AB Chairman, Dr Andries
Treurnicht, have clearly had an impact on the *Broederbond*.
Recent press reports suggest that a struggle for control of the AB
is underway.

The *Broederbond* is organised into 'divisions' of between five and 50 members.
These meet regularly to 'discuss everything to do with Afrikaners, particularly
economic affairs'. An executive council acts as the directing body of the
organisation, and is elected at an annual congress. Nobody can apply to join
the organisation: new members are recruited by existing members, and all
new recruits are thoroughly discussed by all the divisions. In this sense the
AB is a self-chosen elite, which exercises enormous influence through its
network of members. It also has a 'youth' organisation for under 35 year olds,
the *Ruiterwag* (Horseguards), with nearly 5,000 members. It is clear *Broederbond* policy to infiltrate its members into all key organisations in 'national
life', where they are expected to pursue AB policies. This has led to frequent
(but not necessarily correct) allegations, that the *Broederbond* is South
Africa's 'secret government'. It does, however, clearly exercise an enormous
influence through this extensive membership network. Today it has
approximately 12,000 members, including almost every member of the South
African Cabinet, senior state bureaucrats, military officers and businessmen.

The First 30 Years
The *Broederbond* was formed in Johannesburg in June 1918, by a small
group of clerks and clergy, to 'promote the interests of the Afrikaner nation'.
It argued that 'politically and economically the Afrikaner has been reduced
to a slave in the land of his birth' by British imperialist domination, and
involved itself mainly in cultural work and the promotion of the Afrikaans
language. Although it became a secret organisation in 1921, throughout the
1920s it remained a small and generally insignificant group. As an almost
exclusively urban petty bourgeois organisation confined in this period to the
Transvaal, where Afrikaner nationalism was then dominated by emerging
capitalist farmers and was heavily rural in its concerns and orientation, the AB
had no clear conception of its role. It experienced great difficulty in maintaining a stable, disciplined membership.

The abandonment of a republican programme by the Nationalist Party in
1928 began the process of transformation of the AB into the vanguard
organisation of Afrikaner nationalism through its self-conception as 'the
silent moving force in the life of the Afrikaner community'. It extended its
membership to the three other provinces, and set out to capture control of
all existing Afrikaner organisations. This was largely achieved through the
establishment of its self-acknowledged 'public front' in 1928 when the
Broederbond formed the *Federasie van Afrikaanse Kultuurverenigings*

(Federation of Afrikaner Cultural Associations, FAK — see entry p.270).

However, at this stage, the petty bourgeoisie was still a very minor force within a nationalist movement dominated by capitalist farmers. In June 1934, the Nationalist Party split. The majority faction representing capitalist farmers in the northern provinces, 'fused' with the strongly pro-imperialist and pro-monopoly South African Party, now to form the United Party led by the former NP Prime Minister, Gen. J.B.M. Hertzog (see p.157). The minority, representing capitalist farmers and small Afrikaner finance capitalists in the Cape, and the petty bourgeoisie and smaller farmers in the northern provinces, refused to join in 'fusion' and formed the *Gesuiwerde* (Purified) Nationalist Party, led by Dr D.F. Malan.

In the northern provinces, the *Gesuiwerde* NP was extremely weak, particularly in the Transvaal. This reflected the isolation and disorganisation of the northern Afrikaner petty bourgeoisie. In this context, the extra-parliamentary and petty bourgeois *Broederbond* began to emerge as the dominant force in northern Afrikaner nationalism. It reorganised and purged itself, and pursued three clear forms of activity which gave shape to the development of Afrikaner nationalism over the following two decades. First, it engaged in substantial ideological debate, to redefine the ideology of Afrikaner nationalism. Refined through the prism of 'reformed' Calvinism, the emerging *Broederbond* ideology of 'Christian nationalism' embodied a rigid ethnic exclusivism, an anti-British republicanism and a growing concern with developing the principles of 'apartheid'. Outside of the rarified intellectual debates through which this 'Christian nationalism' emerged, the *Broederbond* organised two broad social movements which gave this ideology a concrete class content, and gradually permeated it into the consciousness of Afrikaans-speakers of all classes. Beginning in 1934, the AB initiated a struggle to take over key unions in the white labour movement. Its expressed aim was to wean Afrikaner workers away from established trade unions and white labour-based political organisations and ideologies of class in order to cultivate a mass base for northern Afrikaner nationalism. This was in keeping with a major tenet of its new ideology which argued that 'British imperialism' had subjected Afrikaans-speakers of all classes to oppression and exploitation and that all Afrikaners had identical interests. Any ideology of class, but above all, communism, was an ungodly attack on the 'Afrikaner nation'.

This analysis was given an even clearer class content in the 'Afrikaner Economic Movement', organised jointly by the *Broederbond* and the Cape life assurance company, SANLAM (see entry p.70). Its clearly stated aim was to transform 'the Afrikaner' (i.e. the Afrikaner petty bourgeoisie) 'from a spectator in the business life of the country', into the owners of capital and employers of labour. This attempt to generate a class of Afrikaner financial, industrial and commercial capitalists was to be built on the surplus profits of Afrikaner capitalist farmers and the savings of Afrikaner workers and petty bourgeoisie. Its success thus depended on the mobilisation of an alliance of Afrikaners of all classes.

During the war, in the face of bitter and often violent struggles for

dominance between the two Afrikaner nationalist political organisations,
the NP and the Nazi-inspired *Ossewa Brandwag* (Oxwagon Sentinels), the
Broederbond did succeed in organising an alliance of class forces within the
various organs of the economic movement. This laid the basis for the
Nationalist Party to organise these forces politically in 1948, and so come to
power. But throughout this period, the AB had been involved in conflicts
with the more capitalist oriented Afrikaner nationalists in the Cape, who gave
Afrikaner nationalism a much more openly capitalist interpretation.

The Broederbond Under NP Government
Once the Nationalist Party was in power, the relationship between it and the
Broederbond changed. For the first ten years of NP rule, the *Broederbond*
confined its role largely to providing support for the NP and remained outside
the party political sphere. The first two NP Prime Ministers, D.F. Malan and
J.G. Strijdom, were not leading *Broederbond* members and fought to keep it
out of the growing internal conflicts within the NP. However, with the
accession to the prime ministership of a long time member of the AB executive
council, H.F. Verwoerd, in 1958, the relationship between the NP and the AB
changed. Verwoerd's period of leadership, 1958–66, saw intense class-based
conflicts within Afrikaner nationalism (see NP entry p.142). In these struggles,
Verwoerd relied heavily on the *Broederbond*, then under the leadership of
Dr P.J. Meyer, and used it successfully against his major opponents in the Cape
NP.
   Most visibly, the *Broederbond* was the key mobilising organisation in the
campaign, 1958–60, to turn South Africa into a republic – finally achieved
in May 1961. Less visibly, it was used to check attempts by the Cape NP to
effect minor modifications in apartheid policy, such as its proposal to include
so-called 'coloured' MPs as 'coloured' representatives in parliament. Although
the then leader of the Cape NP, Dr E. Dönges, had long been an important
Broederbond figure, this conflict between the Cape NP leadership and the
dominant Verwoerd/Meyer faction in the *Broederbond*, 1960–6, further
weakened the influence of the AB *vis-à-vis* the Cape NP.
   With the assassination of Verwoerd in September 1966, the factional
conflict in the Afrikaner nationalist class alliance burst open into bitter
struggles between the so-called *verligtes* (moderates) and *verkramptes*
(reactionaries). This essentially pitted groups identified with the interests of
emerging Afrikaner monopoly capital on the one hand against the petty
bourgeoisie, small farmers and white labour on the other (see p.143). The
verkramptes tried to use the AB as their major vehicle to attack *verligtes*.
However, in a long struggle, *verligtes* won the support of centrist elements
around Vorster. This alliance captured control of the AB and then used it
to purge the *verkramptes* both from the NP in 1969, and for those who
joined the newly-formed *Herstigte Nationale Party* (see entry p.153), from the
Broederbond itself in 1972.
   The pro-Vorster, centrist group totally dominated the *Broederbond* in
the period 1970–6. During this period it was converted into a tame support

organisation for Vorster's policies. However, the intensification of the mass challenge to the apartheid state after 1972 and the growing economic crisis after 1975 resulted in a major crisis for the NP, for its dominant Vorster faction and for the capitalist class as a whole. This reopened severe conflict between class forces within the Afrikaner nationalist alliance over the types of policies necessary to deal with the crisis. These conflicts partly gave rise to the 'Muldergate' scandal and the consequent election of P.W. Botha as NP leader and Prime Minister in 1978 (see p.144).

The adoption of the Total Strategy by the Botha regime further intensified these struggles (see p.145). In 1979, in an attempt to weaken the influence of the opposition to his policies within the *Broederbond*, Botha appointed its then Chairman (and leading Botha supporter) Dr Gerrit Viljoen, to the Cabinet. However, this move backfired as it enabled the far right to recapture control of the leadership structures of the *Broederbond*. Under its new Chairman, Professor Carel Boshoff, the *Broederbond* became a major vehicle of far right opposition to the Botha regime. Its long-standing policy of exclusive support for the NP was abandoned, and various organisations, including *Aksie Eie Toekoms*, were formed within the *Broederbond*. Acting through its acknowledged 'public arm', the FAK, the *Broederbond* convened a '*Volkskongress*' (congress of the Afrikaner *volk*) in early 1982, which resoundingly rejected the recommendation by the government appointed de Lange Commission for a modification of apartheid in education. This was widely seen as a triumph for the right.

The split in the NP in early 1982 and the formation of the Conservative Party by former AB Chairman, Andries Treurnicht, has led to a sharp struggle for control of the *Broederbond*. Whilst it is still too early to say which faction is dominant, it does appear that the majority favour remaining within the NP, whilst not necessarily supporting the Botha faction.

Federasie Van Afrikaanse Kultuurvereniginge (Federation of Afrikaans Cultural Associations) (FAK)[6]

The leading and acknowledged 'public arm' of the secret *Afrikaner Broederbond* (see entry p.266), the FAK seeks to provide 'direction' and 'central guidance' to all Afrikaans cultural organisations and to prevent the emergence of a state of 'cultural chaos'. Today, nearly 3,000 cultural, religious, educational and other groupings of various types are affiliated to it.

The FAK was formed in 1929 by the *Broederbond*, and has functioned ever since as its public front. During the 1930s and 1940s, when vigorous ideological and strategic divisions existed within Afrikaner nationalist politics, through the FAK, the *Broederbond* was gradually able to assume a large measure of control over the organised development of Afrikaner culture and guide it along chosen paths. This was crucial to the victory of the Nationalist Party in the elections of 1948.

Particularly important in this regard were three sustained campaigns organised by the FAK. The 'economic movement' after 1939 sought to create a class of Afrikaner capitalists on the basis of the surplus profits of Afrikaner farmers and the savings of Afrikaner workers and petty bourgeoisie. In the process, through the FAK subsidiary, the *Reddingsdaadbond* (Rescue Action Society), the FAK and *Broederbond* were able to weld together an alliance of Afrikaans-speakers of all classes. This laid the basis for the political organisation of this alliance by the Nationalist Party after 1945. Secondly, the FAK's Institute for Christian National Education likewise won much support from Afrikaners of all classes. Its activities were important in undermining the then predominant 'South Africanist' ideology amongst Afrikaans speakers, and its replacement by an ethnically exclusive form of Afrikaner nationalism. And thirdly, through a 'people's [sic] congress on the racial question', the FAK played an important role in propagating the apartheid idea amongst Afrikaans speakers, and spreading its message through all cultural organisations.

Since 1948, the FAK has functioned to provide broad support to the policies of the Nationalist government, and to maintain on a cultural front the alliance of Afrikaans-speaking class forces organised by the NP. In this regard it exercises great influence, particularly over Afrikaner churches. The intense divisions within the ranks of the Nationalist Party and *Broederbond* after 1966 also affected the FAK. However, as the main public front of the *Broederbond*, the FAK has followed its line and implemented in public the policies secretly arrived at in the *Broederbond*.

Most recently the FAK organised a '*Volkskongress*' (people's congress) on education, with the clear aim to counter moves to 'reform' apartheid in education. The congress firmly committed itself to the maintenance of apartheid in education. This was a clear intervention in the struggles within the Nationalist Party, in which the *Broederbond* leadership lined up against the Botha faction of the NP. The future policy direction of the FAK depends on the outcomes of struggles within the *Broederbond*.

The Dutch Reformed Churches[7]

The term 'Dutch Reformed churches' (DRCs) refers collectively to the three major Afrikaner Calvinist churches in South Africa: these are the *Nederduitse Gereformeerde Kerk* (NGK – The Dutch Reformed Church), and the two smaller groups, the *Gereformeerde Kerk* (GK – Reformed Church) and *Nederduitsche Hervormde Kerk* (NHK – Dutch Reconstituted Church).

The NGK is often referred to as 'the Nationalist Party at prayer'.

> This points to the fact firstly that most white Afrikaners belong
> to one of the DRCs, and secondly that these three churches, but
> particularly the NGK and GK, played and continue to play a
> vital role in the organisation of Afrikaner nationalism and the
> development of its 'Christian nationalist' ideology and apartheid
> policies. Very large numbers of the clergy of all three churches
> are members of the *Broederbond* (see p.266), leading to charges
> that the churches are controlled by this secret organisation. At
> present these churches are deep in crisis.

The history of the Dutch Reformed churches in South Africa goes back to
the first Dutch settlement at the Cape. The NGK was affiliated to the
Reformed Church in Holland and only began to develop an autonomy in the
19th Century. In 1857 it segregated its congregations. At the time, however,
this may have been seen as a temporary retreat forced by 'the weakness of
some' of its adherents. The schism in the NGK, which finally produced the
GK and NHK, was largely the result of the importation of the theological
disputes of Dutch Calvinism into the South African church. These boiled
down to conflicts between an austere Calvinism based on a strict interpretatio
of the fundamentalist theses of the 1618 Synod of Dort on the one hand,
and an evangelical tendency which developed in Holland and South Africa on
the other. In Holland, the former groups were led by a politician/theologian
who was later to have great influence in the elaboration of Afrikaner nationalis
ideology, Abrahan Kuypers. In the latter half of the 19th Century, the South
African Kuyperians left the NGK, which was then under the domination of
the powerful evangelist, Andrew Murray. This schism gave rise to the militantly
Kuyperian GK, whose members are sometimes known as *'Doppers'* (conservatives), and later, the NHK. Both the NHK and GK are largely, though not
exclusively, based in the Transvaal, whilst the much larger NGK is virtually
the 'national' church of Afrikaans-speakers.

The development of first mining, and later industrial and agricultural
capitalism in South Africa after 1870 slowly broke up and transformed the
rural communities on which these churches were based. These processes
created a profound theological crisis for each of these churches, and
eventually gave rise to new forms of class alliance which produced Afrikaner
nationalism and the Nationalist Party. From the start, DRC clergy and the
organised churches themselves played a crucial role in the ideological and
organisational development of Afrikaner nationalism. The very first genuinely
Afrikaner nationalist organisation, *Die Genootskap van Regte Afrikaners* (the
fellowship of genuine Afrikaners), was formed by one of the founders of the
GK, *Dominee* (Reverend) S.J. du Toit and a number of other dominees in
1875. When the Nationalist Party itself was formed in 1914, it was dismissed
by its Afrikaner opponents as 'a bunch of Hollanders and *Doppers*'. Clergy
from the NGK played a crucial leadership role in the NP and other organs of
Afrikaner nationalism. Best known was perhaps Dr D.F. Malan, who resigned

from the pulpit in 1915 to lead the Cape Nationalist Party. Likewise, after the formation of the *Afrikaner Broederbond* in 1918, Dutch Reformed clergy were prominent as members and leaders.

The Churches and the 'Christian Nationalist' Ideology
The theological crisis and conflicts in Afrikaner Calvinism deepened in the 1920s and 1930s. One result was the growing influence of the Kuyperians, both through the officially 'Kuyperian' GK, and through the development of a strong Kuyperian tendency within the NGK. This continuing theological crisis reflected the changes in the class alliances underpinning Afrikaner nationalism. Following growing conflicts in the Nationalist Party in the 1920s, and its split in 1934 (see entry p.138), a small group of largely GK theologians based at the GK University of Potchefstroom, began a detailed redefinition of Afrikaner nationalist ideology in terms of strict Kuyperian theology. In the early 1930s this group was the dominant force in the *Afrikaner Broederbond*. Through their journal *Koers* (Directions), were first worked out the key ideological concepts which later emerged as 'Christian nationalism'. This group was actively assisted by other Kuyperians within the NGK (and the *Broederbond*) and came to collaborate with a non-Kuyperian *'volkskerk'* (people's church) tendency in the NGK.

This form of Calvinism rested on the assumption that 'God wills the differences between Nation and Nation. And He wills these because He has placed before each People a unique destiny, a unique calling', as Dr D.F. Malan preached in 1911. True Christian duty lay in the fulfilling of this divinely ordained destiny. Out of this grew a theological concept of the immutable exclusiveness of all ethnic nationalities, and a notion of the organic solidarity of the 'divinely created' Afrikaner *volk* — elected by God to fulfill a 'unique calling' in Africa. In the 1930s the unity of this 'divinely created' Afrikaner *volk* was wracked by severe class divisions. The Dutch Reformed ideologists of the period launched a full-scale assault on notions of class struggle and the threat of 'communism'. In the words of one: 'In the cities black and white live together. There is no chance of moral development. Where is our religion and our love for the nation? We reject our own people and they shy from our religion . . . The people are easily exploited. They have but one ideal, bread alone is necessary for life, they know not religious and ethnic feeling'. This gave rise to what was termed 'the Calvinist conception of labour' with a central task to 'combat the devouring cancer of class divisions and incorporate every [Afrikaner] worker as an inseparable part of the body of the *volk*'. This was complemented by a strong insistence on class harmony within the *volk*, a notion which was used to justify Afrikaner capitalism in biblical parables: 'Christ loved the wealthy youth who was a capitalist. The Master had no objection to his capital, but to the purposeless and fruitless way he used it. Christ would have him use his capital to help the poor. Service was the great stipulation the Master laid down for Capital.'

These theological notions of an organically united and separate *volk*, bestowed with a divine 'calling' and destined to develop economic control over South Africa, likewise gave rise to the theological justification for apartheid. An official *Broederbond* paper prepared for the 1944 *Volkskongres* on the 'Racial Question' by the Professor of Theology at Potchefstroom University made clear the 'biblical basis' of apartheid. The book of Genesis, Chapter 11, indicated that after the Tower of Babel incident God had imposed a separate existence on nations and divided and distributed them over the face of the earth. Further 'proof' was found in an interpretation of Deuterenomy 32:8 'When the Most High gave the nations their inheritance when he divided the sons of man, He fixed their bounds according to the numbers and sons of God'. Acts 17:26 put the matter beyond doubt: 'From one single stock He not only created the whole human race so that they could occupy the entire earth, but He declared how long each nation should flourish and what the boundaries of its territory should be'. Moreover, God had established a *hierarchy* of nations in which each had its place and destiny. Some nations were intended to be subordinated to, and serve others.

This 'Christian national' vision had then to be sanctified in state power. In the words of another theologian: 'The Afrikaner Capitalist can only find power in cooperation with other Christian ethnic fellows because our existence as a people was threatened in various ways by imperialists, Jews, coloureds, natives, Indians, Afrikaner renegades and so on'. If controlled by Calvinist Afrikaners, the state would then be used as an instrument of 'moral good', to establish the perfect Christian national society.

In these terms, the Dutch Reformed churches gave strong organised support to the various campaigns of the *Broederbond* in the 1930s and 1940s. Clergy played a vital role in the *Broederbond* attack on white trade unions (see p.247) — at one stage a 'Broad Church Committee' was set up to interfere directly in the affairs of the Garment Workers' Union — in the Economic Movement which sought to create a class of Afrikaner capitalists, and in the *Broederbond*'s struggle for 'Christian national' education. Given the central role of the churches in local Afrikaner communities, this political intervention by the DRC's was an important element in mobilising the class alliance of Afrikaans-speakers which put the Nationalist Party into power in May 1948.

The Churches Under NP Rule

During the first 12 years of NP rule, the various DRCs were 'almost constantly busy trying to interpret, formulate, justify, reconcile and pronounce on the matter of Apartheid and the Scriptures' as one Calvinist history put it. Their work provided the basis for the claim that apartheid is a highly 'moral' system. In a real sense, the Dutch Reformed churches were the single most important publicist and apologist for apartheid. Their clergy also continued to play a central role in the *Broederbond*.

However, the growing mass struggles against, and international censure of, apartheid had their effects on these churches and their theology. In December 1960, in the aftermath of the Sharpeville massacre, the World Council of Churches held a meeting at Cottesloe in Johannesburg with the eight affiliated South African churches — which then included the NGK. NGK delegates concurred with a complex final resolution which in effect condemned apartheid and declared that it had no scriptural basis. The NP leadership under Dr Verwoerd saw this as a serious challenge. The full weight of the Nationalist establishment was unleashed to bring the erring theologians into line. Verwoerd's major ally in this conflict was the then editor of the NGK newspaper, Dr A.P. Treurnicht — later to split from the NP to form the Conservative Party. His major critic was the then Moderator of the Transvaal NGK, Dr Beyers Naude. The conflict was wide ranging. It covered both the 'scriptural basis' of apartheid policy and the links between the churches and the *Broederbond*. The NHK felt compelled to set up an internal commission to investigate *Broederbond* influence in its Church. Finally, the AB and NP mainstream re-established control over the three churches. Naude and a number of other clergy were eventually expelled from their churches, and set up the anti-apartheid Christian Institute in 1963 — itself banned in 1977.

These early conflicts presaged the ideological struggle within Afrikaner nationalism, waged between *verkramptes* and *verligtes* throughout the remainder of the 1960s (see p.150). Though the mainstream of these churches continued to follow the official line, a small number of clergy and individual members began to question both isolated aspects of apartheid, particularly the migratory labour system, and the wider apartheid system itself. However, they remained a very small minority within these churches.

An important aspect of these conflicts was the growing distance between the three major Dutch Reformed churches and the various separate churches for blacks set up by the rigidly segregated DRCs. Until the 1970s, these so-called 'daughter' churches had been led by seconded clergy from the 'mother' churches and slavishly reproduced official rationalisations for apartheid. However, this produced rapidly shrinking congregations and a severe crisis for these churches. In the 1970s, a new aggressive black clergy cut the links between the black Reformed churches and the 'mother' DRC, and developed stringent criticisms of the alleged theological basis of apartheid. Some of the most militant Christian critics of apartheid, such as the members of the '*Broederkring*' (Circle of Brothers), led by Dr Allan Boesak, are drawn from this newly emerging black Reformed tradition. At the end of 1982, Boesak was elected as President of the World Council of Reformed Churches, which strongly condemned apartheid as heresy.

The 1960s and 1970s have seen the almost complete international isolation of the DRCs. The NGK left the World Council of Churches in the 1960s objecting to its financial support for African liberation movements. More significantly from its own point of view perhaps, various international Calvinist groupings have consistently condemned their theological justification of apartheid, and the DRCs have now severed almost all international connections.

The growing crisis of the South African state in the 1970s led to attempts within all these churches to condemn apartheid. Relatively influential groups such as the '*Afrikaner Calvinistiese Beweging*' (Afrikaner Calvinist Movement) have strongly denounced apartheid as 'heretical'. Powerful denunciations of the role of the *Broederbond* have also recently been published by important groups in the NGK.

These developments reflect and express the collapse of the ideological cohesion of Afrikaner nationalism over the past decade. The result has been fairly profound crisis within the DRCs. In the post-1978 conflict within the NP, and its split in 1982, the churches have been deeply divided and unable to develop a coherent and unified position.

SABRA (South African Bureau for Racial Affairs)[8]

A *Broederbond*-influenced, pro-apartheid grouping of 'experts' in 'race relations' which played an important role in formulating and propagating an intellectually 'respectable' version of apartheid theory. It is now a leading *verkrampte* group.

SABRA was established by the *Broederbond* in 1947 as an alternative to the liberal South African Institute of Race Relations (see p.418). It drew together *Broederbond* academic theoreticians of apartheid and the theoreticians in the Nationalist Party itself to hammer out a broad policy framework for the Afrikaner nationalist movement.

During the 1950s, SABRA offered broad intellectual support to the ruling Nationalist Party. However, with the accession to power of Dr Hendrick Verwoerd in 1958, the new Prime Minister began to express reservations about the 'flabby' and allegedly 'still liberal-influenced' thinking of the SABRA establishment. In 1960, the year in which the Afrikaner nationalist establishment was temporarily divided over what course to follow against the mass liberation struggle, (i.e. whether to make concessions as argued by the acting-Prime Minister, Paul Sauer, or intensified repression as was the Verwoerd line), the Verwoerd faction engineered a *Broederbond* purge of the SABRA leadership. This purge of SABRA was strongly opposed by leading elements in the Cape NP. They accused Verwoerd of turning SABRA into a third class organisation, the sole purpose of which was to act as an exhuberant exponent of government policy' rather than a 'serious scientific body'. The new SABRA establishment replied that the part of SABRA 'destroyed by Dr Verwoerd needed to be destroyed because it had fallen under the leftist-radical influence of the South African Institute of Race Relations'.

Following this purge, SABRA became the major intellectual power base of the theoreticians of 'pure apartheid'. The resolutions of its congresses regularly called for the speedy implementation of separate development (see p.204) and the reversal of the influx of blacks into the 'white areas'. It followed an extremely aggressive propaganda policy. In 1966 SABRA initiated a continuing programme aimed at white high school students through conferences, congresses and visits to schools by SABRA officials. This programme covered aspects of apartheid theory, 'threats to South Africa' and the preparedness of youth to reject 'foreign' ideologies. Its lecturers included Afrikaner academics, state officials and MPs. The programme, basically conceived and designed by the *Broederbond*, operated in co-operation with a wide network of church, cultural and other organisations.

SABRA did not escape the extreme power struggles between *verligtes* and *verkramptes* which characterised Afrikaner nationalist politics in the mid to late 1960s (see p.142). When *verligtes* captured control of the *Broederbond* in 1970, for a short period they also dominated SABRA. Professor Gerrit Viljoen became Chairman and the organisation began to distinguish between 'crude apartheid' and 'separate development'. Under Professor Viljoen the idea of 'separate parliaments' was first worked out in SABRA and was later taken up in the 'new constitutional dispensation' proposed by the President's Council (see p.136).

By 1972, however, *verkramptes* were again a leading force in SABRA. Viljoen was replaced by Professor Carel Boshoff as Chairman (Boshoff is the son-in-law of former Prime Minister, H.F. Verwoerd). This provoked the resignation from SABRA of seven members of its Western Cape executive, including a former Vice-chairman. This group openly stated that the new executive 'represents an interpretation of policy direction so reactionary that it offers no perspective on the handling of the challenges which social and economic realities will present in the near future . . . it is not possible to accept a massive flow back of Bantu to the homelands. They will always form a great part of the cities'. When Viljoen himself became *Broederbond* Chairman in 1974, the *verligtes* were unable to recapture control of SABRA. It remained as a leading *verkrampte* voice under Boshoff — who replaced Viljoen as *Broederbond* Chairman when the former was appointed to the Cabinet in 1980.

Under Boshoff, SABRA has devoted much of its energies to secure the expulsion of 'surplus' Africans from the cities, without which it sees 'the survival of the White State' as impossible. In 1980 this was developed into a new schema entitled Project Orange — a plan to create an area in 'white' South Africa from which blacks would be permanently excluded. Blacks would only be allowed to 'drive through' this 'white homeland' and partici-pate in congresses or send sports teams there. They would be forbidden to work or live there. This plan was described by Chairman Boshoff as providing 'a secure base for whites in South Africa'. SABRA has criticised the regime's 'Constellation of States' programme on the grounds that it 'would lead to economic and ultimately, political integration'. The long-standing director of SABRA, Dr C.J. Jooste was appointed editor of the Conservative Party Newspaper, *Die Patriot* in 1982 (see p.149).

Chairman: Professor Carel Boshoff.

Afrikaner Studentebond (Afrikaner Students' League) (ASB)[9]

> Right wing and self-acknowledged 'sectional student organisation'
> formed in 1948 and open only to Afrikaners who profess Protestant
> Christianity and identify with the 'Christian national' ideology of
> Afrikaner nationalism. All Afrikaans-language universities, except
> Stellenbosh, and almost all teacher training colleges are currently
> affiliated.

The ASB traces its origins back to the formation of the *Studenten Werda
Komitee* in 1911, whose objectives were to promote the use of and 'love for'
the Afrikaans language among Afrikaans students. In 1916 the *Komitee*
decided to broaden its objectives to include 'championing of Afrikaans
culture', 'the scientific development of its members' and 'the promotion
of general student interests'. A new organisation, the *Afrikaner Studentebond*
was formed.

With the formation in 1924 of The National Union of South African
Students, NUSAS (see p.381), the ASB declined in significance. The Afrikaans
universities affiliated to NUSAS in 1924 and remained in it until 1933. In
that year, a proposal was made at the NUSAS congress to admit the black
university college, Fort Hare. Although this was rejected (Fort Hare was not
admitted to NUSAS until 1945), the issue provided the *Broederbond* with an
opportunity to agitate for a separate, partisan Afrikaner nationalist student
organisation (see *Broederbond* entry p.266). In August 1933, led by P.J.
Meyer (later Chairman of both the *Broederbond* and South African Broadcasting Corporation), all the Afrikaans centres except Stellenbosh (which
stayed in NUSAS until 1936) withdrew. Later in the year, according to the
official folklore, after listening to 'an inspiring' address on 'Nationalism as a
Philosophy of Life' by the NP leader, D.F. Malan , a new organisation – the
Afrikaans-Nasional Studentebond (ANS – Afrikaner National Students'
League) was formed.

During the war years the ANS played an important role in factional
conflicts within Afrikaner nationalism, identifying with the terrorist and
openly pro-Nazi *Ossewa Brandwag* (Oxwagon Sentinels). When the Nationalist
Party of Malan which favoured a parliamentary struggle and a less fervent
pro-Nazi stance broke with the *Ossewa Brandwag* in 1941, the ANS provided
the *Ossewa Brandwag* with its major public platform. The ANS paper,
Wapenskou (Show of Weapons) became its chief mouthpiece.

The ANS's clear identification with the losing faction led to post-war
intervention by the *Broederbond* and Nationalist Party to restructure the
organisation. In 1948, after the NP election victory, Malan called for an end
to factional conflicts within Afrikaner nationalism behind his slogan 'Bring
together those who belong together because of their inner convinctions'.
The ANS was dissolved and the present *Afrikaner Studentebond* (ASB)

formed.

By 1955 the ASB had succeeded in affiliating all Afrikaans language institutions of higher education. For most of the 1950s and early 1960s it slavishly reflected the current line of the Nationalist Party. With the escalation of struggles within the Afrikaner nationalist alliance between *verligtes* and *verkramptes* (see p.150), the position of the ASB became more complex, reflecting the contradictory position of, and pressures on, the intellectuals of Afrikaner nationalism.

In 1968, Stellenbosh University, with its links to Afrikaner monopoly capital and the Cape Nationalist Party and its consequent *verligte* reputation, disaffiliated, accusing the ASB leadership of being *verkrampte*. When the *Herstigte Nasionale Party* was formed in 1969 (see p.153) many ASB leaders were thought to be sympathetic, but in the end the *Bond* remained within the ambit of the Nationalist Party.

For a short time after P.W. Botha's election as premier in 1978, the ASB seemed to be moving in a more *verligte* direction. Its 1979 congress condemned attempts to break up the Crossroads 'squatter' settlement (see p.365). It also called for Afrikaans children to be taught to 'respect blacks' and published a study defining racism as 'a sinful egoistical attitude of racial superiority and prejudice which can take the form of discrimination and Apartism'. It also discussed admitting so-called coloureds as ASB members.

By 1980, however, the ASB had made a sharp turn back to the far right. It rejected the idea of including blacks in the President's Council, and called for the 'upholding of the principle of homogeneity and differentiation'. A considerable number of delegates walked out when the congress was addressed by an *Inkatha* Youth Brigade leader (see p.387) in conformity with the previous year's policy of 'dialogue' with blacks.

In 1981, it was reported that the organisation had been penetrated by far right terrorist groups, the *Wit Kommando* and *Afrikaner Weerstand Beweging* (see p.156), well known members of whom were prominent at the 1981 congress. It is as yet unclear how the 1982 formation of the Conservative Party will affect the line-up of the ASB.

Polstu (Political Students' Organisation)

Verligte student organisation formed by former ASB members opposed to the latter's sharp turn to the right at its 1980 congress (see ASB entry). Among its leaders are a number of personalities prominent in the ASB leadership during its *verligte* phase.

POLSTU describes itself as a non-racial organisation with the sole qualifications for membership being 'Christianity and a loyalty to South Africa . . .'. It also advocates the implementation of a number of 'reforms' to create a society in which 'all people in South Africa' would have 'equal economic and social opportunities, an equal political decision-making right and free association'. Like a number of earlier 'moderate' student organisations, POLSTU sees itself as a centrist organisation whose role is to provide a political home for the 'silent majority' of (white) students not seen to be catered for by the two 'extremist' white student organisations, NUSAS and the ASB (see pp.381 and 271 respectively).

Whereas most of POLSTU's now defunct centrist predecessors were formed by groups to the right of NUSAS on English-speaking campuses, POLSTU was formed by *verligtes* on Afrikaans speaking campuses as a reflection of the wider crisis of Afrikaner nationalist ideology. Its positions, although somewhat more *verligte* than those of the P.W. Botha faction of the Nationalist Party, are basically located within the same ideological framework as the latter's Total Strategy. For that reason POLSTU has received a certain amount of support from *verligte* Nationalists generally. For example, *Die Transvaler* newspaper suggested in a 1980 editorial that POLSTU was 'exactly what students needed' and that it might generate more 'political energy' than the whole ASB congress.

POLSTU appears to have a fair measure of support on Afrikaans campuses, though it has failed to win endorsement either by Student Councils or mass meetings on any Afrikaans campus. It also seems to have some support among certain 'liberal' (as distinct from 'radical') members of the University of the Witwatersrand Students' Representative Council. It has also sought to co-operate with NUSAS on certain issues. The 1981-2 President of NUSAS claimed that his organisation had 'fairly close working relationships' with POLSTU on those select issues in which POLSTU's aims and activities were compatable with the demands of 'a broad democratic movement'.

BIBLIOGRAPHICAL NOTE

General

As in other chapters, much information was gleaned from a regular reading of the following newspapers: *Rand Daily Mail, The Star, Financial Mail, Sunday Times, Sunday Tribune, The Sowetan, ANC Weekly News Briefing,* and *South African Pressclips* (produced by Barry Streek, Cape Town). Moreover, the *Annual Surveys* of the South African Institute of Race Relations and the Briefings section of the *South African Labour Bulletin* all synthesise various developments covered in this chapter. All of the organisations themselves, with the notable exception of the secret *Afrikaner Broederbond*, also produce their own publications.

1. See 'General' above.
   Davies, R., *Capital, State and White Labour in South Africa, 1900-1960,* Brighton, Harvester Press, 1979.

Hepple, A., *South Africa: Workers Under Apartheid*, London, International Defence and Aid Fund, 1971.

Horrel, M., *South African Trade Unionism: A Study of a Divided Working Class*, Johannesburg, South African Institute of Race Relations, 1961.

Meyer, P.J., *Die Stryd van die Afrikaner Werker*, Stellenbosch, Pro-Ecclesia, 1944.

Naude, L., *Dr A. Hertzog, Die Nasionale Party en die Mynwerker*, Pretoria, Nasionale Raad van Trustees, 1969.

O'Meara, D., 'Analysing Afrikaner Nationalism: The "Christian National" Assault on White Trade Unionism in South Africa 1934–1948', *African Affairs*, 77, 306, January 1978.

Walker, I., and Weinbren, B., *2000 Casualties – A History of Trade Unions and the Labour Movement in the Union of South Africa*, Johannesburg, SATUC, 1961.

2. See 'General' above.

Cronje, S., 'Africans and the TUC' *Africa Magazine*, December 1973.

Ensor, L., 'TUCSA's Relations with African Trade Unions – An Attempt at Control' *South African Labour Bulletin*, 3, 4, 1977.

Hepple, op. cit.

Luckhardt, K. and Wall, B., *Organise or Starve! The History of SACTU*, London, Lawrence & Wishart, 1980.

South African Labour Bulletin 5, 6 and 7, 1980, edition on 'Labour Organization and Registration'.

Walker and Weinbren, op. cit.

3. See 'General' above.

Hepple, op. cit.

Horrel, op. cit.

Report of the Commission of Inquiry into Labour Legislation (Wiehahn Report) *Part I*, Pretoria, RP 47/1979.

4. See 'General' above.

Cooper, C., 'The Mineworkers' Strike' *South African Labour Bulletin*, 5, 3, October 1979.

Davies, R., op. cit.

Naude, L., op. cit.

O'Meara, D., op. cit.

Sitas, A., 'Rebels without a Pause: The MWU and the Defence of the Colour Bar' *South African Labour Bulletin*, 5, 3, October 1979.

5. See 'General' above.

Oelofse, J.D., *Die Nederduitsch Hervormde Kerk en die Afrikaner Broederbond*, report submitted to General Synod 23 April 1964.

O'Meara, D., *Volkskapitalisme: Class, Capital and Ideology in the Development of Afrikaner Nationalism 1934–1948*, Cambridge, Cambridge University Press, 1983.

Pelzer, A.N., *Die Afrikaner Broederbond: Eerste 50 Jaar*, Cape Town, Tafelberg, 1979. This is the official history of the *Broederbond*.

Report of the Commission of Inquiry into Secret Organizations (Botha Commission), Pretoria, RP 20/1965.

Serfontein, J.H.P., *Brotherhood of Power*, London, Rex Collings, 1979.

Wilkens, I. and Strydom, H., *The Super Afrikaaners: Inside the Afrikaner Broederbond*, Johannesburg, Jonathan Ball, 1978.

6. See 'General' above.

All the references in note 5.
Federasie van Afrikaanse Kultuurverenigings, *Referate Gelewer by Geleentheid van die Silwerjubileumkongres van die FAK*, Bloemfontein, FAK, 1955.
7. See 'General' above.
Hexham, I., *The Irony of Apartheid*, New York, Edwin Mellen Press, 1981.
de Klerk, W.A., *The Puritans in Africa: The Story of Afrikanerdom*, London, Rex Collings, 1975.
Moodie, T.D., *The Rise of Afrikanerdom: Power, Apartheid and the Afrikaner Civil Religion*, Berkeley, University of California Press, 1975.
8. See 'General' above.
Pienaar, S., *Getuie van Groot Tye*, Cape Town, Tafelberg, 1979.
9. See 'General' above.
Fick, J.C., 'Afrikaner Student Politics — Past and Present' in van der Merwe, H. and Welsh, D. (eds.) *Student Perspectives on South Africa*, Cape Town, David Philip, 1972.

6. Political Organisations of the National Liberation Movement

THE AFRICAN NATIONAL CONGRESS OF SOUTH AFRICA (ANC(SA))[1] *

The African National Congress is the leading force in the national liberation struggle in South Africa. Based principally on an alliance of class forces amongst the nationally oppressed, the ANC seeks to forge a broad non-racial movement of all democratic elements pledged to the overthrow of the apartheid state. Within this alliance it recognises the 'special role' of the working class as the guarantor that the form of national liberation achieved in South Africa is a democratic state in which the wealth and basic resources are 'at the disposal of the people as a whole'.

The ANC was formed in 1912; for almost 50 years it followed a strategy of non-violent resistance. However, in 1961 it adopted the armed struggle as its principal strategic method of struggle. Its military wing, *Umkhonto we Sizwe* (the Spear of the Nation) remains controlled by the political leadership of the organisation, and armed struggle is combined with other forms of mass organisation — both illegal and semi-legal. The last five years have seen a rapid upsurge of ANC activity inside South Africa, both at the military and mass levels, leading the Minister of Law and Order to lament that 'The ANC is everywhere.'

Current Line and Strategy

The programme of demands of the ANC is contained within the Freedom Charter (see Appendix p.286). Adopted by the ANC in 1956, the

*This chapter includes entries on all non-tribalist and non-collaborationist political organisations which themselves claim to play a role in the national liberation struggle. The inclusion of any particular organisation does not necessarily imply that the authors of this book accept their claim to be a force in this struggle.

Charter basically calls for a democratic state, in which the land and wealth of the country is controlled by the people. These demands are cast within a strategic perspective in the 1959 Strategy and Tactics. Here, the 'present stage' of the South African revolution is defined as 'the national liberation of the largest and most oppressed groups – the African People'. This national liberation is clearly distinguished from chauvinism [and the] narrow nationalism of a previous epoch'. Rather, for the ANC, national liberation from colonial oppression is 'bound up with economic emancipation'. Here the 'special role' of the large and experienced working class is seen as crucial in securing a 'speedy progression from formal liberation to genuine and lasting emancipation'.

In the period since 1976, and particularly after 1978, the ANC has combined military actions with mass mobilisation with visible success. Guerrillas of *Umkhonto we Sizwe* have struck in all areas of South Africa (see p.35 for statistics).

The military strategy of the ANC appears to be concentrated on sabotage attacks against strategic economic and military installations – such as the SASOL refinery, power stations, the *Voortrekkerhoogte* military headquarters, the Koeberg nuclear installation – together with other central apartheid institutions such as Administration Boards, pass records offices, police stations etc. However, in a June 1982 interview, the ANC President, Oliver Tambo, hinted that the success and intensity of this sabotage programme will soon permit the launching of a new phase of armed struggle involving 'more and more confrontation with the enemy forces'.

As a complement to the armed struggle, a number of recent semi-legal campaigns have again generated open mass support for the ANC. In recent years, AN flags have been openly displayed at mass rallies and ANC slogans widely used. A example of this, was the adoption of the slogan 'White Republic – no! Forward to a Peoples' Republic' which marked the 1981 mass campaign against the 20th anniversary of the establishment of a republic in South Africa. Perhaps most significantly, the demands of the ANC programme, the Freedom Charter, have been adopted as a basic blueprint for a future democratic South Africa by a very large number of diverse groupings and class forces, ranging from the Black Sash, open trade unions, student organisations, to church bodies (see Chapters 7, 8, and 9). This does not mean that these are ANC-controlled bodies, but rather demonstrates the extent to which the basic demands of the ANC have come to crystallise a broad democratic opposition to the apartheid system. This has been reflected in increasing international recognition of the ANC as the leading revolutionary force in South Africa. A March 1982 meeting of the Frontline States, in effect granted *de facto* recognition to the ANC as the leading force, despite strong historic links between the ruling parties of Tanzania and Zimbabwe and the Pan Africanist Congress (see p.297). Press reports in 1982 indicated that pressure is mounting within the OAU to grant the ANC sole recognition as the South African Liberation movement.

The History of the ANC: Formation and Early Politics

The current leading role of the ANC is a product of its long history. The ANC was formed in 1912 as the South African Native National Congress and changed its name in 1923. Rejecting the hitherto predominantly tribally-based forms of resistance to colonialism, its founders declared that 'We [the African population] are one people'. Their major aim was to forge a united African nation. In its early years, the ANC was a small organisation based on the traditional chiefs and the small African petty bourgeoisie. Its early aims were limited: to constitute a pressure group to oppose the colour bar and promote interests of Africans. Its methods were strictly constitutional — petitions, deputations and propaganda campaigns. Its dominant moderate elements frequently opposed the development of a mass-based and more radical opposition to the state. A brief attempt by a new President-general, J.T. Gumede to transform the ANC into a 'mass anti-imperialist national liberation movement' and to co-operate with the Communist Party after 1927 came to nothing when alarmed conservatives united to defeat what they called 'such communist inspiration'. Gumede was removed from the leadership in 1930. Throughout the 1930s the ANC was virtually inactive.

The Turn to the Masses

The slow transformation of the ANC from a moderate, petty bourgeois pressure group into a mass national liberation movement began in the 1940s under the leadership of a new President-general, Dr A.P. Xuma. The development of a mass, militant working class movement during the war pushed the African petty bourgeoisie into ever more radical positions. A new democratic constitution was adopted in 1943, together with the ANC's first comprehensive political programme. This demanded a redistribution of the land and 'full political rights' — the first time that the ANC had effectively demanded a universal, non-racial franchise. During this period, the ANC also began to co-operate with the Communist Party on key issues, and African Communists began to enter its leadership. Co-operation likewise began with the national organisations of other oppressed groups, especially with the South African Indian Congress (see p.294).

In 1943, the Congress Youth League (CYL) was formed within the ANC. The CYL became an increasingly dominant strategic and ideological influence within the organisation and eventually took over the leadership in 1949. The 'Africanism' of the CYL stressed that white domination would only be overthrown by mass struggles and African self-assertion — a radical departure from the ANC's constitutionalism. In 1949, the Youth League Programme — known as the Programme of Action — was adopted as the programme of the ANC. This emphasised the African right to self-determination under the banner of 'African nationalism' and set out a policy of boycotts, strikes and civil disobedience. The ANC was to be transformed into a mass organisation through the example of passive resistance.

The Programme of Action was eventually implemented in the 1952 'Defiance Campaign Against Unjust Laws'. This aimed to clog the jails, bring the administration of unjust laws to a halt, and to demonstrate to the people the effectiveness of mass non-violent action. Although the Campaign was eventually broken by strong state repression, it had a number of important political effects.

Firstly, it did generate mass support for the ANC. Within a few months its membership rose from 7,000 to nearly 100,000. Secondly, it saw the beginning of organised joint actions with other political groupings. This eventually gave rise to the Congress Alliance – the co-ordinated politics of the ANC, South African Indian Congress, the Coloured People's Congress, the Congress of Democrats (an organisation of democratic whites) and, after 1955, SACTU – under the leadership of the ANC. Thirdly, the Defiance Campaign stimulated strategic rethinking by part of the ANC leadership, particularly the group around the President of the Transvaal ANC, Nelson Mandela. Mandela argued that the ANC must prepare the basis for semi-underground work and put forward the 'M-plan' for the reorganisation of the movement. This was only implemented in certain regions, however, because of strong opposition from more conservative elements. And fourthly, the Defiance Campaign demonstrated the need for a new, popular programme of demands, which would go beyond the Programme of Action.

The latter gave rise to the convening of 'the Congress of the People' by the Congress Alliance in June 1955. Here, the 3,000 delegates from all regions adopted the Freedom Charter as the basic demands of the people of South Africa (see Appendix p.314). The Freedom Charter was adopted by the ANC itself in 1956. As a mass, popular organisation, the ANC now possessed a comprehensive programme drawn up by the people, for a democratic society. The main demands of the Freedom Charter were as follows:

The People Shall Govern
All National Groups have Equal Rights
The People Shall Share in the Country's Wealth
The Land Shall be Shared Among those who work it
All Shall be Equal before the Law
All Shall Enjoy Equal Human Rights
There Shall be Work and Security for All
The Doors of Learning and Culture Shall be Opened
There Shall be Houses, Security and Comfort
There Shall be Peace and Friendship.

The new mass politics of the ANC during the 1950s was evident in a number of other campaigns. Particularly in its attempt to combat the introduction of Bantu Education in 1954 (which was to provoke the Soweto uprising 20 years later), the organisation sought not only to rally popular opposition but began to provide the first forms of alternative educational schemes. These, like other campaigns, were finally broken by ever more stringent state repression – yet the ANC was able to exhibit an increasing capacity to mobilise hundreds of thousands of Africans. This itself began to pose serious questions about the limits of non-violent struggle by the late 1950s, and on the ways in which the ANC should lead the masses.

These changes during the 1950s were not without effect within the organisation. The transformation of the ANC into a mass movement, the formation of the Congress Alliance and the adoption of the Freedom Charter, all provoked fierce internal ideological struggle. A minority right wing faction calling themselves 'Africanists', argued that the new leadership under Chief Albert Luthuli had abandoned the 'genuine' African nationalism of the 1949 Programme of Action and had become the tools of the 'white communists' of the Congress of Democrats. The 'Africanists' opposed joining with the democratic organisations of non-Africans in the Congress Alliance, violently rejected the Freedom Charter – and especially its provision that 'South Africa belongs to all who live in it' and 'socialistic' economic clauses – and opposed what they called general 'leftist influence' in the ANC. Following years of disruptive agitation within the organisation, they finally left the ANC in 1958. Led by R.M. Sobukwe and P.K. Leballo, they formed the Pan Africanist Congress in April 1959 (see entry p.297).

The mass campaigns and radicalisation of the ANC in the 1950s led to increasing state action against it. The 1950 Suppression of Communism Act was explicitly directed not just at the Communist Party but at any mass opposition to the state. In a May Day rally organised by the ANC in 1950 to protest against the Act, a number of workers were shot dead by the police. In the early 1950s, prominent ANC office holders including its Secretary-General, Walter Sisulu, and Deputy-President, Nelson Mandela, were banned from holding office in the organisation, and its President-General, Chief Albert Luthuli was restricted to rural areas of Natal for long periods. Police broke up the 1955 Congress of the People on its second day and confiscated all documents. The following year, the Freedom Charter was used by the state as basis of a charge of treason against 156 leaders of the Congress Alliance. The five year Treason Trial ended in the acquittal of all accused, but had the effect of removing the top ANC leadership from daily political activity at the time of gathering mass struggles. In April 1960, at the height of an ANC anti-pass campaign, and in the wake of the Sharpeville massacre a few days previously, the ANC was declared an 'unlawful organisation'.

The banning of the ANC forced it underground. This eventuality had been forseen as early as 1953 and the 'M-plan' formulated to provide for illegal existence. In some areas, particularly in the Eastern Cape, where the M-plan had long been implemented, the ANC was able to maintain an effective underground operation. In other areas, however, the transition from a highly visible mass organisation to an illegal, clandestine movement proved much less effective. Despite the banning of the organisation, throughout 1960 it continued with efforts to organise legal opposition, in particular an 'all in' conference in Pietermaritzburg, to demonstrate the depth and range of African opposition to the regime.

The Turn to Armed Struggle

The banning of the ANC marked an irrevocable turning point in its history. The mass campaigns of the 1950s had been based on a strategic principle of non-violent resistance (for which the ANC President-General, Chief Luthuli, was awarded the Nobel Peace Prize in 1960). Underlying this was still a belief that sufficient whites could be won over to non-racialism to rid South Africa of apartheid. This vision had been questioned in some quarters in the late 1950s. The reaction of the state in 1960, the bannings, State of Emergency and policy of Prime Minister Verwoerd, to erect 'walls of granite' against attempts to undermine apartheid, finally shifted this non-violent strategy. In 1960 a number of prominent ANC and Congress Alliance leaders were sent abroad to form an external mission under the then Deputy-President, Oliver Tambo. Finally, in 1961, together with the South African Communist Party, ANC leaders formed a military wing, *Umkhonto we Sizwe*, with Nelson Mandela as its Commander-in-Chief. Large numbers of cadres left the country for military training.

The early actions of *Umkhonto* were based mainly on sabotage attacks against state installations. They were designed to prepare the masses for the new, violent means of struggle. Again, the state responded with massive violence, and new Draconian laws. In July 1963 the underground network of the ANC and *Umkhonto* was effectively broken when police captured virtually the entire leadership in a raid on the Rivonia underground headquarters. In the ensuing 'Rivonia trial' a number of the top leadership, including Mandela, Sisulu and Govan Mbeki were sentenced to life imprisonment.

Inside South Africa, the Rivonia trial was followed by a fairly lengthy period of political inaction. The underground machinery had been severely damaged if not destroyed, much of the leadership and the middle level cadres were imprisoned and the ANC was unable immediately to recover the initiative or rebuild itself. For the rest of the 1960s, the external mission of the organisation became the primary focus of the ANC.

In the early 1960s, after the collapse of a short-lived 'South African United Front' with the PAC, the external mission developed a number of basic alliances with other African liberation movements and other international bodies. During this period the ANC was closely identified with FRELIMO, MPLA, PAIGC, SWAPO and ZAPU, all of which at this stage had similar international perspectives and broad positions. Much assistance too was forthcoming from the socialist countries and particularly the Soviet Union.

The major thrust of ANC military activity in the 1960s was the 'Wankie campaigns' of 1967–8. Waged jointly with the forces of ZAPU, these campaign aimed to infiltrate guerrillas into South Africa by traversing Zimbabwe.

However, the guerrillas were soon discovered and a number of major engagements were fought against the Rhodesian security forces. These incursions were eventually contained when the Rhodesians persuaded the South African regime to send in large-scale reinforcements, and very few ANC guerrillas reached South Africa. Criticism of the Wankie campaigns was widespread within and outside the ANC.

At a more general level, the turn to armed struggle itself, and the particular experience of the Wankie campaigns, prompted further ideological development within the ANC. At a consultative conference held at Morogoro in Tanzania in 1969, the previous policy of maintaining separate organisations for various national groups was abandoned and the external mission of the ANC was opened to all democrats. The aims and strategy of the national revolution were defined more clearly — the theory of 'Colonialism of a Special Type' was adopted as official policy. This views South Africa as an 'internal colony' in which the white colonisers exploit the black colonised in a capitalist system. The revolution is then seen as having a number of 'phases'. The broad purpose of the military struggle in the first phase of the revolution was defined as 'the complete political and economic emancipation of all our people' along the lines set out in the Freedom Charter. However, the Strategy and Tactics document adopted at Morogoro lays great stress on 'economic emancipation' and the 'possibility of a speedy transition from formal liberation to genuine and lasting emancipation'. It further stresses the 'special role' of the working class as the guarantor of this transition and one which 'constitutes a reinforcing layer in our struggle for liberation and Socialism'.

This continuing leftward turn provoked a very small faction (known as 'the group of 8') into the formation of the 'ANC (African Nationalist)' in 1975, arguing that the Morogoro decisions led to domination by white leftists and the replacement of genuine nationalism by 'class struggle'. On the other hand, in 1979, another minute faction calling itself the 'Marxist Workers' Tendency in the ANC' argued that the ANC is 'petty bourgeois dominated' and called for it to be transformed into a working class party on a 'socialist programme'. Both the right wing and ultra-leftist sects argue that the ANC is under 'Moscow domination'. The ANC reply to these splinter sects was that it represents an alliance of class forces in this 'present stage' of the South African revolution, and that the main task of this phase is to unite together on as broad as possible a front of democratic, progressive forces to overthrow the apartheid state. Moreover, it argues that its commitment to the nationalisation of the monopoly industries, the large farms and the mines and banks, contained in the Freedom Charter, reveal clearly what sort of South Africa this national liberation movement envisages.

The early 1970s saw a slow upsurge of mass struggles inside South Africa. Two streams were particularly important. First was the steady growth in militancy and organised strength of black workers, who had been relatively passive since the effective state destruction of the internal organisation of SACTU in the mid-1960s. And second was the growth of largely student-based Black Consciousness organisations (see p.302). This growing mass challenge to the state was ignited by the Soweto uprisings of June 1976 and the general strikes which followed. The period since Soweto has seen an unprecedented upsurge in ANC activity at all levels, military and public. The result has been to push the regime into the defensive, behind its Total Strategy (see p.38), and developing military concept of 'area defence' (see p.184).

A crucial element in the regime's response has been intensified repression, directed both at ANC activists and other participants in mass struggles. A number of captured ANC guerrillas have been sentenced to death (unlike the ANC, the apartheid state has refused to ratify the provisions of the Geneva Convention guaranteeing prisoner of war status to combatants in guerrilla warfare). Large numbers of ANC and non-ANC political prisoners have died in police detention. Other activists with ANC connections, such as Griffiths Mxenge, have died in mysterious circumstances. Externally, the regime has initiated the assassination of a number of ANC militants such as Joe Gqabi and Ruth First in southern Africa countries. In various ways it has sought to weaken support from the governments of the region for the ANC. These manoeuvres have ranged from the so-called 'land concession' to Swaziland, destabilisation in most countries, to outright military intervention such as the attack on ANC residences in Matola, Mozambique in January 1981, and in Maseru, Lesotho in December 1982.

Despite this repression and attacks by the apartheid state, ANC activity and support appears to be increasing steadily, leading the regime's Minister of Justice to complain that 'the ANC is everywhere'.

The editor of a pro-apartheid newspaper, *Beeld*, argued in 1982 that the regime would be forced to negotiate with the ANC. The escalation of ANC activity has led to increasing international recognition of the ANC as a likely future governing party from groupings as diverse as the Frontline States and sectors of American business.

Important leaders:
President-General: O.R. Tambo
Secretary-General: A. Nzo
Treasurer-General: T. Nkobi
Nelson Mandela, Walter Sisulu, Govan Mbeki, all serving life sentences, are all key ANC leaders.

THE SOUTH AFRICAN COMMUNIST PARTY (SACP)[2]

An underground, cadre party, the SACP, has the 'supreme aim' of the establishment of a socialist South Africa. Its *immediate* aim is the carrying out of a national democratic revolution to 'overthrow the colonialist state of white supremacy and establish an independent state of national democracy in South Africa'. This national liberation of the people is seen as the 'indispensable' basis for the advance . . . to a socialist and communist future'. The CP is allied in this national revolutionary struggle with the African National Congress (see p.283).

Current Theoretical Line and Strategy

The current programme of the SACP was adopted in 1962. Its central theoretical proposition characterises South Africa as a system of 'Internal Colonialism', — 'the combination of the worst features both of imperialism and of colonialism with a single national frontier', maintained in the interests of all whites, but particularly the monopolies which 'are the real power'. In this 'white colonialist system' the task of the Communist Party 'is to lead the fight for the national liberation of the non-white people, and for the victory of the democratic revolution'. For the CP, the main aims and line of the national democratic revolution are defined in the Freedom Charter. Whilst declaring that the Freedom Charter is 'not a programme for socialism', the party pledges 'unqualified support' for the Charter as 'its aims will answer the pressing and immediate needs of the people and lay the indispensable basis for the advance of our country along non-capitalist lines to a socialist and communist future'.

This perspective implies further cementing the alliance between the CP and the ANC, with the latter as the organisation of an alliance of classes amongst the oppressed. Whilst all classes amongst the black oppressed have an interest in ending national oppression 'they do not share the same goal of the fundamental transformation of a liberated South Africa'. For the CP, 'the inevitable victory of the national liberation movement can only be truly meaningful and guaranteed if the capitalist system of exploitation, which is the true foundation and purpose of racist oppression, is destroyed'. This implies that within the broad alliance for national liberation 'the working class must be the leading revolutionary force. This means that the Party . . . must ensure that the end result of the present phase of our struggle is the winning of People's power and the creation of a state in which the working class in town and countryside, and in alliance with the poor peasants, will be the leading force'.

The current strategy of the CP is based on the armed struggle waged by *Umkhonto we Sizwe* (see p.288). This is seen as a guerrilla struggle under the firm control of the political leadership. Recent issues of the CP journal the *African Communist* have carried a debate on 'arming the masses' and the Party has come out strongly against the insurrectionist strategies advocated by some of its critics.

History 1921–1950

The Communist Party of South Africa (CPSA as it was called until 1950) was formed in July 1921 by the revolutionary wing of the white working-class movement. Much of its early history was characterised by a struggle to resolve for itself the relationship between the national question on one hand, and socialist revolution on the other. This was a question both of theory and of the practical political relationship of the Party and its members to the various national organisations.

The first Programme of the CP defined its immediate goal as 'the overthrow of the capitalist system'. Advanced white workers were seen as the shock troops of this socialist revolution. The questions of racism and national oppression would be solved under the dictatorship of the proletariat, which would free all South Africans from oppression and exploitation. In this vision the national movements were defined as 'bourgeois' organisations, following a reformist rather than revolutionary nationalist path.

By 1928, however, the vast majority of CP members were Africans. After a fierce struggle within the Party over the national question, the Sixth Congress of the Communist International intervened. As a result, the CPSA adopted the position that the national question was at the 'foundation of the revolution', whose moving force was the black peasantry, allied with, and led by, the working class. Under the slogan of 'the independent Native Republic as a stage towards a workers' and peasants' Republic', the CP was now to work within the 'embryonic national movements', especially the ANC, to transform it into a 'fighting nationalist revolutionary organisation against the white bourgeoisie and British imperialists, based on trade unions and peasant organisations etc'.

The period after the adoption of the Native Republic Programme was one of deep sectarianism and membership shrank from 1,750 in 1928 to 150 in 1935. Attempts to influence the ANC, after a brief period of success under the radical Gumede leadership of the ANC 1927–30, floundered when conservative elements captured control of the ANC in 1930. Likewise, great progress in organising African workers into independent trade unions also floundered during the Depression, under intense state repression and the expulsion of most leading trade unionists from the Party. For much of the 1930s, the CP was in decline.

Resuscitation began towards the end of the 1930s, as the CP concentrated on building a united front of all groups (not just the peasants and workers of the 1928 Programme), against fascism. During the Second World War, the intensification of mass struggles at all levels, and particularly the rapid growth of a militant African trade union movement, stimulated the rapid growth of the CPSA. CP candidates were elected to various municipalities, and also to parliament as 'Native Representatives'. Co-operation with the ANC on specific issues, such as the formation of an African Mine Workers' Union, and an anti-pass campaign, began anew.

During this period, the CP resisted attempts by Trotskyist and other groups to by-pass the still largely reformist ANC, and establish a more 'radical' Non-European Unity Movement (see p.310). Leading CP members such as Moses Kotane and J.B. Marks were elected to the ANC National Executive. CP leadership of the trade union struggle during this period culminated in a strike of 100,000 African mineworkers in August 1946. Though the strike did not achieve any of its demands, it significantly altered the direction of the national liberation struggle, leading to a turn to the masses by the ANC.

By the end of the 1940s the CP was moving towards a new theory of the South African revolution. The 1950 Congress argued that 'the distinguishing feature of South Africa is that it combines the characteristics of both an imperialist state and a colony within a single, indivisible geographical, political and economic entity'. This led to the conclusion that '. . . the national organisations must be transformed into a revolutionary party of workers, peasants, intellectuals and petty bourgeoisie . . . in alliance with the class conscious European workers and intellectuals'. This was to be achieved by 'relating the struggle against racial discrimination to the struggle against capitalism by showing that the colour bar is primarily a technique of exploitation for private profit, by emphasising the unity of interests that exist between workers of all races and by ensuring the dominant role of class conscious workers in the national movement'.

In May 1948, the Nationalist Party came to power pledged to 'destroy communism'. The Suppression of Communism Act of 1950 outlawed the Communist Party. Dominated by what its official history terms, 'a certain tendency to legalistic illusions', the CP had taken no effective steps to prepare for illegal work. The Central Executive Committee decided by a majority vote to disband the CP in June 1950. However, most former members remained active within the national and trade union movements, and after some debate, the Party was reformed underground in 1953, now as the South African Communist Party (SACP).

The CP Underground 1953 to the Present

The SACP defined its prime task after 1953 as that of 'combining legal mass work with the illegal work of building the Marxist-Leninist Party'. The re-formation of the CP was not announced publicly until 1960, although a theoretical journal, the *African Communist*, first appeared in 1959. The Party concentrated on working within the various organisations of the Congress Alliance, and transforming them in the direction outlined by the 1950 Central Committee report. This led to frequent attacks by the 'Africanist' element in the ANC, who argued that the Congress Alliance was 'Communist dominated'.

After the banning of the ANC in April 1960, new strategic perspectives were imperative. In 1961, the CP and ANC leaders together formed a military organisation, *Umkhonto we Sizwe* (MK) (Spear of the Nation) to 'carry on the struggle for freedom and democracy by new methods'. Initially, this involved a sabotage campaign, but by 1962 the Party was moving towards a theory of guerrilla war. The formation of MK marked the beginnings of the armed struggle now based on a new formal organisational alliance between the Communist Party and the ANC. The formation of *Umkhonto* was complemented by adopting a new programme at the underground 1962 Congress. This developed the position of 1950 into the 'Theory of Internal Colonialism' (see above p.291) and pledged the Party's support for the immediate demands set out in the Freedom Charter. Here too the Party's conception of guerrilla struggle was elaborated.

Together with the ANC, the SACP suffered a series of reverses in the 1960s. In 1963 the entire High Command of *Umkhonto we Sizwe*, including many senior CP cadres, were arrested at Rivonia, sentenced to long terms of imprisonment, and the underground organisation effectively smashed. In 1966, another crucial CP leader, Braam Fischer, was also sentenced to life imprisonment. The recovery from these blows was slow and only became apparent after the Soweto uprising. An assessment of the current strength of the CP is extremely difficult, given its nature as an underground cadre party allied to the ANC. Critics of both the ultra-left and right have argued that the CP 'controls' the ANC.

On the one hand, nationalists of the PAC and the 'Group of 8', have argued that 'our national struggle has been hijacked by the white communists of the SACP'. On the other hand, various Trotskyist sects have alleged that the CP has abandoned working class politics and developed a petty bourgeois nationalism. To this, the CP replies that as an organisation of overwhelmingly African working class members, its vanguard role consists of strengthening 'the national movement as the major mass organisational force'. As such it retains its separate identity and independence, and works to ensure the leading role of the working class in the national struggle.

Leaders:
Chairman: Dr Yusuf Dadoo
General Secretary: Moses Mabhida
Many important CP leaders are imprisoned.

POLITICAL ORGANISATIONS BASED ON THE INDIAN COMMUNITY: SOUTH AFRICAN INDIAN CONGRESS; NATAL INDIAN CONGRESS; TRANSVAAL ANTI-SA INDIAN COUNCIL COMMITTEES[3]

The first of the above named organisations operated from the 1920s until the mid-1960s, becoming in its later years a member of the ANC-led Congress Alliance. The latter are internally operating progressive organisations formed in the 1970s and 1980s which

> have been prominent in the struggle against the puppet, state-sanctioned South African Indian Council and attempts to 'co-opt' classes within the Indian community as part of the 'Total Strategy'.

Political organisation within the Indian community dates back to the formation of the Natal Indian Congress by Mahatma Gandhi in 1894. The NIC developed the tactic of passive resistance, later used in the independence struggle in India, in campaigns against discriminatory legislation affecting persons of Indian origin. The SA Indian Congress itself was formed in 1920 as a merger of Indian Congresses of Natal, the Transvaal and the Cape.

For nearly a quarter of a century from its foundation, the SA Indian Congress was, like the ANC, dominated by 'moderates' seeking essentially better terms for a petty bourgeois minority within the existing form of state. It began to change, however, following the passage of two laws – the 'Pegging Act' of 1943 and the 'Ghetto Act' of 1946 – by the Smuts government. The former Act prohibited the further acquisition of land in the Durban area by persons of Indian origin; the latter demarcated certain areas in which persons of Indian origin were totally prohibited from owning land.

Although both measures limited property rights and thus hit particularly at petty bourgeois interests, the Acts were correctly seen as the first move in an offensive by the state to intensify the national oppression of all persons of Indian origin. They thus had the effect of mobilising resistance from a broader range of class forces than those most immediately affected.

Within the SA Indian Congress the leadership passed, as in the case of the ANC, to more radical elements favouring mass action. When it became known in 1944 that the then Chairman of the SA Indian Congress, A.I. Kajee, had been negotiating with Smuts for a suspension of the 'Pegging Act' in return for acceptance of a licencing board to 'control' the occupation by Indians of houses formerly occupied by whites, a storm of protest erupted both within the Congress and the Indian community at large. Younger leaders such as Dr Yusuf Dadoo, currently chairman of the SA Communist Party, and Dr G.M. Naicker, denounced the agreement as tantamount to 'voluntary segregation'. They formed an Anti-Segregation Council to agitate for adult suffrage on a common roll. Within a short time, the anti-segregation faction won control of the Congress and Naicker became Chairman of the Natal Indian Congress, whilst Dadoo became President of the Transvaal section. Under its new leadership, the SA Indian Congress organised a number of passive resistance campaigns and a strike of Indian workers and traders in 1946.

Another important development during this period was the search for unity in struggle with other nationally oppressed groups. Prior to 1943 the SA Indian Congress had opposed any such moves. Afterwards, however, it sought to form alliances with organisations representing 'coloureds' and Africans. At first, for a brief period, it sought to do this through the Non-European Unity Movement, (see p.310). However, under the leadership of Dadoo and Naicker, it left the Unity Movement, complaining that its leadership wished to 'isolate the African National Congress' and turned instead to the ANC. An important indication of the new pattern of alliances came in 1947 with the signing of the Xuma-Dadoo-Naicker pact providing for joint action between the SA Indian Congress and the ANC.

The 'radicalisation' of the SA Indian Congress and drive for unity continued after the coming to power of the Nationalist Party regime in 1948. The SA Indian Congress took a prominent part in the Defiance Campaign of 1952 and eventually in 1953 joined with the ANC, the Coloured People's Congress and the Congress of Democrats, to form the Congress Alliance.

Throughout the 1950s and 1960s, the SA Indian Congress participated in all the various struggles waged by the Congress Alliance. A number of its leaders were charged along with leaders of other Congresses in the Treason Trial of 1956–60. With the formation of *Umkhonto we Sizwe* in 1961, a number of SA Indian Congress militants became involved in the sabotage campaign. Not surprisingly, the SA Indian Congress became a victim of the wave of repression launched by the state, particularly after Sharpeville. Although, like SACTU, the SA Indian Congress itself was never banned, many of its leaders were jailed, imprisoned or exiled and its activities paralysed. This remained the situation until 1971, when a group led by Merwa Ramgobin revived the Natal Indian Congress as an internally operating force. The NIC's current President is George Sewpersadh, who was banned between 1972 and 1978, and has since been detained several times.

The NIC has campaigned against the puppet South African Indian Council and against all proposals to incorporate persons of Indian origin in some new 'constitutional dispensation' which excludes other nationally oppressed groups. In 1979 it was prominent in setting up the Anti-Constitutional Proposals Committee, but without doubt its most important activity to date was its role in the campaigns against the elections for the puppet South African Indian Council in 1981.

The NIC took the lead by promoting the establishment of Anti-SAIC committees throughout Natal and the Transvaal. The Anti-SAIC campaign rapidly became a mass movement raising wider issues than the Indian Council. Using the Freedom Charter as its shadow constitution, the Anti-SAIC movement set out as its main ideal the 'uniting of all people interested in a democratic South Africa'. Personalities such as Albertina Sisulu, wife of jailed ANC leader Walter Sisulu, and Albertina Luthuli, widow of former ANC President-General Albert Luthuli, addressed meetings at which ANC symbols were prominent.

In terms of immediate objectives the Anti-SAIC campaign scored a notable success: in the 'elections' held in November 1981, a derisory 10% poll was recorded and in some constituencies the poll was as low as 2%.

In May 1983 the Transvaal Indian Congress was revived. Both the Natal and Transvaal Indian Congresses have been prominent in the establishment of a United Democratic Front to oppose the implementation of the three chamber parliament proposed by the regime (see p.132).

THE PAN AFRICANIST CONGRESS OF AZANIA (PAC)[4]

The PAC is the second organisation recognised by the Organization of African Unity (OAU) as a force in the South African liberation struggle. It was formed in 1959 when the 'Africanist' element left the ANC, claiming that it was controlled by 'leftists' and the whites and Indians of the Congress Alliance, and voicing strong objections to the Freedom Charter. In the 1960s, the PAC officially adopted 'Maoism'. It waged a campaign of vilification against the ANC, the South African Communist Party, and the Soviet Union – which it claimed was manipulating the South African struggle. By 1972 it was pleading for a united front with the ANC, whilst intensifying its attacks on the SACP, 'white Marxist confusionists' and the Soviet Union. In 1978 this also involved a sharp attack on Angola, described by a PAC journal as a 'social-fascist' state.

Based on a strong Pan-Africanist ideology, the PAC identifies its 'ultimate goal' as the achievement of 'Africanist Socialist Democracy'. This is defined politically as 'government of the Africans, by the Africans for the Africans'; economically as 'the rapid extension of industrial development in order to alleviate pressure on the land . . . [and] a policy guaranteeing the most equitable distribution of wealth'; and socially as 'the full development of the human personality'.

After its banning in 1960, the PAC claimed responsibility for a series of attacks by an organisation calling itself *POQO* ('ourselves'). Grandiose plans for an 'armed uprising' in 1963 were 'betrayed' (in the words of an official PAC publication) by its Acting-President, Potlako Leballo, and the remnants of its underground organisation destroyed. Since then the PAC has been best known for its bitter and generally violent internal struggles, involving the death of a number of prominent PAC cadres. Following the murder in 1979 of a member of its Presidential Council by loyalists of another faction, the then Chairman of the PAC told the OAU Liberation Committee that the PAC had split into 'two well-armed factions waging open war against each other', and that gangsterism and gross indiscipline were rife in the organisation. An attempt to purge and restructure the PAC under a new Chairman, John Pokela – appointed in 1981 – has not ended the violent struggles. A member of its Central Committee resigned in 1982 claiming that there were, 'irreconcilable differences' in the leadership, and that the PAC was 'falling apart'.

Early Roots

The roots of the PAC go back to the formation of the 'Africanist' movement
within the ANC Youth League in the 1940s (see p.285). While the Youth
League's 'Africanism' represented a number of different tendencies, the PAC
stood firmly in the tradition of its strongly individualist and strongly anti-
communist trend. The adoption of the Youth League's Programme of Action
as the official ANC Programme in 1949 marked the first step in a move
towards the masses by the ANC. However, the direction this took in the 1950s
– involving organisational co-operation with other democratic movements,
institutionalised in the Congress Alliance, a growing stress on the organisation
of African workers and finally the adoption of the Freedom Charter by the
ANC as its official programme in 1956 – aroused very sharp opposition. A
small faction led by Potlako Leballo, A.P. Mda and Robert Sobukwe, labelled
themselves 'Africanist' and launched a fierce struggle within the ANC for a
policy of 'authentic African nationalism'.

Their differences with the mainstream of Congress were many. They
charged that the 'nationalist' orientation of the ANC's 1949 Programme of
Action had been abandoned by a new 'leftist' leadership under Chief Luthuli.
They were violently opposed to the formation of the Congress Alliance,
alleging that whites and Indians had taken over the direction of the struggle
and that these 'aliens' were interested only in preventing the 'indigenous'
African majority gaining their rightful control of 'Azania' (as they termed
South Africa). This was mingled with a militant anti-communism, and the
allegation that due to the 'infiltration' of the ANC by the allegedly 'white'
Communist Party – through the Congress of Democrats – the genuine
nationalist struggle had been hijacked. In the words of Potlako Leballo,
later to be the PAC Acting-President and Chairman for some 17 years,
Africans 'know these people to be leftists and when they want to fight for
our rights these people weaken us. This is because they use campaigns for
their own ends and also because the government will not listen to our requests
and demands because of their own outlook.'

These differences were finally concretised in the violent rejection by the
'Africanists' of the Freedom Charter. They objected firstly to its provision
that 'South Africa belongs to all who live in it black and white', and secondly
to the 'leftist' economic clauses of the Charter, which called for the
nationalisation of the mines, banks, monopoly industries and large farms.
A later PAC journal condemned the Charter as 'the most notorious document
ever to be produced in the entire colonial history of Africa. It is a fraudulent
document which attempts to betray the national aspirations of the Black
people of Azania'. Beyond these policy differences, there were wide divergences
on strategy and tactics. Accusing the ANC leadership of inactivity, the
'Africanists' called for 'planned programmatic ACTION'. Opposing the ANC's
economic campaigns, their journal, the *Africanist*, argued that the focus of
this action should be 'our immediate battle for STATUS . . . next year we
are going to put a stop to the terms "Boys and Girls" . . . (in shops) we will

demand OUR STATUS as customers'.

Formation and Strategy

The 'Africanists' were strongest in the Transvaal. When their attempt to take over the Transvaal ANC leadership collapsed in November 1958, they split from the ANC and formed the PAC in April 1959. Its new President, Robert Mangaliso Sobukwe spelled out the PAC's differences with the ANC as follows: 'To us the struggle is a national struggle. Those of the ANC who are its active policy makers, maintain . . . that ours is a class struggle. We are according to them oppressed as WORKERS, both white and black . . .We claim Afrika for the Africans; the ANC claims South Africa for all'. Proclaiming 'Africanism' to be 'a Third Force', its 'historic tasks' were defined in strongly Pan Africanist terms, aiming at the creation of a United States of Afrika', and the achievement of 'Africanist Socialist Democracy'.

The PAC strategy for liberation was based on a perception of the need to bring about a 'mental revolution' amongst Africans, in which they would lose their 'slave mentality'. Its major campaign was therefore the campaign for status. Answering accusations that his organisation was more concerned with status, 'being addressed as Sirs and Mesdames', than the economic plight of the African people, Sobukwe replied that

> such allegations can only come from those who think of the African as an economic animal – as a thing to be fed – and not as a human being . . . [these] people have no idea whatsoever of the African personality.

This status campaign went hand in hand with a powerful rhetorical militancy, which led ANC leaders to accuse the PAC of 'black racialism'.

Throughout 1959 the PAC sought to build an organised base for itself. Its first and only congress was told that it had 31,000 members, but also that apart from the Western Cape, its organisation was extremely weak. The bulk of support for the PAC was drawn from younger elements of the African petty bourgeoisie and lumpenproletarians. The PAC's attempts to organise workers reveal very clearly its class orientation at the time. Its 'Secretary of Labour', J.D. Nyaose formed the Federation of Free African Trade Unions of South Africa (Fofatusa) in June 1959, with the assistance of the anti-communist ICFTU (see p.253). Fofatusa aimed to represent African workers on an 'all-African' basis, in an organisation free from 'leftist infiltration'. It attacked SACTU for its recognition that politics and trade unionism were inseparable in South Africa, and argued that SACTU was the tool of the 'Congress Multiracialists'. Fofatusa affiliated to the ICFTU in 1959, but was never to prove a viable organisation.

The existence of the PAC as a legal organisation was short-lived. After refusing an ANC invitation to join the national anti-pass campaign to begin on March 30 1960, it announced its own such campaign for the 21st of March under the slogan 'no bail, no defence, no fine'. Police opened fire on a PAC demonstration at Sharpeville killing 69 people. Most PAC leaders were arrested when they handed in their passes to the police. In April 1960, together with the ANC, the PAC was declared an unlawful organisation.

PAC Underground and in Exile

Possessing only a skeletal organisation, and with most of its leaders imprisoned, the PAC was unable to organise effectively underground. Its centre of activities shifted to outside South Africa. In 1962 a 'consultative conference' decided to organise for an armed uprising in 1963. Armed attacks on whites and policemen by groups calling themselves *POQO* were claimed to have been organised by the PAC. The planned uprising was 'betrayed' when the Acting-President Leballo (Sobukwe was in prison) called a press conference in Maseru, Basutoland, at which he announced that the PAC had mobilised 150,000 people for an uprising in 1963. Large numbers of PAC supporters were arrested, and a number were sentenced to death for their part in *POQO* attacks. The last known attempt of the PAC to infiltrate guerrillas into South Africa occurred in 1968 when a column of 12 men entered Mozambique. A press statement by Leballo and David Sibeko alerted the regime, and the column disappeared.

The characteristic features of PAC politics in exile have been those of intense sectarianism and bitter internal division. Rapidly forgetting its attacks on 'leftists', class analysis generally, and the 'rigid totalitarianism' for which Sobukwe had condemned Chinese communism in 1959, in the wake of the Sino-Soviet split the PAC officially adopted 'Maoism'. It occasionally labelled itself the 'Marxist-Leninist vanguard party of Azania', but did not produce a coherent class analysis of South African society. For the PAC, South Africa remained a colony in which a 'foreign conqueror' exploited and oppressed the 'indigenous owners'. It continued to uphold the ANC's 1949 Programme of Action as the correct revolutionary programme for South Africa, later expanding this to include the 1928 Programme of the Communist Party, drawn up by the Comintern — ignoring the fact that the latter guaranteed the rights of 'national minorities' (previously anathema to the PAC) and called for an alliance of black and white workers together with the African peasantry and 'revolutionary' petty bourgeoisie against imperialism and its black allies. A new programme entitled the 'New Road of Revolution' was also adopted, but subsequently 'banned' by the Acting-President. Much literature of the PAC makes no reference to this 'programme'.

A central facet of this 1960s 'Maoism' lay in the vilification of the ANC as white and Moscow controlled. Its ally, the SACP was attacked as:

> a handful of false communists whose career and business in life is
> thwarting, frustrating and defeating the unity of our national liberation

movement, preventing the Azanian Revolution, oppressing some African leaders in the Azanian struggle and ensuring the permanence of white supremacy and privilege in our country. The SACP has never done a stitch of good work in our country throughout its years of existence. Having failed to bring us liberation, it is perpetually making certain that nobody else will do so. It is reactionary through and through.

Together with this sharp sectarianism went a claim that the PAC virtually controlled the Black Consciousness movement. This was allegedly shown by the use of the PAC name for South Africa — Azania — by the BCM, and in its stress on psychological liberation and exclusion of whites.

Internal Struggles

This sectarianism was complemented by a series of bitter internal struggles which have racked the PAC from 1962 to the present. It is impossible to trace all these. Many centred on the personality, politics and financial probity of the Acting-President after 1962, Potlako Leballo.

The most serious of these struggles erupted in 1977 following the arrest, and later trial, of what seemed to have been the entire underground PAC apparatus in South Africa. This caused a deep strategic division within the PAC. One group around the chief of the 'High Command' of the PAC 'army', Templeton Ntantala, favoured a policy of protracted 'peoples' war'. A group around Leballo, allegedly based mainly on new recruits from the Soweto uprising, were said to favour armed confrontations with the apartheid state within the cities of South Africa. The Leballo group engineered a coup, and despite their minority position within the PAC central committee, expelled the Ntantala faction. This latter group then formed itself into the Azanian People's Revolutionary Party (APRP) and claimed that Leballo and at least two other members of the PAC Central Committee had long been in the pay of various western intelligence groups.

In May 1979, Leballo's hitherto closest allies, David Sibeko and Vusi Make finally engineered their own coup. Leballo was removed from the chairmanship (which he had assumed after the death of Sobukwe in 1978) and replaced by a three-man 'Presidential Council'. A month later, a member of this Council, Sibeko, was assassinated by pro-Leballo elements. The new PAC Chairman, Vusi Make told the Liberation Committee of the OAU that the PAC was split into two well-armed warring factions and that gangsterism and indiscipline were rife within the organisation. Attempts were made to purge all Leballo supporters, but without much success. In early 1981, Make was himself replaced as Chairman by John Pokela, and a reorganisation of the PAC announced. The APRP members were readmitted, but Leballo apparently retained strong support within the PAC camps. A number of attempts on the life of Pokela have been reported (and not all of them denied). In April 1982, former SASO President and the then PAC Director of Foreign Affairs and permanent UN Representative, Henry Isaacs, resigned from the Central Committee and the PAC claiming that 'irreconciliable differences' in the leadership were leading to the 'falling apart' of the PAC.

The organisation is now in profound crisis. Since the 1960s the organisation has shown no signs of an effective presence inside South Africa and its recognition by the OAU as a 'South African Liberation Movement' is in jeopardy. The Frontline States have effectively ignored it, despite historic links between the PAC and the ruling parties in Zimbabwe and Tanzania. Throughout the growing disintegration of the PAC in the 1970s, it has advocated a 'united front' of all 'African revolutionaries'. This position received strong support from Nigeria, Libya, Tanzania and other states within the OAU. At one stage, in 1979, unity of the ANC and PAC was formally recommended by the OAU Liberation Committee. The beleagured Pokela leadership continues to advocate this programme, claiming that it is presently involved in talks about the creation of a united guerrilla front with the ANC. (However, it continues bitter attacks on the ANC programme, its ally the SACP, and 'white Marxist confusionists' within the ANC.) This is hotly denied by the ANC, which, since the failure of a short-lived 'United Front' in the 1960s, has refused to countenance joining the 'splittist forces' of the PAC, arguing that it was not the ANC's task 'to carry PAC people on its back into the battle front'.

THE BLACK CONSCIOUSNESS MOVEMENT (BCM)[5]

The term conventionally used to describe both the ideology of 'Black Consciousness' developed primarily by black students after 1968, and the various organisations and groupings which sprang up in its wake, until the banning of all major BC organisations in October 1977.

The central tenet of Black Consciousness held that Blacks (by which was meant Africans, Indians and so-called coloureds), had to liberate themselves psychologically and shed the slave mentality induced both by institutionalised racism and white liberalism. This implied a rejection of all 'white', i.e. Eurocentric, values and the inculcation of a positive 'black' world view. Only blacks could liberate blacks through the harnessing of the collective energies of all blacks in 'solidarity-in-action'.

All Black Consciousness organisations accepted the proposition that 'in all matters relating to the struggle towards realising our aspirations, whites must be excluded'. This was eventually concretised in a 30 point 'Black Communalism' programme, adopted in April 1976.

Throughout the period from its inception in 1969 to the banning of all the then existing BC organisations in October 1977, the BCM was based primarily on the urban black petty bourgeoisie. It did seek, however, to develop a wider base in the community. As a loose amalgam of organisations and tendencies, the BCM always assumed a contradictory character; some BC organisations and prominent leaders frequently gave vent to reformist and pro-capitalist sentiments and encouraged the growth of black business. On the other hand, the BCM came to mobilise militant, and sometimes mass, opposition to the apartheid regime – seen most clearly in its central influence in the Soweto uprisings of June 1976. Shortly before the October 1977 bannings of all BC organisations, certain elements were moving towards an analysis of South African capitalism in class terms and open support for the liberation movement. The BCM played a vital role in shattering the long period of political passivity which followed the smashing of the underground organisation of the liberation movement in 1964.

Following the banning of the Black Consciousness organisations in 1977, new organisations developed. While one of these (AZAPO – see p.308) remains largely within the formulations and prescriptions of the old BCM, other and particularly student organisations have now acknowledged that BC was an important stage in the development of an analysis for liberation, but one which has now been superceded by a class analysis of South African capitalism (see entries on AZASO and COSAS, pp.308 and 371). Finally a small rump established an exile group known as the Black Consciousness Movement of Azania (BCMA).

Formation and Early Development: 1969–1972

The Black Consciousness movement emerged in the late 1960s with the birth of the South African Students Organisation (SASO) in 1969. Dominated by a new generation of student activists, it marked the first break in the long period of political passivity after the suppression of the liberation movement in the early 1960s. SASO was formed by black students previously affiliated to the National Union of South Africa Students (NUSAS), but who had grown tired of what they saw as the paternalism of its dominant liberalism and its major concern with issues affecting white students. As one spokesman put it: 'It does not help us to see several quiet black faces in a multi-racial gathering which ultimately concentrates on what the white students believe are the needs of black students'. SASO initially recognised NUSAS as the national students' organisation, but withdrew completely in 1970 to unite black students to confront the problems they encountered both as students and as part of the oppressed community. It pledged to promote community awareness, capabilities, achievement and pride.

For its first three years of existence, SASO's major focus was on winning the support of all black students. This was primarily achieved through mobilising students in terms of the emerging Black Consciousness philosophy. Black Consciousness was described as:

> an irreversible process of self-understanding and self-assertiveness of black people in the face of an oppressive socio-political structure imposed by the white government; a philosophy that translates itself into active opposition to government policies intent on estranging black people from themselves and therefore an active resistance to every form of injustice meted out to blacks, a philosophy which expresses and ensures black solidarity.

This implied a rigid exclusion of all whites from participating in its activities; the role of sympathetic whites was 'to fight for their own freedom, educate their white brothers and serve as lubricating material'.

This early period of the development of BC was marked by intense ideological discussions. SASO's members came from varied political backgrounds ranging from the ANC, the PAC, Unity Movement and the Liberal and Progressive parties. The role and policies of all these groups were hotly debated by the new black student leadership. The line which eventually emerged reflected a number of different political tendencies. However, the dominant tendency took a sharply anti-class line. This was best summed up by the late Steve Biko, sometimes known as 'the father of Black Consciousness': '[some people] tell us that the situation is a class struggle rather than a race one. Let them go to Van Tonder in the Free State and tell him this. We believe we know what the problem is and will stick by our findings'.

Turn to the Community: 1972–1975

The emergence of SASO was at first mistakenly welcomed by the state as a manifestation of 'separate development' theory. As a result, SASO was given a measure of official recognition at the strictly controlled black universities, teacher training colleges and seminaries. However, the organisation's increasingly militant posture and anti-state rhetoric brought head-on confrontation in 1972. A militant speech by an important SASO leader, Onkgopotse Tiro, led to massive student expulsions and prolonged students' strikes on all black campuses. The result was to propel SASO into attempts to move out of its narrow student base. Its 1972 conference discussed 'at length, the gulf between the intellectual elite and the people of the ordinary black community'.

A number of new organisations were formed to implement closer community links. The Black Peoples's Convention (BPC) was established as a general political wing of the BCM. Its early aims were limited to inculcating black pride and self-help, to break the white stranglehold on privilege and opportunity, eradicate racial prejudice and create a truly 'plural society in which all shall be equal before the law'.

Following the 1972–3 strikes in Durban, the Black Allied Workers' Union (BAWU) was set up on an explicitly Black Consciousness programme to win workers' support for the movement. BAWU was strongly opposed to mobilising workers in terms of their class interests, but emphasised rather their common oppression with all blacks. Stressing the personal development of workers, BAWU argued that it was not its intention 'to hold the economy of the country to ransom by organising illegal strikes and making unreasonable demands for political reasons, but to raise the productivity of black workers by sponsoring training courses and training centres for black youth'.

Despite extravagant membership claims and strong financial support from the US Labor Movement (AFL-CIO), BAWU never emerged as a significant force in the mushrooming trade union movement of the period. Its General Secretary, Drake Koka, had strong links with various social-democratic organisations in Europe, and particularly, West Germany.

The post-1972 turn to the community also saw the establishment of the Black Community Programmes. These aimed to generate self-help programmes especially in the rural areas, and thus to forge links of 'solidarity in action' between urban intellectuals and 'the ordinary black people'. Other important areas of BC activity during this period were in theatre and other cultural programmes and the elaboration of 'Black Theology'. This latter was based on the question that 'in terms of our own experience as blacks in South Africa, to what extent is Jesus Christ identified with the plight of the black oppressed masses?'

The period 1972–5 saw Black Consciousness move out of its narrow student base, to establish itself as perhaps the predominant political influence amongst the black petty bourgeoisie as a whole. Its influence extended far beyond the membership of its own organisations. Even the collaborationist elements which sat in the political structures created by the apartheid regime felt compelled to adopt the terminology of Black Consciousness. Soweto Urban Bantu Councillor David Thebahali, for example, claimed to support BC efforts 'to overcome a feeling of psychological insecurity that had been induced by whites and to stand on their own feet, working for self-help, self reliance and self-determination'.

But the interpretation of these activities differed widely. For some, they were a call to establish black business. Thus in an ironical echo of the strategy of the Afrikaner nationalist *Reddingsdaadbond* of the 1940s, which aimed to establish Afrikaner capital by mobilising all Afrikaners on a nationalist basis, Steve Biko argued:

> we need to take another look at how best to use our own economic power, little as it seems. We must seriously examine the possibility of establishing business cooperatives whose profits will be ploughed back

into community development programmes. We should think along such
lines as the 'buy black' campaign once suggested in Johannesburg and
establish our own banks for the benefit of the community.

The National African Federated Chambers of Commerce (NAFCOC – see
p.119) openly used BC sentiments to attract savings to its African Bank,
arguing that the black businessmen should have prior access to black money:
'The black business sector, although keenly interested in the buying power
of their people, are not in a position to compete against the better trained
and more competitive white retail outlets . . . It is the black people themselves
who must solve this problem'.

The overall economic policy of the mainstream of the BCM was elaborated
in the 'black communalism' programme adopted by the BPC in 1976. This
modified version of traditional African economic life was essentially a
programme for a mixed economy with some state regulation of key sectors.
The state would govern the use of land, set up communal villages and rent
land to private farmers and other institutions. Some centralised planning
would be instituted, 'strategic industries' and 'major corporations' would fall
under state regulation. Private undertakings would also be encouraged. Trade
unions would be recognised on a 'craft basis'.

Some of the different emerging tendencies and conflicts in the BCM came
into the open at a convention called in December 1974 to achieve black
solidarity and outline a 'programme of action for the liberation of blacks'.
At this Black Renaissance Convention, the militants of SASO and BPC
clashed strongly with more moderate delegates. The organising secretary of
the Convention accused them of 'doctrinaire blacker than thou-ism', and of
dividing the conference. By 1975, the very ideological successes of the BCM
and its achievement of a level of 'black solidarity' intensified the strong
contradictions within its often amorphous formulations and prescriptions
and clear strategic divisions emerged.

Its most militant sections remained the students and particularly the
school students organised in the South African Students' Movement (SASM).
With the formation of locally based Students' Representative Councils in
many areas, the BC movement played a crucial role in pushing forward a
struggle against the imposition of the Afrikaans language under Bantu
Education.

The outbreak of the Soweto uprisings in June 1976 led to even deeper
involvement with these committees and the formation of other BC organisations such as the Black Parents' Association (BPA). The Soweto uprisings to
some extent also revealed the limitations of the BCM ideologically and
strategically. Most significant here was the crucial initial failure to organise
the support of hostel-based migrant workers for the students' struggle, a
failure which the police were able to use to manipulate some hostel workers
into violent attacks on the striking students. This was overcome later when a
clear recognition emerged of the need to organise workers in terms of their
own specific interests and positions, and led to two highly successful general

strikes in August and September 1976.

Bannings and the Rethinking of Black Consciousness: Post-1977

The Soweto uprisings and the brutality of the state response crystallised
further political developments within the BC movement. Many individuals
left the country to join the ANC or, on a smaller scale, the PAC. Internally,
it led to a rethinking of the class-race issue. SASO attacked the formation of
the Urban Foundation (see p.122) in October 1976 as an attempt to divide
blacks along class lines. But the clear efforts by the state and monopoly
capital to win the support of the black middle class raised the class issue
squarely within the BCM. The 1976 SASO Congress attacked 'this aspiring
black middle class' for trying 'to compete with capitalistic concerns . . . on
the basis that Black markets should be left to the Black entrepreneurs. All
they are saying is that blacks should be exploited by blacks . . . This black
middle class aligns itself with imperialism.' The conclusion was reached that
the BCM needed to 'look at our struggle not only in terms of colour interests
but also in terms of class interests' — an advance on the bitterly anti-class
positions of the early 1970s.

The Black Consciousness movement had been subject to strong repression
from the early 1970s. In 1972, eight of its leaders were banned, and in
various trials the state has attempted to link the BC movement alternatively
to the ANC, PAC and Communist Party. The most important trial took place
after SASO/BPC ignored a ban on its rally called to celebrate the installation
of a Frelimo-dominated transitional government in Mozambique in September
1974. Nine prominent BC leaders were charged with sedition and ultimately
sentenced to lengthy prison terms. Following the Soweto uprisings, state
action against the BC movement intensified, culminating in the banning of
18 Black Consciousness organisations and a large number of its leaders in
October 1977. The month before the banning, Steve Biko was killed whilst
in police custody.

The period between the Soweto uprisings and the banning of the BC
organisations was in many ways the high point of the black consciousness
movement. It not only produced rapid political rethinking within its ranks,
but also intensified attempts by various imperialist interests to turn the BCM
into a 'third force', as an alternative to the ANC and PAC. While it would be
untrue to suggest that these forces in any way controlled the Black Consciousness movement, the Geneva-based International University Exchange Fund
(IUEF) in particular gave the BC movement a great deal of support as part of
its 'third force strategy'.

The banning of the BC organisations led to new developments: many of
its leading younger cadres left the country to join the ANC or PAC; a minority
group in exile also tried to start an alternative to these two established
organisations. In 1979 the Black Consciousness Movement of South Africa
was formed in London, later changing its name to the BCM of Azania. It

described BC as an 'ideology of liberation', accepted the major role of the working class in the struggle for liberation and recognised the 'necessity for waging a mass-based armed struggle'. Since its inception, however, the BCMA has been rent with internal divisions. Some of its most important leaders have now gone over to the ANC, and the BCMA appears to be a spent force, though it maintains offices in London, New York, Bonn, Lesotho and central Africa.

The internal reorganisation of the BCM began in 1978 with the formation of the Azanian People's Organisation (AZAPO), which itself gave birth to other organisations. However, a clear organisational split has now emerged between those organisations which remain wedded to a strict BC ideology, and others which have come to embrace a class analysis of South Africa and the Freedom Charter, arguing that Black Consciousness has served its purpose and 'we must move forward' (see pp.370-1).

Some of the early and influential leaders of the BC movement were:
Steve Biko (died in detention)
Barney Pityane (in exile)
Harry Nengwenkhulu (in exile)
Goolam Abrams
Strini Moodley (released from Robben Island in 1982)
Aubrey Mokoape (released from Robben Island in 1982).

THE AZANIAN PEOPLE'S ORGANISATION (AZAPO)[6]

> Currently the leading Black Consciousness organisation within
> South Africa, AZAPO is based predominantly on black
> intellectuals and urban petty bourgeoisie.

AZAPO was formed in May 1978 'to fill the leadership gap' after the wholesale banning of all Black Consciousness organisations in October 1977. The executive committee were all detained soon afterwards, and the organisation only really got off the ground in September 1979. AZAPO was conceived as a national organisation. Its five expressed aims were to conscientise and mobilise black workers through Black Consciousness; to work for an education system which 'responds creatively' to the needs of the people; to interpret religion 'as a liberatory philosophy relevant to black struggle'; to expose the exploitative and oppressive apartheid system; and to work for black unity and the 'just distribution of wealth and power to all'.

In pursuit of these aims, AZAPO has tried to organise support activities for various mass struggles, ranging from strikes to rent and bus boycotts. It has also concentrated much effort on organising commemorative activities around important events in the calendar of the national liberation struggle. In mid-

1982, it played a leading co-ordinating role in the organisation of black opposition to, and boycott of, a tour of South Africa by an international soccer team. This united opposition to the infringement of the sports boycott of South Africa was successful in prematurely ending the tour.

From the outset, AZAPO has been marked by sharp internal ideological debate. Its formation conference in May 1978 expressed the need 'to correct the errors of the past black consciousness movement' by taking Black Consciousness to the black masses. However, the definition of the black masses within the organisation has provoked strong differences, leading to the dismissal of the first AZAPO President, Curtis Nkondo, by the Executive. Two issues have been central here — the role of democratic whites in the national liberation struggle, and the relationship between class and national struggles. On the first issue, the majority tendency within AZAPO has clung to the original Black Consciousness line that all whites should be excluded from the national liberation struggle because they are 'part of the problem'. On the class question, in 1980 AZAPO arrived at the uncomfortable compromise position that all blacks are workers and are exploited as such by whites who are all 'capitalists'. This line has now been sharply criticised by other formerly Black Consciousness organisations. Thus in 1982, the students' organisations AZASO and COSAS (see pp.370 and 371) formally abandoned Black Consciousness arguing that it has 'served its purpose' and 'we must move forward'. The organisations committed themselves to 'class analysis' and expressed their support for the demands of the Freedom Charter. They also criticised AZAPO for clinging to Black Consciousness, provoking some conflict between the organisations.

Partly in response to these criticisms, and also provoked by the critique of being isolated from mass struggles, the second AZAPO Congress, held in March 1982, decided to 'speak with the community'. Seeking to go beyond its largely petty bourgeois and Soweto base, AZAPO resolved to strive for 'a big membership'. It is reported to have established branches in the eastern and northern Transvaal, the Vaal complex, the Orange Free State and the Eastern Cape.

From its birth, AZAPO has been subject to state repression. Its first executive committee was detained for a long period. Individual leaders have been forced into exile, where some have joined the ANC. On numerous occasions government ministers have accused AZAPO of furthering the aims of the ANC. The organisation has denied these allegations. Indeed, its Black Consciousness philosophy makes it uncomfortable with the ANC's line to build a non-racial democratic movement to overthrow apartheid and it thus opposes certain provisions of the Freedom Charter. However, AZAPO has acknowledged the 'important role' played by the ANC.

Until 1983 AZAPO did not appear to be making much headway, but at its 1983 conference a number of prominent, former Robben Island political prisoners took over its leadership. These included some of the Black Consciousness leaders imprisoned after the 1975 ' SASO' trial (see p.307), as well as former members of the unity movement. This new leadership has reaffirmed its opposition to the Freedom Charter of the ANC and continues to bar whites from membership of the organisation. Under this new leadership AZAPO can be expected to be more ideologically combative.

Present leadership:
    President: Lybon Mabasa
    Vice-President: Saths Cooper
    National Organiser: Sefako Nyaka
    General Secretary: Muntu Myeza
    Publicity Secretary: Ismael Mkhabela

THE SOUTH AFRICAN YOUTH REVOLUTIONARY COUNCIL (SAYRC)[7]

Also known as the Azanian Youth Revolutionary Council (AYRC), it is based in Nigeria — which was reported in 1981 to be backing the organisation financially. It is made up of those members of the Soweto Student Representative Council (SSRC) who, in the wake of the 1976 Soweto uprising and the banning of the SSRC by the South African government in 1977, fled abroad and did not align themselves with either the ANC or PAC. These elements continued using the name of the SSRC to canvas support in the United States and western Europe, as well as Nigeria and other West African states. In July 1979, Tsietsi Mashinini, the first President of the SSRC, was replaced by Khotso Seatlhoho, and the organisation adopted its present name. The AYRC later claimed to have formed a military wing. The organisation did not, however, appear to be making much progress. It only reappeared in the limelight with the arrest of its President by the security police in 1981 after he had returned to South Africa clandestinely, reportedly along with other members of the AYRC, with the objective of recruiting people to undergo military training.

   In 1982, Khotso Seatlhoho and Mary Loate were tried and convicted under the Terrorism and Internal Security Acts. Seatlhoho was sentenced to ten years imprisonment and Loate to five. Nothing further has been heard of the organisation.

THE UNITY MOVEMENT OF SOUTH AFRICA (UMSA)[8]

Formerly known as the Non-European Unity Movement (NEUM) the Unity Movement was for many years regarded as South Africa's 'Trotskyist' movement. Today it is the smallest of the three organisations claiming to lead the national liberation struggle in

South Africa. Unlike the ANC and PAC, it is not recognised by
the Organization of African Unity, which has been one of the
factors hindering its development of an effective external mission.
Inside South Africa, its remaining base of support is confined to
small groups within the Western Cape. These continue the long-
standing Unity Movement policy of 'boycott' of all racist institutions, and of only selective involvement in mass activity not directly
initiated by itself when it considers this will advance its own
claim to leadership of the liberation struggle.

Formation

The Unity Movement was formed in 1943, in a period of great upsurge
of mass struggles. The rapid development of a militant African trade union
movement, and a spate of strikes, pushed the African petty bourgeoisie into
more radical positions, and affected all classes of the oppressed population.
These processes raised fundamental questions about the character of the
national liberation struggle, the classes which were to lead this struggle, and
its organisational form. During this period, the previously moderate African
National Congress and the South African Indian Congress began to transform
themselves. The Unity Movement was formed by various elements dissatisfied
with the weakness of the ANC, and who sought to build a wider alliance of all
nationally oppressed groups in South Africa, together with various Trotskyist
forces which hoped to build an alternative mass movement to those influenced
by the Communist Party. Concretely, the NEUM was created by a merger of
the All African Convention (AAC – a federal body set up in 1935 to oppose
the state's new Land Act and disenfranchisement of Cape Africans), and a
militant coloured federation known as the Anti-CAD (Anti Coloured Affairs
Department). The South African Indian Congress was also initially associated
with the NEUM. However, reflecting the ideological divisions of the time,
the Indian Congress withdrew from the NEUM in 1944 when its new Dadoo-
Naicker leadership argued that instead of trying to 'isolate the ANC and revive
the defunct AAC', a better approach would be to 'strengthen existing liberatory
organisations by making them live and active bodies'.

Political Line and Strategy up to Sharpeville

The aim of the NEUM was 'the liquidation of the National Oppression of the
Non-Europeans in South Africa, that is the removal of all the disabilities
and the restrictions based on the grounds of race and colour, and acquisition
by the Non-Europeans of all those rights which are at present enjoyed by the
European population'. The founding congress adopted the '10 Point Programme'
calling for equal franchise rights, free and equal education, civil liberties and
personal security, a redivision of the land, and 'revision' of the legal code,

taxation, and labour laws in accordance with the principle of equality.

The Trotskyist elements within the NEUM saw the 10 Point Programme as a series of 'transitional demands', i.e. demands which would win mass support but which the ruling class could not concede, and which would thus generate mass support for the more revolutionary demands of the working class.

To its leadership, the NEUM represented an alliance of class forces. This was to be organised within a federal structure which would both provide for centralised direction and allow the various affiliated organisations and class forces to retain a measure of autonomy. This federal strategy was one of the hallmarks of the NEUM, which was to be open to all groups 'genuinely willing to fight segregation and to accept its programme'. While the organisation advocated unity between all oppressed groups, it insisted on what it called 'principled unity'. It was only willing to accept unity on the basis of its own 10 Point Programme. Its strategic perspective of struggle was based on a notion of 'non-collaboration', organised around the tactic of the boycott of all racist institutions. Prospective members were asked a single question: 'Do you believe in the 10 Point Programme?', and the test of this was 'does he apply the principle of non-collaboration?'.

Throughout its history, despite ambitious claims for mass support, the Unity Movement has remained based predominantly in the Western Cape, with some support in the Transkei in the 1950s. In the 1940s and 1950s, it drew its main support from African teachers organised in the Cape African Teachers' Association which was affiliated to the AAC, and from the predominantly coloured Teachers' League of South Africa.

The three overriding NEUM principles, federalism, 'principled' unity on the 10 Point Programme, and non-collaboration, formed the basis for a vigorous struggle against the ANC and its allied organisations. In 1948, unity talks between the ANC and the AAC (a leading NEUM affiliate) broke down when the ANC rejected federalism, although it accepted both the 10 Point Programme and non-collaboration. Throughout the 1950s the Congress Movement was attacked as 'quislings', and mass action organised by the ANC and its allies was dismissed by the NEUM as 'spectacular stunts' and condemned for being 'unprincipled' and 'unprepared'.

In practice, the NEUM did not involve itself in mass organisation, and confined itself largely to ideological work. Its Anti-CAD wing in particular, under the domination of its Trotskyist leadership, followed what it described as a Marxist line, based on the following proposition: 'We, the non-European oppressed, must never confuse the European worker, aristocrat of labour though he may be today, with the European ruling class'. For the Anti-CAD, economic exploitation, national or colour oppression, sprang from the same root. The white worker must willy-nilly find his real allies — African and coloured workers — on the basis of the 10 Point Programme. The door was to be kept open for white workers as the Anti-CAD had no desire 'to replace the white Herrenvolk by a black Herrenvolk'. This was reflected in the NEUM definition of 'Who constitutes the South African nation? . . . The nation consists of the people who were born in South Africa and have no other country except South Africa as their motherland.' The ANC policy of 'multi-racialism' was criticised for reproducing the theory of four nations (African, coloured, Asian and European) in South Africa.

By the mid-1950s, a split was emerging in the NEUM between a faction loyal to I.B. Tabata (based mainly in the AAC) and that grouped around Hosea Jaffe in the Anti-CAD. The so-called 'Jaffeites' adopted an openly leftwing position, and produced a 'Marxist' critique of the 10 Point Programme, describing it as 'bourgeois'. This brought criticism from the AAC against those who 'saw only class oppression and denied the reality of colour oppression'. Marxist terminology was similarly condemned for exposing the NEUM to possible state repression under the Suppression of Communism Act. In the late 1950s, the Teachers' League which dominated the Anti-CAD, pulled out of the NEUM and 'killed off the Anti-CAD'.

Post-Sharpeville

The split in the NEUM thus took the form of a division between the African leadership of the AAC and the so-called coloured leadership of the Anti-CAD. To counter this, the Tabata leadership formed an individual membership organisation affiliated to the NEUM, in January 1961. This was the African Peoples' Democratic Union of South Africa (APDUSA). APDUSA strongly critcised the 'two-stage' theory of the revolution associated with the Communist Party. Echoing Trotsky's theory of Permanent Revolution, it proclaimed the need for 'an ongoing, uninterrupted revolution'. Its constitution declared that 'the democratic demands and aspirations of the oppressed workers and peasants shall be paramount in the orientation of APDUSA, both in its short term and long term objectives'. Despite the fact that South Africa's rural population has long been effectively proletarianised, APDUSA claims to be the only South African political movement which stresses 'the crucial role' of the peasantry as the 'largest section of the population' and the 'most oppressed and most exploited class'. However, 'it is the leadership of the proletariat in the conduct of the struggle for democratic rights that will ensure the continuity of the revolution — uninterrupted to its socialist goal'.

Neither the NEUM nor any of its affiliated organisations were included in the ban on the ANC and PAC in April 1960. However, the Unity Movement was unable to capitalise on the vacuum in political leadership created by the campaign of state terror in the early 1960s. Some APDUSA militants were imprisoned on Robben Island. Many of its most important leaders left South Africa and petitioned the OAU in vain for recognition as a liberation movement.

Within South Africa the Unity Movement remained a small, Western Cape-based pressure group. It also appeared to maintain some influence within one Cape trade union. In the recent upsurge of mass struggles in South Africa, these remnants of the Unity Movement have rigidly adhered to 'boycott' tactics. They have attacked attempts to build mass-based community organisa-tions and have again concentrated on undermining what they see as ANC influence on emerging mass struggles.

President: I.B. Tabata.

APPENDIX

FREEDOM CHARTER, adopted by the Congress of the People, 26 June 1955
PREAMBLE
We, the people of South Africa, declare for all our country and the world to know:
That South Africa belongs to all who live in it, black and white, and that no government can justly claim authority unless it is based on the will of the people;
That our people have been robbed of their birthright to land, liberty and peace by a form of government founded on injustice and inequality;
That our country will never be prosperous or free until all our people live in brotherhood, enjoying equal rights and opportunities;
That only a democratic state, based on the will of the people can secure to all their birthright without distinction of colour, race, sex or belief;
And therefore, we, the people of South Africa, black and white together — equals, countrymen and brothers — adopt this FREEDOM CHARTER. And we pledge ourselves to strive together, sparing nothing of our strength, and courage, until the democratic changes here set out have been won.

THE PEOPLE SHALL GOVERN!

Every man and woman shall have the right to vote for and stand as a candidate for all bodies which make laws.
All the people shall be entitled to take part in administration of the country.
The rights of the people shall be the same regardless of race, colour or sex.
All bodies of minority rule, advisory boards, councils and authorities shall be replaced by democratic organs of self-government.

ALL NATIONAL GROUPS SHALL HAVE EQUAL RIGHTS!

There shall be equal status in the bodies of state, in the courts and in the schools for all national groups and races;
All national groups shall be protected by law against insults to their race and national pride;
All people shall have equal rights to use their own language and to develop their own folk culture and customs;
The preaching and practice of national, race or colour discrimination and contempt shall be a punishable crime;
All apartheid laws and practices shall be set aside.

THE PEOPLE SHALL SHARE IN THE COUNTRY'S WEALTH!

The national wealth of our country, the heritage of all South Africans, shall
be restored to the people;
The mineral wealth beneath the soil, the banks and monopoly industry shall
be transferred to the ownership of the people as a whole;
All other industries and trade shall be controlled to assist the well-being of
the people;
All people shall have equal rights to trade where they choose, to manufacture
and to enter all trades, crafts and professions.

THE LAND SHALL BE SHARED AMONG THOSE WHO WORK IT!

Restriction of land ownership on a racial basis shall be ended and all the land
re-divided amongst those who work it, to banish famine and land hunger;
The state shall help the peasants with implements, seed, tractors and dams to
save the soil and assist the tillers;
Freedom of movement shall be guaranteed to all who work on the land;
All shall have the right to occupy land wherever they chose;
People shall not be robbed of their cattle, and forced labour and farm prisons
shall be abolished.

ALL SHALL BE EQUAL BEFORE THE LAW!

No one shall be imprisoned, deported or restricted without a fair trial;
No one shall be condemned by the order of any Government official;
The courts shall be representative of all the people;
Imprisonment shall be only for serious crimes against the people, and shall
aim at re-education, not vengeance;
The police force and army shall be open to all on an equal basis and shall be
the helpers and protectors of the people;
All laws which discriminate on grounds of race, colour or belief shall be
repealed.

ALL SHALL ENJOY EQUAL HUMAN RIGHTS!

The law shall guarantee to all their right to speak, to organise, to meet together,
to publish, to preach, to worship, and to educate their children;
The privacy of the house from police raids shall be protected by law;
All shall be free to travel without restriction from countryside to town,
from province to province and from South Africa abroad;
Pass laws, permits and all other laws restricting these freedoms shall be
abolished.

THERE SHALL BE WORK AND SECURITY!

All who work shall be free to form trade unions, to elect their officers and to
make wage agreements with their employers;
The state shall recognise the right and duty of all to work, and to draw full
unemployment benefits;
Men and women of all races shall receive equal pay for equal work;
There shall be a forty-hour working week, a national minimum wage, paid
annual leave and sick leave for all workers and maternity leave on full pay for

all working mothers;

Miners, domestic workers, farm workers and civil servants shall have the same rights as all others who work;

Child labour, compound labour, the tot system and contract labour shall be abolished.

THE DOORS OF LEARNING AND OF CULTURE SHALL BE OPENED!

The government shall discover, develop and encourage national talent for the enhancement of our cultural life;

All the cultural treasures of mankind shall be open to all, by free exchange of books, ideas and contact with other lands;

The aim of education shall be to teach the youth to love their people and their culture, to honour human brotherhood, liberty and peace;

Education shall be free, compulsory, universal and equal for all children;

Higher education and technical training shall be opened to all by means of state allowances and scholarships awarded on the basis of merit;

Adult illiteracy shall be ended by a mass state education plan;

Teachers shall have all the rights of other citizens;

The colour bar in cultural life, in sport and in education shall be abolished.

THERE SHALL BE HOUSES, SECURITY AND COMFORT!

All people shall have the right to live where they choose, to be decently housed, and to bring up their families in comfort and security;

Unused housing space to be made available to the people;

Rent and prices shall be lowered, food plentiful and no one shall go hungry,

A preventive health scheme shall be run by the state;

Free medical care and hospitalisation shall be provided for all, with special care for mothers and young children;

Slums shall be demolished and new suburbs built where all have transport, roads, lighting, playing fields, creches and social centres;

The aged, the orphans, the disabled and the sick shall be cared for by the state;

Rest, leisure and recreation shall be the right of all;

Fenced locations and ghettos shall be abolished, and laws which break up families shall be repealed.

THERE SHALL BE PEACE AND FRIENDSHIP!

South Africa shall be a fully independent state, which respects the rights and sovereignty of all nations;

South Africa shall strive to maintain world peace and the settlement of all international disputes by negotiation — not war;

Peace and friendship amongst all our people shall be secured by upholding the equal rights, opportunities and status of all;

The people of the protectorates — Basutoland, Bechuanaland and Swaziland — shall be free to decide for themselves their own future;

The right of all the peoples of Africa to independence and self government shall be recognised, and shall be the basis of close cooperation.

Let all who love their people and their country now say, as we say here:
'THESE FREEDOMS WE WILL FIGHT FOR, SIDE BY SIDE, THROUGH-
OUT OUR LIVES, UNTIL WE HAVE WON OUR LIBERTY.'

BIBLIOGRAPHICAL NOTE

General

The best general historical overview of the trends in the development of the
liberation movement is H.J. and R.E. Simons, *Class and Colour in South
Africa, 1850–1950*, Harmondsworth, Penguin, 1969. A different perspective
on these developments is found in I.B. Tabata, *The All African Convention:
The Awakening of a People*, Johannesburg, Peoples' Press, 1950 (republished
in 1974, by Spokesman, Nottingham). These two books cover the period up
to the 1950s. The four volume series, *From Protest to Challenge*, edited by
T. Karis, and G. Carter contains a valuable if uneven collection of documents
of the major movements up to 1964. This series also has a useful bibliography
and chronology. A detailed analysis of the 1950s is found in T. Lodge, *Black
Politics in South Africa Since 1945*, Johannesburg, Ravan Press, 1983.

During the 1940s and 1950s various elements of the Congress Movement
published newspapers and journals. Important among these were: the *Guardian*
(banned but published under various other titles, most importantly, *New Age*);
Inkululeko; Freedom; Fighting Talk; Africa South. The 'Africanist' element
in the ANC published irregularly the *Africanist*. The Teachers' League publication, the *Torch*, generally reflected the positions of the NEUM. The specific
references cited in this chapter are divided into a) the sources used to write
the entry, and b) material for those who wish to pursue further reading.

Specific entries:
1. a) See 'General' above.
     ANC, *ANC Speaks: Documents and Statements of the African National
     Congress 1955–1976*, 1977.
     ANC, *Unity in Action: A History of the African National Congress
     1912–1982*, London, 1982.
     O'Meara, D., *Class and Nationalism in African Resistance: Secondary
     Industrialisation and the Development of Mass Nationalism in South
     Africa 1930–1950*, M.A. dissertation, Sussex University, 1973.
     Walshe, P., *The Rise of African Nationalism in South Africa: The African
     National Congress 1912–1952*, London, Hurst, 1970.
   b) *Sechaba* (official organ of the ANC).
     Dawn (organ of *Umkhonto we Sizwe* – military wing of the ANC).
     Mayibuye (an ANC journal).
     Voice of Women (VOW) (organ of the Women's Section of the ANC).
     The *African Communist* (organ of the South African Communist Party).
2. a) See 'General' above.
     Bunting, B., *Moses Kotane: South African Revolutionary*, London,
     Inkululeko Publications, 1975.
     Lerumo, A., *Fifty Fighting Years*, London, Inkululeko Publications,

1972 (the official history of the SACP).

SACP, *South African Communists Speak, 1915–1980*, London, Inkululeko Publications, 1981. (Basic documents of the SACP.)

b) The *African Communist* (SACP organ).

Inkululeko (contemporary SACP underground publication in South Africa).

Brooks, A.K., *From Class Struggle to National Liberation: The Communist Party of South Africa 1940–1950*, M.A. dissertation, Sussex University, 1967.

3. a) See 'General' above.

Helman, E. (ed.), *Handbook of Race Relations in South Africa*, London Oxford University Press, 1949.

Lerumo, A., op. cit.

South African Institute of Race Relations, *Survey of Race Relations in South Africa*, Johannesburg, SAIRR, annual.

b) Pahad, E., *The Development of Indian Political Movements in South Africa, 1924–1946*, D. Phil. dissertation, Sussex University, 1972.

Ginwala, F., *Class Consciousness and Control*, D. Phil, Oxford University 1975.

Tayal, M., 'Ideology in Organised Indian Politics 1890–1948', paper to conference on South Africa in the Comparative Study of Class, Race and Nationalism', SSRC, New York, 1982.

4. a) See 'General' above.

Gibson, R., *African Liberation Movements*, London, Oxford University Press, 1970.

Ikwezi (pro-PAC journal published in London).

PAC, *Policy and Programme of the PAC*, Dar es Salaam, n.d.

PAC, *Pan Africanist Congress of Azania: Two Official Documents and an Interview with Theo Bidi of the PAC*, New York, n.d.

PAC, *One Azania, One Nation, One People: Speeches and Documents of the Pan Africanist Congress*, Quebec, 1977.

Ntantala, T., 'The Crisis in the PAC' Dar es Salaam, mimeo, 1977.

b) *Azania News* (PAC organ).

The *Africanist* (PAC journal).

Gerhardt, G.M., *Black Power in South Africa*, Berkeley, University of California Press, 1978.

5. a) See 'General' above.

Black Community Programmes, *Black Review*, Lovedale, Lovedale Press (annual published between 1974 and 1977).

Nengwekhulu, H.R., 'The Meaning of Black Consciousness in the Struggle for Liberation in South Africa', in D.L. Cohen and J. Daniel (eds.), *Political Economy of Africa*, London, Longman, 1981.

No Sizwe, *One Azania, One Nation: The National Question in South Africa*, London, Zed Press, 1979.

South African Institute of Race Relations, *Survey of Race Relations in South Africa*, Johannesburg, annual.

van Der Merwe, H. and Welsh, D., *Student Perspectives on South Africa*, Cape Town, David Philip, 1972.

b) Biko, S., *The Testimony of Steve Biko, Black Consciousness in South Africa*, London, Granada, 1979.

Gerhardt, G.M., op. cit.

6. a) See 'General' above,
South African Institute of Race Relations, *Survey of Race Relations in South Africa,* Johannesburg, annual.
  b) The *Sowetan.*
ANC Weekly News Briefings.
7. a) Ibid.
8. a) See 'General' above.
APDUSA, June 1980.
No Sizwe, op. cit.
Simons, H.J. and R.E., op. cit.
Tabata, I.B., op. cit. (the official history by UMSA).
  b) *APDUSA* (journal of major remaining UMSA affiliates).

7. Democratic Trade Unions

INTRODUCTION

As indicated in Chapter 5, the South African trade union movement is divided into two distinct sections. First there are unions based mainly on white labour, but also to a lesser extent on a minority of more skilled so-called 'coloured' and Indian workers. These unions have fought for privileges for a minority of workers within the apartheid cheap labour system. Until very recently they have either totally excluded Africans from membership, or, as in the case of TUCSA (see p.250) confined them to separate 'parallel' organisations. These unions have generally fought for some form or other of job colour bar and have supported in various ways the racially exclusive form of state. These organisations are discussed on pp.241–65.

This chapter deals with a different group of unions – those based mainly on African workers, and which are not subsidiary organisations of racist unions*. Until 1979, such unions were totally excluded from the 'industrial conciliation' system. Today, although based mainly on African workers, with some notable exceptions, these unions are open to, and in many cases actually include, members of other races. For that reason they are better described as democratic unions rather than African unions. These unions differ from each other in a number of ways: some are general unions, others industrial unions; some belong to federations, others are unaffiliated; some emphasise factory floor organisation, others the need to build links with community organisations; some have tended to limit themselves to economic struggles, while others have grappled in various ways with the problem of how trade unions can contribute to the development of working-class political practices articulated within the broader liberation struggle. This chapter does not categorise the democratic unions. Rather, it presents basic information about the policies and practices of the most important existing such unions. The list presented here is not exhaustive – a number of smaller, but important, democratic unions are not covered.

---

* For this reason, although TUCSA 'parallels' have a large African membership, they are treated as organisations supportive of the ruling class and discussed in Chapter 6.

Before dealing with the individual unions, an outline of the history of democratic trade unionism in South Africa is given in order to present some of the central issues now facing the democratic trade union movement.

THE HISTORY OF DEMOCRATIC TRADE UNIONISM IN SOUTH AFRICA[1]

Growth and Repression, 1920–1970

Large scale trade union organisation among black workers dates back to the 1920s. Prior to this there had been a number of strikes by black workers, but attempts to organise them into unions had been sporadic and largely unsuccessful. The exception was a small number of so-called 'coloured' artisans who had been admitted into white-controlled craft unions in the Western Cape since the end of the 19th Century.

The first major trade union embracing black workers was a general union open to workers in all industries and of all races – the Industrial and Commercial Workers' Union of Africa (ICU). The impetus to its formation came from a successful strike by dockers and railwaymen in 1919. In July 1920, the ICU held its opening congress in Bloemfontein, and in 1921 elected Clements Kadalie as National Secretary. The ICU grew extremely rapidly; by the mid-1920s it was clearly the largest and most influential organisation of the oppressed, claiming 100,000 members. However, it declined equally rapidly in the late 1920s. The leadership split, communists were expelled, different regional centres broke away and the mass base melted away. By 1930 the ICU had virtually ceased to exist.

In the late 1920s and early 1930s, former ICU members and other activists began organising industrial unions of African workers. Many of these did not survive long. The depression of the 1930s, and the migrant character of the overwhelming majority of the African labour force made union organisation difficult. More importantly, so did the response of capital and the state. Unions including as members 'pass bearing natives' were explicitly denied formal recognition under the industrial legislation. They could not participate in the negotiating machinery set up under the 1924 Industrial Conciliation Act. More significantly, they were denied facilities to organise at the work-place and were subject to a variety of harrassments by state officials and police.

Nevertheless, an embryonic trade union movement based principally on African workers did succeed in establishing itself during these years. In 1941, many of these unions grouped together to form the Council of Non-European Trade Unions (CNETU). By September 1945, CNETU claimed a national membership of 158,000 in 119 unions.

The 1940s was a period of heightened mass struggle (see p.16). It climaxed in the 1946 African miners' strike led by the CNETU-affiliated African Mine Workers' Union. Between 75,000 and 100,000 miners struck work for four days demanding a minimum daily wage of ten shillings and other benefits. Although the state repressed the strike with great violence (12 miners were killed and hundreds injured), this was South Africa's largest strike in terms of the numbers involved. It had the effect of radicalising the African National Congress (see p.285). It also marked the highpoint of the crisis created for the ruling class by the heightened challenge of the masses (see p.16).

The state's decisive response to this challenge came after the election of the Nationalist Party government in 1948. The new regime launched a major offensive against the organisations and living standards of the masses (see p.21). It rejected the findings of its own 1951 Commission of Inquiry into Industrial Legislation which recommended a strategy to incorporate African unions into a separate, highly controlled negotiating system. Instead, in the words of the then Minister of Labour, the state sought 'to bleed' the African trade unions 'to death'. The 1953 Bantu Labour Settlement of Disputes Act specifically prohibited the recognition of African trade unions. African workers were supposed to negotiate with employers on an individual basis through works' and liaison committees. By February 1971, only 28 such committees had been established, many of which were hardly functioning. The principal intention of the Act was to serve as a basis for an attack on democratic unions. These unions were subject to a wide range of harrassments; leaders were systematically restricted or banned and any form of strike action brutally suppressed.

The state's attack on the democratic unions was assisted by the actions of collaborationist unions. As early as 1947, African unions affiliated to the Trades and Labour Council (often on the basis of less than full membership) found their position challenged. In 1954, African unions were voted out of the Council which then restyled itself as TUCSA (see p.248).

This betrayal prompted democratic unions to seek unity amongst themselves. In 1955, in the face of the impending Industrial Conciliation Act (see p.248) and rejection by the TLC, various former CNETU unions together with some unions now excluded from the TLC and other progressive unions formed themselves into the South African Congress of Trade Unions (SACTU – see p.329).

From the outset, SACTU identified itself with the national liberation struggle: it became part of the Congress Alliance led by the ANC. It participated in the political strikes (stay-at-homes) organised by the ANC in the 1950s, as well as putting forward wage and other demands. As part of the Congress Alliance it was subject to the intensified repression of the 1960s, and effectively disappeared as a legal trade union centre. Its largest affiliate, the Food and Canning Workers' Union (see p.342), managed to survive the repression of the 1960s.

The Development of Democratic Trade Unionism After 1973

At the end of 1972, the black trade union movement inside South Africa consisted of two former SACTU affiliates (the Food and Canning Unions) and a number of TUCSA 'parallels'. This situation was changed dramatically by the mass strikes which broke out in 1973. The causes and overall impact of these strikes are discussed pp.33–4. Here it is necessary to note merely that the period following the 1973 strikes saw the formation of new democratic trade unions and support organisations. By the end of 1975 there were 21 unregistered unions of African workers with a membership around 40,000. Four of these unions, embracing 20,000 members, were TUCSA 'parallels'. Six of the others were affiliated to the Trade Union Advisory and Coordinating Council (TUACC – see p.334), set up in late 1973 to co-ordinate unregistered trade unions in Natal. Seven other belong to the Urban Training Project (UTP – see p.345) based in the Transvaal. Four were unaffiliated. By 1980, two federations of democratic unions had been formed, FOSATU and CUSA (see pp.332 and 345). Total membership of all democratic unions reached over 100,000 rising to 247,000 at the end of 1981. Yet this latter figure represents only 18% of the African work-force in industry, construction, commerce and transport. Moreover, the organisation of African mineworkers is only just beginning, whilst African workers in agriculture and domestic service remain totally unorganised.

The following list indicates the unions and federations in open existence at the end of 1981:

FOSATU – Federation of South African Trade Unions (Membership: signed-up – 95,000; paid-up – 60,000)

MAWU	Metal and Allied Workers' Union
CWIU	Chemical Workers' Industrial Union
NUTW	National Union of Textile Workers
T&GWU	Transport and General Workers' Union
E&AWU	Engineering and Allied Workers' Union (expelled in February 1982)
SF&AWU	Sweet, Food and Allied Workers' Union
PW&AWU	Paper, Wood and Allied Workers' Union
G&AWU	Glass and Allied Workers' Union
NAAWU	National Automobile and Allied Workers' Union
J&GWU	Jewellers' and Goldsmiths' Union
EPSF&AWU	Eastern Province Sweet, Food and Allied Workers' Union

CUSA – Council of Unions of South Africa (Estimated membership: 49,000)

BC&AWU	Building, Construction and Allied Workers' Union
LC&DWU	Laundry, Cleaning and Dyeing Workers' Union
SACWU	South African Chemical Workers' Union
T&AWU	Transport and Allied Workers' Union
FB&AWU	Food, Beverage and Allied Workers' Union
SE&AWU	Steel, Engineering and Allied Workers' Union
CCAWUSA	Commercial, Catering and Allied Workers' Union of South Africa (since disaffiliated)

UAMW	United African Motor Workers (Natal and Transvaal)
UAMW&WU	United African Motor and Allied Workers' Union of Natal.

Unaffiliated, democratic unions

AFCWU	African Food and Canning Workers' Union	10,000 members
FCWU	Food and Canning Workers' Union	
SAAWU	South African Allied Workers' Union. Claimed 70,000 members	
GWU	General Workers' Union. 10,000 members.	
GAWU	General and Allied Workers' Union	
MACWUSA	Motor Assembly and Component Workers' Union of South Africa. 2,700 members.	
BMWU	Black Municipal Workers' Union	
MWASA	Media Workers' Association of South Africa	
CTMWA	Cape Town Municipal Workers' Association.	

The State Response – The Wiehahn Strategy

The emerging democratic unions after 1973 were not recognised in terms of industrial legislation. They could not participate in negotiating bodies set up under the Industrial Conciliation Act, and were denied facilities to organise at the work-place. However, such unions were not formally proscribed. This meant that they were left free to determine their own constitutions and internal mode of operating, and were not subject to the controls over union constitutions applied to the registered unions. While the democratic trade union movement remained weak, this incidental consequence of unregistered status did not perturb the capitalist class much. However, under conditions of rapid expansion of democratic trade unions it was seen as a potential threat to the apartheid state.

Accordingly, the Wiehahn Commission of Inquiry was appointed in 1977 to make recommendations, *inter alia*, for future state strategy towards the democratic unions. Its first report was published in May 1979; it set out the 'problem' from the state's point of view as follows:

> Registered trade unions are under certain statutory restrictions and obligations designed to protect and nurture a system that has proved its success in practice. The Industrial Conciliation Act of 1956, provides for [*inter alia*] . . . the strict control of constitutions and membership; and a prohibition of affiliation with any political party or granting of financial assistance to a political party . . . Black trade unions are subject neither to the protective and stabilising elements of the system, nor to its essential discipline and control: they in fact enjoy much greater freedom than registered unions, to the extent that they are free if they so wish to participate in politics and to use their funds for whatever purposes they see fit. (paragraphs 3.35.4; 3.35.5)

This vision of unlimited 'freedom' for black unions was a myth. SACTU attempted to exercise such freedom in the 1950s and 1960s but soon found itself hounded by bannings, imprisonment and detentions until it was forced underground. However, what had now come to perturb the ruling class was the possibility that — given the relative absence of state control over the organisational structure and operation of non-registered unions — they might eventually become a vehicle for organised political opposition.

In this situation the Commission argued that the ruling class had to choose between two alternatives: 1) to prohibit all forms of trade union organisation by blacks; or 2) to try to subject black unions to a greater degree of official control. The majority of Commissioners rejected the first of these alternatives firstly because such

> a prohibition would undoubtedly have the effect of driving black trade unionism underground and uniting black workers not only against the authorities, but, more importantly, also against the system of free enterprise in South Africa' (paragraph 3.36.8)

Moreover, it was considered that such a course might adversely affect foreign investment in South Africa and possibly lead to sanctions against the country.

The Wiehahn Commission thus recommended a strategy aimed at incorporating the black trade union movement into a rigidly controlled industrial relations system. This

> would have the beneficial effects of countering polarisation and ensuring a more orderly process of collective bargaining, in addition to exposing black trade unions more directly to South Africa's trade union traditions and existing institutions, thus inculcating a sense of responsibility and loyalty towards the free market system. (paragraph 3.35.25)

Concretely, the Commission recommended that unions including black workers be formally recognised and encouraged to participate in negotiations in statutory bodies and Industrial Councils, but only if officially registered. Registration would depend on, *inter alia*, applicant unions being considered 'bona fide' by state officials, who would be obliged to 'take into account all factors relating to the maintenance of peace, harmony and the national interest'. Moreover, union constitutions would have to be approved by the registrar. They would be subject to a probationary period of 'provisional registration' during which their activities would be monitored. Any form of political activity would be prohibited.

The basic strategy recommended by the Wiehahn Commission was accepted by the government and enacted in the 1979 Industrial Conciliation Amendment Act — itself amended several times since and finally renamed the Labour Relations Act. The clear strategic objective of this legislation has been to get democratic unions to register and to incorporate them into the highly centralised and bureaucratic Industrial Council bargaining system (see p.246).

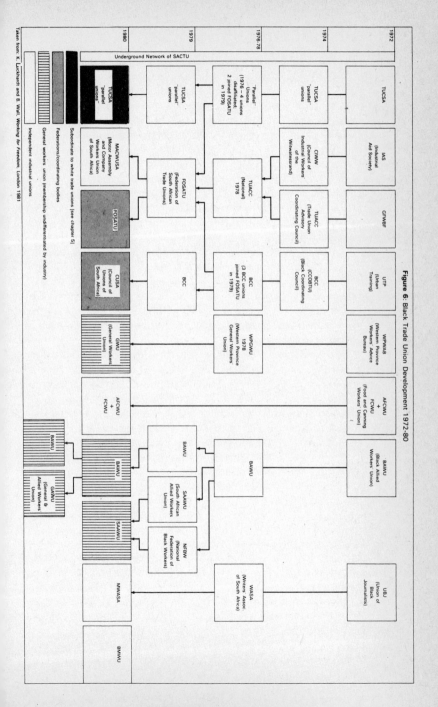

Figure 6: Black Trade Union Development 1972-80

The Unions' Response to Wiehahn

The enactment of the Wiehahn legislation raised major strategic and tactical questions for the democratic unions. The Wiehahn package was a combination of concessions and controls. Unions had now to decide whether they could take advantage of the concessions without becoming subject to the constricting effects of the controls. One of the most important initial questions was that of registration; strong differences emerged over this question. The TUCSA 'parallels' rapidly sought registration as a means of advancing their position *vis à vis* other unregistered unions. CUSA remained uncritical of the strategy, and most of its member unions registered. FOSATU criticised the system and recognised that the intention behind the legislation was to control the labour movement. Nevertheless, following certain amendments to the draft legislation, FOSATU decided to apply for registration – as non-racial unions – on 'tactical' grounds to 'test' the system. FOSATU has since argued that although the controls exist on paper they have no real effect in practice, and that by conceding the right to organise, registration has enabled it to advance. Other unions, however, refused to register. Some argued that the controls constituted a real interference in the democratic procedures they are trying to develop. Others have taken the position that registration amounts to collaboration with apartheid.

To a certain degree, the registration question has now been superceded by a 1981 amendment to the Labour Relations Act. This allowed the registrar of trade unions to intervene in the affairs of both registered and non-registered unions. However, the issue of industrial councils remains a live question. For some time there was a greater degree of unanimity on this issue. All democratic unions agreed in August 1981 that the system was bureaucratic and that democratic unions should stay out. CUSA and FOSATU affiliates already in Industrial Councils agreed to review their position. FOSATU, however, has subsequently embarked upon a policy of making tactical use of Industrial Councils, arguing that the major problem with the Councils arose not from inherent structural characteristics of the system, but the practices of their members; such practices could be changed. CUSA unions have now also entered Industrial Councils.

The other major issue to have arisen within the democratic trade union movement is that of unity between the various groupings. Prompted by a renewed offensive by capital and the state, discussions on this question began in earnest in 1981. The bosses' offensive had a number of aspects. One was an intensified effort by all major capitalist organisations to persuade or cajole unions into the Industrial Council system (see pp.38 and 110). Secondly, the 1981 amendment to the Labour Relations Act gave the registrar the right to intervene in any union. Finally, officials of a number of the more militant unions were detained. One of them, Dr Neil Aggett died under suspicious circumstances while in detention – an event which led to one of the first strikes over non-work place issues for many years – a widely supported national 30 minute work stoppage.

This bosses' offensive prompted democratic unions to seek greater unity. A number of 'unity conferences' have been held. At the first of these, in August 1981, unions agreed to support one another in the event of attacks by the bosses or state, and to resist attempts to cajole them into Industrial Councils. At the second such conference in April 1982, a proposal was made to form a new federation of democratic unions. However, while all groups agreed on the need for greater unity, serious differences emerged over how this should be achieved and what form it should take. FOSATU proposed 'disciplined' unity around a programme to build up factory floor organisation as a key step towards the eventual emergence of a working-class political movement (see p.336). CUSA did not attend because it argued in favour of a federation of black unions, expressing opposition to the principle of non-racialism. MACWUSA/GWUSA walked out of this second conference arguing that a firm commitment against registration or any form of 'collaboration' with the official system had to be the starting point for any unity programme. This position initially drew some support from SAAWU and GAWU, and for some time it seemed that all these unions might form a federation open only to unregistered unions. The Food and Canning Unions and the General Workers' Union continued to oppose registration. Yet they pushed hard for a form of unity which would include FOSATU — though on terms providing for greater autonomy for affiliates than envisaged in FOSATU's 'disciplined unity' proposal.

A further unity conference was held in April 1983 and appears to have broken this deadlock. Seven union groupings, together representing 200,000 workers — viz., FOSATU, GWU, Food and Canning Unions, SAAWU, GAWU, the Cape Town Municipal Workers' Association and the Commercial, Catering and Allied Workers' Union — set up a 'feasibility committee' to prepare proposals for a new federation. In May 1983, CUSA appeared to change its mind and announced it would join in these deliberations. MACWUSA/GWUSA has, at the time of writing, not yet finally decided whether or not to participate.

SOUTH AFRICAN CONGRESS OF TRADE UNIONS (SACTU)[2]

> Underground trade union organisation allied with the African National Congress. From its formation as a trade union federation in 1955, SACTU refused to confine itself to narrow economistic forms of trade unionism. It argues that workers' struggles for improved living standards cannot be separated from the struggle for political rights and liberation. Since 1964 SACTU has been forced to operate underground and in exile. Its cadres currently operate both within openly existing trades unions and independently in support of a 15 point programme of demands.

SACTU was formed in 1955 following the decision of the Trades and Labour Council to exclude unions with African members and to reconstitute itself as the racially exclusive TUCSA (see p.248). SACTU was based initially on the minority of progressive unions which opposed the dissolution of the TLC, together with the majority of the unions grouped in the Council of Non-European Trade Unions (see p.322).

From the outset, SACTU rejected 'non-political', economistic forms of trade unionism. The policy statement adopted at its first annual conference in 1955 declared:

> SACTU is conscious of the fact that the organising of the mass of workers for higher wages, better conditions of life and labour is inextricably bound up with a determined struggle for political rights and liberation from all oppressive laws and practices. It follows that a mere struggle for the econo rights of all the workers without participation in the general struggle for political emancipation would condemn the trade union movement to uselessness and to a betrayal of the interests of the workers.

This position led SACTU to associate from the outset with the Congress Alliance.

Another of SACTU's important affiliations is to the World Federation of Trade Unions which it joined in 1955 at a time when the rival, pro-imperialist International Confederation of Free Trade Unions was collaborating with TUCSA to set up the puppet FOFATUSA (see p.253). Ironically, the motion to affiliate was proposed by Lucy Mvubelo who subsequently defected to TUCSA and is currently one of the foremost proponents of 'parallel unionism'.

During the 1950s and 1960s, SACTU affiliates organised workers in, among others, the food, canning and metal industries of the Western Cape; the automobile and rubber industries of the Eastern Cape (often regarded as SACTU's most militant area); the metal and textile industries of the Transvaal; the textile, chemical, garage and stevedoring sectors of Natal; as well as a number of agricultural workers, railway workers and (through general workers' union) various other workers throughout the country. When its membership peaked in 1961, SACTU had 46 affiliated unions with a total membership of 53,323 (of whom 38,791 were Africans, 1,650 Indians, 12,384 so-called coloureds and 498 whites).

Among the most important of SACTU's campaigns during these years was the '£1 [R2] a-day' campaign which demanded a legislated national minimum daily wage of £1 for all workers. This demand directly challenged the basis of the apartheid cheap labour system and mobilised a large number of workers until the heightened repression after 1962 made the continuation of the campaign impossible. This and other campaigns apart, SACTU affiliates were involved in struggles in individual factories. Important among these were a series of struggles by the African Food and Canning Workers' Union in the Western Cape which wrung concessions from employers despite the general climate of repression. Finally, as a member of the Congress Alliance,

SACTU was also involved in the organisation of the mass political strikes (stay-at-homes) called in support of the demands of the Alliance (see p.286).

SACTU's open existence within the country came to an end during the wave of repression 1962–4. Unlike the ANC and the Congress of Democrats, SACTU itself was never formally proscribed. However, its meetings and other activities were constantly banned and its leaders subjected to restriction; SACTU leaders were among the accused in the 1956–60 Treason Trial. In 1963 and 1964 alone, over 30 SACTU officials were jailed, whilst a further 48 were placed under banning orders preventing them from carrying on the functions of the organisation.

For some time after 1964, finding itself in a situation in which many of its leading cadres were forced into exile, SACTU concentrated on international solidarity work. It publicised conditions of workers under apartheid and campaigned for the withdrawal of foreign capital, trade boycotts and the isolation of the regime. It also fought for the exclusion of officials of the regime and racist trade unions from international bodies such as the International Labour Organization (ILO). In 1964 it succeeded in forcing the withdrawal of the apartheid state's nominee, and in 1973 secured TUCSA's exclusion as a body representing South African workers.

During the phase of resurgence of mass action after 1973, SACTU reconstituted itself as an underground organisation operating within the country. SACTU cadres currently operate both within the existing unions and independently seek to promote the 15 point programme, reproduced below, which links workers' struggles over immediate demands to the broader struggle for national liberation.

South African Workers Demand

1. We demand the immediate recognition of the right of all workers to form and join trade unions of their choice.
2. We demand the abolition of the pass laws and of the migratory labour system.
3. We demand the unconditional right to strike for all workers in support of their demands.
4. We demand a national minimum wage for all workers, regardless of race or sex, of R75 per week, indexed to inflation.
5. We demand the abolition of all discrimination in the workplace on the grounds of sex or race, and an end to job reservation.
6. We demand free and compulsory education for all children regardless of colour or creed, and extended training facilities for all workers. We demand the abolition of discrimination in education and training, including apprenticeships.
7. We demand an eight-hour working day for all workers, with a total of 40 hours basic work (excluding overtime) per week.
8. We demand that workers should not be compelled to work overtime.

And when overtime is worked, the total number of hours worked per week, including overtime, should not exceed 50 hours. Workers should be paid double their normal rate for overtime worked during the week, and two-and-a-half times the normal rate on weekends and public holidays.

9. We demand four weeks paid leave per year for every worker.
10. We demand that every worker be entitled to twenty-one days sick leave per year with full pay, to be extended in cases of serious illness.
11. We demand that all workers should enjoy full medical benefits.
12. We demand unemployment pay and injury compensation for all workers, without exception or time limit, and fixed at 100 per cent of current salary.
13. We demand that all workers should be eligible for retirement at 60 years of age, on full pension.
14. We demand that women workers be able to participate fully in all aspects of production, without discrimination in wages, training, job allocation or pension benefits.
15. We demand full political rights for all South Africans.

President: Stephen Dlamini
General Secretary: John Gaetsewe.

FEDERATION OF SOUTH AFRICAN TRADE UNIONS (FOSATU)[3]

A militant non-racial federation of unions embracing workers across South Africa in many industries. A number of FOSATU unions have been involved in important struggles to establish the right of workers to organise.

FOSATU has been the major force among the democratic unions arguing for registration under the Labour Relations Act on 'tactical grounds'. It emphasises building up a strong factory floor based organisation and concentrating on work-place as distinct from 'community' issues. It argues that trade unions should not be tempted into 'seeking a role in the wider struggle' at the expense of building an 'effective worker organisation'. This it sees as the only strategy to avoid the workers' movement being 'highjacked by elements who will in the end have no option but to turn against their worker supporters'.

FOSATU has argued for a 'disciplined unity' among democratic trade unions, rather than *'ad hoc'* or 'loose' unity over specific issues. However, in 1983 it agreed to investigate the possibility of forming a new federation with six other democratic union groupings.

Formation

On its formation in April 1979, FOSATU became the first non-racial trade union federation to operate above ground since SACTU in the early 1960s. Preliminary discussions to set up a federation began in December 1976. The first meeting was held in March 1977, at which were represented the Trade Union Advisory Coordinating Council (TUACC), the Black Consultative Council (BCC) (see p.345), the Council for the Industrial Workers of the Witwatersrand (CIWW), the National Union of Motor Assembly and Rubber Workers (NUMARWOSA), the Union of Automobile Workers (UAW), the Food and Canning Unions (p.342) and the Western Province Workers' Advice Bureau (WPWAB) (see p.339). The Black Allied Workers' Union and TUCSA 'parallels' refused to attend (see pp.305 and 254).

The Food and Canning Unions and WPWAB later decided not to affiliate as they felt unions needed more development at a grassroots level before a federation was formed. The majority of BCC unions also later withdrew. When FOSATU was finally established some two years after the first meeting, it consisted of four TUACC unions, three from the BCC, two former TUCSA 'parallels' (which left TUCSA to join FOSATU), and some independent unions. Most affiliated unions were unregistered, but four were registered under the Industrial Conciliation Act.

By the end of 1982 FOSATU had 13 member unions. These represented workers in the metal, chemical, textile, transport, sweet, food, paper, wood, glass, and motor industries, jewellers and goldsmiths (see p.324). Two of these unions, The National Union of Textile Workers and the Metal and Allied Workers' Union had organised on a national basis, while the National Automobile and Allied Workers' Union was the dominant union in the motor vehicle industry. Total FOSATU union membership rose from 50,000 at the end of 1980 to 94,000 during 1981. The Federation is particularly strong in the East Rand, Durban and Port Elizabeth, and weak in the Western Cape.

As laid out in its constitution, FOSATU's main aims and objectives can be summarised as follows:
1) to secure social justice for all workers;
2) to strive to build a united labour movement independent of race, colour, creed or sex;
3) to bring together all spliter groups and craft unions into broadly based industrial unions;
4) to secure decent standards of living;
5) to comment on, advance or oppose any policy affecting workers' interests;
6) to win recognition and negotiating rights.
The constitution also provides for decentralised decision making to guard against the creation of unresponsive bureaucracies and permit workers to exercise maximum control.

A number of FOSATU unions have been involved in important struggles to establish the right to organise. In 1982, its affiliated Metal and Allied Workers' Union was involved in a number of strikes in the Witwatersrand metal industries seeking the right of workers to negotiate at factory level rather than exclusively through Industrial Councils. Out of these struggles has emerged a powerful shop stewards' organisation.

However, FOSATU's importance in the current South African trade union scene goes beyond the size of its membership or involvement in particular strikes. FOSATU represents a distinct strategic position within the democratic trade union movement. In analysing this, it should be noted that the Federation is no monolith, but contains a number of different and competing ideological tendencies. The analysis below sets out the broad position of the dominant tendency within FOSATU up to the end of 1982.

FOSATU's Strategic Position

The assumptions underlying FOSATU's approach were in many senses a synthesis of the experience and practice of the two largest constituent bodies which later merged into FOSATU — The Natal and Transvaal based TUACC, and the Eastern Cape motor unions, NUMARWOSA and UAW.

The practice of TUACC 1975-9 was built on an analysis of the South African economy as dominated by monopoly capitalism. TUACC concentrated on shop floor organisation in multinational companies. In a situation in which workers' organisation was seen to be weak, it could be protected by organising mainly in those undertakings most susceptible (for many reasons, including international pressure) to signing recognition agreements with unregistered trade unions. This was presumed to increase the companies' interest in obtaining state recognition of trade unions. Underlying this strategy was a concern with recognition by the state as a major goal of the independent trade unions. Recognition agreements, such as that signed between the British-owned Smith & Nephew and the NUTW in 1974, became the overriding objective of this perspective.

Hand in hand with this view of weak working class organisation, there also developed a mistrustful attitude towards the politics of community organisations — whose struggles were beginning to assume some significance in the mid-1970s. This was provoked firstly by a fear that state reaction to any trade union involvement with community struggles would jeopardise the workers' organisations. It stemmed secondly from a view that because the working class was weak it should be wary of petty bourgeois-dominated community organisations, whose allegedly predominantly nationalist ideological orientation could dilute worker organisation in the factories. This reflects a strong line of 'no politics within the trade union movement' which grew up in FOSATU.

The two Eastern Cape motor unions, on the other hand, were registered unions belonging to Industrial Councils. In 1965 the membership of these unions had removed a bureaucratic leadership and instilled a more democratic practice. These unions brought to FOSATU their experience in the Industrial Councils and particular conception of workers' power operating within the existing industrial relations system, which was to have strong influence in

FOSATU. They argued that if based on strong factory floor organisation and democratic control by the membership, independent trade unions could successfully use Industrial Councils for their own ends.

The draft legislation arising out of the Wiehahn report posed a sharp problem for the entire democratic trade union movement. Initially, the state proposed to exclude migrant and contract workers from the new forms of 'recognition' now to be granted to African trade unions. All the major independent trade unions opposed this, leading to its eventual withdrawal. However, by focusing primarily on the issue of migrant workers, not much attention was paid to the new forms of control being introduced by the state. When the state conceded the rights of migrant workers to join unions, the unions in CUSA (a body generally regarded as being to the right of FOSATU) announced that they would seek registration. FOSATU, the Food and Canning Unions and Western Province General Workers' Union met to try to work out a common strategy. They agreed that the proposed legislation violated the 'internationally accepted principles' of the 'right of all workers to join unions of their choice and the right of workers to unrestricted control of their unions'. Yet they differed on the practical strategies to follow.

The eventual FOSATU position of 'tactical registration' as non racial unions to 'test the system' was based on a number of considerations. The first was that the position of the democratic unions was weak. As the FOSATU General Secretary put it in 1981: '. . . we are not in a position of strength, let's face. Look at the percentage of the labour force which is organised — I mean it's peanuts, man'. FOSATU thus concluded that registration would offer some protection both from the threat of state repression and the TUCSA 'parallels'.

Moreover, FOSATU argued that if member unions could register on their own terms as non-racial unions, and if they could maintain unity, the controls could be rendered ineffective. This was partly based on the view of the two registered Eastern Cape motor unions that the existing registration process was largely a formality. In the words of the FOSATU General Secretary: 'The controls are there on paper, but nobody bothers us . . . All the registrar wants are returns and membership fees. There are no real problems'.

Thus, while FOSATU acknowledged that the registration procedure laid down by the state was far removed from the goals it had fought for, and in some senses represented a withdrawal of rights enjoyed by the non-registered unions, it decided to 'test' the procedures by trying to register its members on its own terms as non-racial unions. This decision was extremely controversial among the democratic unions.

Critics pointed to a contradiction in FOSATU's position: on the one hand, the state is depicted as all-strong, with a capacity to repress trade unions, while on the other hand, the official industrial relations procedures and institutions are reduced to a paper tiger. FOSATU's early clear separation of economic from political struggles, and distance from the latter, also provoked sharp debate.

This has gone through a number of stages. Some elements within FOSATU

were strongly opposed to any form of political involvement. However, prior
to the 1982 FOSATU congress, its leadership did argue that 'you can't
divorce economics from politics'. Yet it strongly opposed trade union involvement in political struggles outside the factory. FOSATU General Secretary
Joe Foster argued in 1981 that

> you can't fight the state and the employers at the same time . . . Who
> are the enemy? The bosses are the enemy — and these are the people
> one should actually direct attention to.

This view has been criticised as economistic in that it elevates struggles at the
point of production against employers to the most important political task of
the working class.

This view secondly reflected a certain suspicion of the national liberation
movement: 'I can't see that the national liberation movement is striving for the
same type of society as us' argued Foster in 1981. The position has both a left
and right face. The former argues that the 'petty bourgeoisie' are

> afraid of the movement of black workers: they wish either to restrict
> it within a narrow terrain, or more usually, to dissolve it in a mass
> political movement dominated not by the workers but by the petty
> bourgeoisie. According to them the workers are only useful as a kind
> of battering ram for a movement they themselves seek to lead.

The right wing view in fact sees no connection between trade union struggles
for higher wages and better working conditions with the broader workers'
struggle to transform the social conditions of production, and argues that the
former is the only legitimate form of activity.

In the course of debates with other trade union bodies, FOSATU's original
argument about the necessity of registration to protect weak working-class
organisations gradually gave way to an assertion both that the controls are
meaningless and that the state's industrial relations institutions can be used by
the workers. The new system of registration is seen as a 'real concession under
pressure' which grants 'real rights' to trade union bodies. This view was an
important factor propelling two FOSATU unions — MAWU and the NUTW —
to apply to join the metal and textile Industrial Councils respectively in
1982.

FOSATU's general strategic line produced a distinct position of the question
of trade union unity. In a speech to the FOSATU congress held shortly
before the second unity conference in April 1982 (a speech subsequently
adopted as official policy), General Secretary Foster drew a clear distinction
between FOSATU and what he termed 'community based unions'. The latter
he accused of seeking 'a role in the wider struggle' at the cost of building
'effective worker organisation'. Tribute was paid to groups involved in the
'wider struggle', particularly the ANC, but he argued that there had never
been 'a working class movement' in South Africa. This could only arise by

concentrating initially on factory organisation and work-place issues. This was not 'economism', he argued, as 'FOSATU's whole existence is political'. To build such a workers' movement, 'clear political direction' was necessary. FOSATU would provide this by consolidating factory floor organisation. This would prevent the workers' movement being 'highjacked by elements who will in the end have no option but to turn against their worker supporters.'

This position was likewise controversial. Nevertheless, throughout 1982 closer co-operation developed between FOSATU on the one hand, and the Food and Canning Unions and GWU on the other. In April 1983, together with six other union groupings, FOSATU agreed to enter a feasibility committee to investigate forming a larger federation.

General Secretary: Joe Foster
President: Chris Dlamini.

SOUTH AFRICAN ALLIED WORKERS' UNION (SAAWU)[4]

> A militant trade union based mainly in the Eastern Cape. In 1980 and 1981, SAAWU was the fastest growing trade union body in South Africa. Its membership rose from 5,000 in March 1980 to a claimed 70,000 by the end of 1981.

SAAWU was formed in March 1979 following a split in the Black Consciousness Black Allied Workers' Union (BAWU) (see p.305). Dissatisfied with BAWU's racially exclusive constitution, a dissident faction 'expelled' most of BAWU's executive on the grounds that they 'had misrepresented the union', and reconstituted themselves as SAAWU. SAAWU was initially based in Durban; in early 1980 it moved its major activities to East London where workers were 'totally un-trade unionised'. It consciously sought to establish 'a powerful base' in the East London area prior to expanding elsewhere. Its rapid growth dates from this move, and has been concentrated mainly in the East London area.

SAAWU began as a general workers' union with the long-term aim of developing into a federation of industrial unions. By 1981 it had organised in the chemical, sweet, beverage, transport and other industries; 23 'sub-unions' had affiliated. In that year a further split from BAWU led the Natal-based National Federation of Black Workers with 26 claimed affiliates to join SAAWU. This rapid growth created problems in consolidating factory floor organisation. Nevertheless, the union fought a number of recognition battles with employers, winning several of these. In 1981 it became involved in a major recognition dispute with the Wilson-Rowntree sweet company.

SAAWU vigorously rejects registration under the Labour Relations Act. It sees registration as part of 'all those draconian laws which amount to genocide against the working class, and the black workers in particular. We can't participate in our own exploitation and oppression'.

Although it grew out of a Black Consciousness organisation, SAAWU takes a strong non-racial class line. It argues that: 'In any capitalist society there are always two contending forces — the bourgeoisie and the proletariat. The state will always side with the bosses'. It sees the lines of struggle in South Africa in clear class terms:

> We are aware that workers see the bosses as whites and we must show them that bosses are people that are exploiting them. Quite a sizeable number of blacks are becoming employers and people must not see them as our brothers . . . people must not be fooled just because they are black — they are exploiters.

As a working-class organisation, SAAWU sees the aims of South African workers as 'the total liberation of the working class and the toiling masses in this country'. It emphasises non-racialism in the context of a leading role for the working class:

> South Africa's future is in the hands of its workers — only the workers in alliance with all other progressive-minded sections of the community can build a happy life for all South Africans. But workers should be the vanguard.

As a trade union body it argues that its fight for workers demands cannot be restricted only to economic issues. 'Our fate was decided for us long ago by politicians. If we want to solve the problem we must act politically — there is no other way'. SAAWU participates in community politics and struggles, with its major base in East London's Mdantsane township.

Beyond its stress on working-class non-racialism, SAAWU emphasises the need for workers to directly control trade union organisation behind the twin principles of 'mass participatory democracy' and 'collective leadership'. On this basis it sought unity with all other progressive working-class organisations, arguing that 'unity should be the watchword of the union movement'. In East London, SAAWU has co-operated closely with the African Food and Canning Workers' Union and the GWU. It also played an important role in convening the first unity conference in August 1981. Following the collapse of the second unity conference in April 1982 over the registration issue, for a while it appeared as if, together with MACWUSA, GWUSA and GAWU, SAAWU was working towards the formation of a trade union federation excluding all registered unions. However, a year later, SAAWU was one of seven groupings which set up a feasibility committee to explore the possibility of forming a new union federation.

SAAWU draws a distinction between its long-term aims of 'total liberation'

and immediate aims. Its programme of immediate demands included (early 1980):
1) a national minimum wage of R50 per week, linked to the rate of inflation;
2) four weeks annual paid leave;
3) restrictions of maximum hours of overtime, none of which were to be compulsory;
4) minimum monthly wage of R80 for domestic workers;
5) the implementation of codes of conduct by foreign companies.

The union declared 1980 'the Year of the Worker' and called for the abolition of the pass laws, the migratory labour system, the Group Areas Act and Separate Amenities Act.

SAAWU has been a principal target of state repression: many of its leaders are regularly arrested and detained and their homes have been attacked. In one incident, the mother and uncle of Thozamile Gqweta died in an arson attack on his home. At their funeral, shots aimed at Gqweta killed a friend standing next to him. East London's Mdantsane township technically falls into the Ciskei Bantustan, and SAAWU has campaigned strongly against the fraud of Ciskei 'independence'. As a result, the puppet Ciskei regime of the Sebe brothers has launched a particular reign of terror against SAAWU. Over 200 of its members and leaders have been detained by the 'Ciskei Central Intelligence Service' and the Bantustan's 'Chief Minister' declared that he would 'have no mercy on SAAWU'.

President: Thozamile Gqweta
Secretary: Sam Kikine.

GENERAL WORKERS' UNION (GWU) (Formerly Western Province General Workers' Union)[5]

Unregistered militant union originally based in the Western Cape, but which now has a presence in all major coastal centres as well as in several industries in the Transvaal.

The GWU places a strong emphasis on workers' control and internal democracy. It strongly opposed the Wiehahn labour legislation. It favours forging links with community organisations and other progressive unions. Early in 1983 it hosted the conference at which seven union groupings, including the GWU, set up a feasibility committee to investigate the possibility of forming a new federation of democratic unions.

The Western Province General Workers' Union was formed in Cape Town in 1978; open to workers of all races in any industry, it adopted its present name to mark its expansion out of the Western Cape in 1981. It grew out of the Western Province Workers' Advice Bureau (WPWAB) which was formed in 1972. Under apartheid laws, in the Western Cape 'preference' in employment is given to so-called coloured labour, which thus constitutes the great bulk of Cape Town's working class. Many so-called coloureds are members of conservative, bureaucratic unions. The WPWAB favoured a general union over industrial unions, arguing that the latter divided workers along industrial lines. Early organising efforts were concentrated on the minority of African workers in the Western Cape. These were mainly migrants who often moved from one industry to another and who were concentrated in two large townships. However once it had organised Cape Town stevedores it saw the need to organise stevedores on a national basis, and moved into other centres.

The GWU now has members in various industries in the Western Cape and the coastal cities of Port Elizabeth and East London; more recently, it began organising in Durban and the Witwatersrand. Together with meat workers in the Western Cape, the stevedores of four of the major ports (Cape Town, Durban, Port Elizabeth and East London) provide the union with one of its strongest bases. The GWU claimed a membership of 10,000 at the beginning of 1982.

The GWU is a prominent advocate of internal democracy and effective workers' control over the running of the union. It sees effective mass participation by members as the union's only possible long term defence against state repression. Thus it argues that: 'The political question of the day in South Africa is the struggle for democracy'.

> Correct political practice consists in nothing else than uniting all the oppressed people in the struggle for democracy. Our political practice consists first and foremost in our absolute adherence to internal democracy and in our willingness to cooperate openly and democratically with all other organisations who share our democratic goals. In the final analysis that is why there can be no compromise over the question of internal democracy.

This position led the GWU to strongly oppose registration under the Labour Relations Act. It argued that:

> . . . the requirements for registration presuppose that the workers voluntarily relinquish exclusive control over their union . . . In essence . . . the constitutional format of the union is rendered so complex by the process of registration that it effectively removes the function of drawing up the constitution from the hands of the workers and places it in the hands of legal experts . . . Registration thereby becomes a process which removes direct control of the union from the hands of the members. It is therefore not a neutral technical exercise devoid of influence on the union's internal operation. Rather it is a process which

permits state involvement in the union's internal affairs . . .

The GWU similarly opposed the Industrial Council system, arguing:

> . . . we cannot compromise on the question of the relation between the
> workers' representatives on the shop floor and the union; or, accordingly,
> on the relation between shop floor representatives and management.
> This is the nub of union activity and we cannot envisage accepting a
> system whereby shop floor representatives are restricted to 'discussing'
> day-to-day trivia on the shop floor, whilst their union is reduced to
> concerning itself bureaucratically with the annual round of Industrial
> Council negotiations over all substantial issues and in the policing, in
> cooperation with the bosses of the Industrial Council, of these agree-
> ments.

However, the GWU sees its position on these questions as tactical and based on
a concrete analysis of current conditions of class struggle rather than a
dogmatic 'boycottism' (as some of its critics have alleged). Early in 1980
it stated that:

> If there were to be concessions taking into account certain of our
> previously stated objections to the initial moves of the state, they will
> of course be seriously examined and our position in relation to the
> industrial legislative framework will shift accordingly.

These positions are reflected in negotiating practice. The union does not
emphasise formal recognition for itself as such from employers — rather, it
stresses *de facto* recognition and negotiation with elected Workers' Committees
which the union assists in organising.

The GWU has argued strongly that the way to defeat TUCSA 'parallels'
was not through registration but by offering workers a democratic and
militant alternative. It claims this position was vindicated in the 1979 stevedores strike, when the mass of Cape Town's stevedores supported the GWU,
despite a management attempt to foist a TUCSA 'parallel' on them.

The other major strike in which the union was involved was the meat
workers' strike in 1980. This was the first strike in recent years to involve
black workers in different firms across a single industry. It also generated a
high degree of community support as community organisations supported
the workers by boycotting red meat. For the duration of the strike, African
and coloured butchers also refused to sell red meat. In terms of its immediate
demands — recognition by the meat companies of Workers' Committees —
the strike was not a success. Strikers were dismissed and union officials
imprisoned. However, the GWU emerged from the strike with even stronger
support. In 1982 the union was involved in a major struggle with the state-
owned SATS (see p.96) when it tried to organise dockworkers employed
by SATS in the Port Elizabeth harbour. SATS refused to recognise GWU

Workers' Committees. Many observers believe that the state sought to provoke the union into a national dock strike in order to break it. The GWU mobilised strong international and local support, but eventually resisted this provocation. Though the union admitted defeat on the question of organising dockworkers, it held on to its base among the stevedores.

The GWU has also been prominent in the promotion of trade union unity. In early 1982, in the interest of 'creating greater unity among emergent trade unions', the GWU resolved not to organise workers in certain industries in which other democratic unions already had an effective presence. While the GWU continues to refuse to register itself, it has opposed the position of those unregistered unions which refuse to have links with registered union groupings such as FOSATU. It appears to agree with the fairly widespread view that following the 1981 Labour Relations Act, the registration debate has been superceded (see p.328). Along with the Food and Canning Unions, it struggled for unity with FOSATU on a formula which allows greater autonomy to individual unions than is envisaged in FOSATU's 'disciplined unity' position. The GWU is one of the seven union groupings which agreed in April 1983 to investigate the formation of a new federation.

General Secretary: Dave Lewis.

FOOD AND CANNING WORKERS' UNION AND AFRICAN FOOD AND CANNING WORKERS' UNION (FCWU and AFCWU – known jointly as the Food and Canning Unions)[6]

> Long-standing militant and progressive unions, based mainly in the Western and Eastern Cape. They regard themselves, and largely function as, a single union. Both were leading members of SACTU in the 1950s and 1960s, and maintain that tradition of progressive unionism.

The Food and Canning Workers' Union was formed in the Western Cape in 1940. The canning factories were located predominantly in the rural areas and workers in this industry were subject to particularly harsh conditions and low wages. The FCWU rapidly won much support and engaged in a series of struggles. It also emerged as a leading progressive force within the then co-ordinating centre, the Trades and Labour Council (see p.263).

The FCWU was open to workers of all races. Given the composition of the work-force in the canning factories, the majority of its members were so-called coloureds with a small African minority. Significantly, the overwhelming majority of workers in this low wage industry were women and the FCWU was notable for the leading role played by its women members.

From inception, the FCWU was registered under the Industrial Conciliation Act. The Act barred membership in registered unions to 'pass bearing natives'. Though African women did not have to carry passes in the 1940s, the union had a number of male African members, and after 1945 it was subjected to 'a campaign of harrassment by the Department of Labour'. Its offices were raided and it was threatened with de-registration unless it expelled African members. After much internal debate, a separate African Food and Canning Workers' Union was formed to enable the union to survive. The two unions acted jointly, met together, dealt with employers together and refused to attend conferences separately.

The Food and Canning Unions were prime targets of the intensified repression against working-class organisations under the Nationalist regime after 1948. A series of general secretaries and other leaders of both unions were removed from office by the state and banned. Nevertheless, during this period the union grew in influence, establishing a thriving branch on the East Rand, and won a number of important strikes throughout the country. Many of its leaders also played important roles in the South African Federation of Women (see p.366), the African National Congress (p.283) and, above all, SACTU.

The Food and Canning Unions were founder members of, and perhaps the most important single force in, SACTU. Their membership comprised almost one third of the total membership of SACTU affiliates. Many Food and Canning leaders — such as Ray Alexander, Elizabeth Mafekeng, Frances Baard, Oscar Mpetha, Mabel Balfour, Mary Moodley and others — were important SACTU leaders, and the campaigns and struggles of the Food and Canning workers formed a crucial part of SACTU's history. With the further removal of many of its leaders from office in the early 1960s, SACTU's role as an open trade union centre was effectively ended. However, the Food and Canning Unions survived this period of intense repression and maintained both the support of Cape workers and the tradition of progressive unionism.

With the flowering of the new wave of democratic trade unions in the 1970s and 1980s, the Food and Canning Unions have again emerged as a strong force. They rejected the Wiehahn strategy of registering new democratic unions. They also see a link between trade union and community struggles. This was especially exemplified in the long 1979 Fattis & Monis strike, in which the co-ordination of the unions' activity with a community boycott of the company's products led to a significant victory for the union. Food and Canning Unions have also been active in trying to organise a united front of all democratic unions. This goes hand in hand with attempts to unite the two unions into one — in keeping with their effective practice. Their long-standing commitment to the principle of the non-racial organisation of workers is bearing fruit — in 1980 and 1981 the first whites since the 1940s joined the union.

Militants of the Food and Canning Unions were prominent victims of the wave of detentions launched in late 1981. Among those detained was Dr Neil Aggett, Transvaal regional secretary of the Food and Canning Unions, who was later murdered in detention.

The response to Aggett's death symbolised the extent of the growing mass struggle in South Africa. Over 100,000 workers affiliated to all major democratic trade unions stopped work for 30 minutes in the first strike over non-work place issues for many years. His funeral was attended by over 15,000 people, including representatives of community and other progressive organisations as well as trade unionists. Prominently displayed were symbols and slogans of the liberation movement. Both the strike and the funeral indicated the non-racialism characteristic of the present phase of the mass struggle as black workers identified a progressive white as 'a man of the people'.

At the trade union level, Aggett's death also accelerated the drive for unity. Together with the GWU, the Food and Canning Unions opposed the line of a number of unregistered unions which refused to have links with registered unions. In 1983, the Food and Canning unions were one of seven groupings which agreed to investigate the formation of a broader federation.

General Secretary: Jan Theron.

GENERAL AND ALLIED WORKERS' UNION (GAWU)[7]

GAWU is a non-racial general workers' union formed in 1980 following the disintegration of the Black Allied Workers' Union in the Transvaal. It organises in the brush and copper industries, in mining house offices, and cleaners, scooter drivers, petrol and transport workers.

GAWU describes its policy as 'one of mass participatory democracy and collective leadership. The members must understand what trade unionism is, and, as members, participate in the leadership of the union.' It rejects registration on the grounds that: 'The state is against all progressive trade unions and still relies on the same means as it did with SACTU in the past'.

GAWU also emphasises involvement in community issues. Since November 1981 it has come under attack by the state and its President and a number of its leaders have been detained.

The union favours unity between unions in a 'progressive front'. In 1982 it was linked with MACWUSA/GWUSA and SAAWU in refusing to co-operate with registered unions. However, in 1983 it was one of the seven groupings which agreed to investigate the feasibility of forming a new broad federation of democratic trade unions.

President: Samson Ndou.

COUNCIL OF UNIONS OF SOUTH AFRICA (CUSA)[8]

> Trade union federation grouping nine unions with a claimed
> membership of about 49,000 in 1982. CUSA describes itself as
> 'black orientated and controlled'. It is open only to blacks and
> criticises other unions for their non-racial position. The group
> generally promotes a non-political approach to trade unionism.
> It is cultivated by several leading monopolies and has links with
> western trade union organisations.

CUSA grew out of the activities of the Urban Training Project (UTP) formed
in 1970 by former officials of the African Affairs Department of TUCSA.
This department had been disbanded in 1968 when TUCSA expelled its handful of associated African unions (see p.249). The UTP was established as 'an
educational institution or service organisation', strongly committed to keeping
politics out of labour organisations. The UTP initially encouraged, on tactical
grounds, participation in works committees (see p.323). With the wave of
strikes and emergence of unions after 1972, the UTP's attention shifted to
union organisation.

UTP training activities contributed to the formation of a group of unions
which, together with some TUCSA 'parallels', constituted themselves in 1978
as the Black Consultative Committee of Trade Unions (BCC). The BCC in
fact permitted dual membership both of itself and TUCSA. The BCC unions
initially participated in the preliminary discussions which eventually led to the
formation of FOSATU (see p.332). However, only three BCC unions eventually
joined FOSATU. Six BCC unions in fact participated in a seminar in Gaborone
in October 1978 organised by the African American Labour Centre, and
addressed by the US ambassador to Pretoria. This was timed to coincide with
a seminar which led to the formation of FOSATU.

CUSA itself was formed in September 1980, after which dual membership
with TUCSA was ended. Like the BCC, it adopted a black exclusivist ideology
and is critical of unions which maintain a non-racial perspective. Yet, through
its continuing links with the UTP, CUSA has a number of white advisers. It
also has links with pro-capitalist union groupings in the western countries,
particularly the AFL-CIO.

CUSA has generally promoted a form of trade unionism which does not
challenge the capitalist system. The major ideological force within CUSA, the
UTP, explicitly defines its 'first and foremost concern' as the promotion of
'a healthy relationship with the employers'. CUSA's approach to negotiations
gives a leading role to officials rather than shop stewards. Questioned on the
difference between CUSA's perspective and that of FOSATU, the General
Secretary of CUSA's National Union of Mineworkers replied:

> They [FOSATU] are talking about working-class struggle — and we talk

about the workers' struggle. This is, I guess, an ideological difference.
Affiliation to CUSA means that we uphold the black leadership concept.
We ourselves as a union want to uplift the workers so they can get
into leadership positions as we believe that this country is going to be
run by 'black people'.

CUSA cautiously welcomed the Wiehahn legislation. Most affiliates soon
applied for registration, and almost all are now registered. Its leaders frequently
appear at business conferences as the acceptable black trade union voice. They
are strongly cultivated by certain monopolies.

On the other hand, CUSA affiliates have been involved in a number of
strikes. Growing worker militancy, plus pressure from other union groupings,
have led CUSA to identify from time to time with militant positions. It
attended the first unity conference in August 1981 and agreed to a resolution
critical of the Industrial Council system. Some CUSA unions were also
involved in the 1982 national work-stoppage to protest the death while in
detention of Neil Aggett.

In the latter part of 1982 CUSA announced the formation of a National
Union of Mineworkers, and obtained permission from the Chamber of Mines
to begin organising African miners — who had remained unorganised since
the collapse of the influential African Mine Workers' Union following the
1946 African mineworkers' strike. If CUSA succeeds in establishing a base
in this crucial sector, it will be placed in a powerful strategic position within
the trade union movement.

CUSA attended the April 1983 meeting which decided to investigate the
formation of a new union federation. It was initially not represented on the
feasibility committee. However in May 1983 it decided to join in the
exploratory talks.

General Secretary: Phirowshaw Camay.

THE MOTOR ASSEMBLY AND COMPONENT WORKERS'
UNION OF SOUTH AFRICA (MACWUSA)
GENERAL WORKERS' UNION OF SOUTH AFRICA (GWUSA)[9]

MACWUSA organises in the motor industry in the Eastern Cape
and Durban. It emerged out of a conflict between some Ford
workers and the leadership of the UAW in 1980. GWUSA was
formed by MACWUSA in 1980. Both unions have close links with
PEBCO (see p.359). They strongly oppose links with registered
unions, arguing that the basis for unity should be the total rejection
of the official industrial relations system. Both emphasise linking
factory floor struggles to those workers confront in the wider community

The Port Elizabeth-East London area has witnessed some of the most militant and protracted workers struggles after 1979. MACWUSA was formed in October 1980 as a result of dissatisfaction of Ford workers with the role of the FOSATU-affiliated UAW during the 1979 Ford strike. The UAW leadership refused to support a mass demand for a strike over the dismissal of Thozamile Botha for refusing to resign from the presidency of PEBCO (see p.360). The union leadership argued that this was a community issue in which the union should not be involved. Workers at the Cortina plant nevertheless came out on strike and accused the UAW leadership of siding with the management. The Cortina workers then held a meeting which 'dismissed' the UAW leadership. However, they did not advise other plants of the meeting, and the UAW secretary refused to recognise this as a constitutional meeting and declined to hand over the books of the union. The Cortina workers then resolved to form a new union. Its inaugural congress was held in February 1981 and attended by more than 8,000 workers and members of the community.

MACWUSA remains based on particular plants in the Eastern Cape car industry, with a small presence in Durban and Pretoria. It is very hostile to, and competitive with, the FOSATU-affiliated National Automobile and Allied Workers' Union (into which UAW merged in 1981). In 1982 MACWUSA members continued working during a strike called by NAAWU.

The union places much emphasis on rank and file organisation and participation by members in decision-making and control of the union. It has rejected registration as a state ploy to divide workers and as tantamount to acceptance of the apartheid system.

Soon after its formation, MACWUSA was approached by workers in various industries with requests for help in organising themselves. Given that its organisational activities are confined to the motor industry, MACWUSA then formed GWUSA in May 1981. Like MACWUSA, GWUSA is based mainly in the Eastern Cape.

The militant stance of MACWUSA led to confrontation with the state soon after its formation. Most of its important leaders were detained in June 1981. Soon after their release in April 1982, they were banned.

MACWUSA/GWUSA attended the first two trade union unity conferences, but walked out of the second. They subsequently criticised attempts to seek unity with registered unions, arguing that 'unions should first agree on the principle of totally rejecting Industrial Councils and registration because these were government created institutions'. It walked out of the unity conference because proposals to create a new federation of autonomous unions would have allowed registered unions to 'stay registered if they wished'. For a while it appeared as if MACWUSA, together with SAAWU and GAWU, was moving towards the formation of a new federation of unregistered unions. These moves were blocked when both SAAWU and GAWU joined the feasibility committee to establish a federation of registered and unregistered unions. MACWUSA/GWUSA voted against this resolution and are not represented on the committee. However, a Pretoria branch of GWUSA broke away in May 1983 and announced its intention to join in these discussions.

Important leaders:
  Dumile Makhanda
  Dennis Neer
  Government Zini.

MEDIA WORKERS' ASSOCIATION OF SOUTH AFRICA (MWASA)[10]

> Militant unregistered and unaffiliated union of employees in the media and communications industries, open only to blacks. MWASA grew out of organisations linked to the Black Consciousness movement and is still strongly influenced by Black Consciousness ideology. MWASA has been involved in several struggles in the newspaper industry. Several of its leaders have been banned and/or detained.

MWASA was formed in 1980 as a union open to all black employees in the media and communications industries. It succeeded the Writers' Association of South Africa, which catered only for journalists – which itself succeeded the Union of Black Journalists, banned with other Black Consciousness organisations in 1977. Since its formation, MWASA has sought to transform itself from a journalists' organisation into a black media workers' union. It claims some success in this. Its October 1982 conference was informed that less than 10% of its 2,000 members were journalists. However, the organisation recognised that its leadership remained dominated by journalists, with power concentrated in the national executive. It planned a reorganisation at its 1983 congress to change this situation.

   Shortly after its establishment, MWASA became involved in a prolonged strike. In the latter half of 1980, workers on the *Post* newspaper struck over a wage claim. When the *Post* management conceded, the strike spread to *Cape Herald* workers who demanded a similar settlement. In November 1980, MWASA called a national strike in support of *Herald* workers, demanding payment of salaries for the period on strike and negotiation with MWASA representatives. The *Cape Herald* management conceded on the wage claim but refused to pay salaries for the period of the strike. Most *Herald* workers returned to work, but MWASA tried to maintain the strike for a further two months, calling for a boycott and news blackout of Argus and SAAN newspapers (see p.407) by blacks. During this strike, a number of MWASA activists, including its President, were banned. The registration of the *Post* (one of the more anti-apartheid commercial papers) was cancelled by the state, and the *Post* was replaced by the more moderate *Sowetan*. The strike and the boycott were called off early in 1981.

MWASA has been criticised for calling a national strike and boycott over strike pay when the main demand (wages and conditions) had been won. This divided workers to the advantage of the bosses and the state. The failure to liaise with community organisations, to form support groups or to recognise that other workers relied on media reports to publicise their own struggles has also been criticised. The Natal Indian Congress and SAAWU further criticised MWASA for discounting the potential support from more progressive white journalists. This enabled reactionary elements to gain absolute control of the South African Society of Journalists during the disputes, and 15 white journalists who struck in support of MWASA — and were repudiated by the union — were then victimised by management.

MWASA survived the state repression following the 1980/1 strike and is a growing force among media workers. In 1981 it refused to testify before the Steyn Commission of Enquiry into the media (see p.415) on the grounds that its leaders were banned and in detention and that the Commission had a clear brief to recommend stronger control over the press. Towards the end of 1981, a number of MWASA activists were detained, including its already banned President. In 1982, its then National Secretary was sentenced to 18 months imprisonment for refusing to testify in the trial of SAYRC leaders (see p.310).

MWASA's Western Cape section attended the April 1982 trade union unity conference. However, the organisation's Black Consciousness stance makes it hostile to the principle of non-racial trade unionism and MWASA was not represented on the feasibility committee established in April 1983 to investigate a broader union unity.

President till banned in 1982: Zwelakhe Sisulu (son of jailed ANC leader, Walter Sisulu)
Current President: C. Ngqakulu
National Secretary: Thami Mazwai (imprisoned for 18 months in 1982).

THE MUNICIPAL AND GENERAL WORKERS' UNION OF SOUTH AFRICA (MAGWU), formerly the Black Municipal Workers' Union (BMWU)[11]

The BMWU was best known for its involvement in a strike in July 1980 which paralysed Johannesburg municipal services for four days. The strike was ruthlessly suppressed and a number of BMWU leaders put on trial. Since then a dispute within the leadership led to the formation of a breakaway union in the Eastern Cape.

The BMWU was formed in June 1980 as a union of black, mostly migrant workers employed by the Johannesburg City Council. It was set up in direct opposition to an 'in house' union that management sought to foist on workers At its first executive meeting the question of registration was discussed. According to one participant the conclusion was reached that:

> The long and the short of it is that after registration the union becomes an impotent giant, and that without registration it becomes a non-existent giant, in that management can lawfully ignore it.

However, the union finally decided to 'risk registration' in order to 'take advantage of the three months laid down by law that a newly formed union has to wait before applying for registration', to get the union established.

This strategy was, however, overtaken by events. A long simmering dispute at the Orlando power station erupted into a spontaneous strike one month after the BMWU was formed. The City Council sacked 640 workers, saying it would recruit replacements in the Venda Bantustan. The BMWU then called a strike of all municipal workers demanding improved wages and conditions, reinstatement of the dismissed workers and recognition of the union. Johannesburg's municipal services were paralysed for four days. The City's Management Committee responded in traditional apartheid fashion by transporting striking workers back to the Bantustans. Three BMWU leaders were charged under the Riotous Assemblies Act and the sabotage section of the General Laws Amendment Act. They were acquitted in March 1981.

The BMWU's experience in the 1980 strike led to a change in its stance on registration, to which the union is now strongly opposed. BMWU leaders were active in the 1981 anti-Republic day campaign. The union works closely with SAAWU and GWUSA and it attended all three unity conferences. After the collapse of the second unity conference it moved closer to the anti-registration grouping. It is not now represented on the feasibility committee to investigate the formation of a new federation.

Towards the end of 1981 a dispute arose within the leadership over administration. This also appeared to have ideological overtones. The pro-Black Consciousness Secretary, Philip Dlamini and Treasurer, Joseph Mlangeni broke away to form their own union in the Eastern Cape with a claimed membership of 9,000. In 1982 Dlamini was charged with furthering the aims of the PAC. The BMWU President, Joseph Mavi was killed in a car crash following the second unity conference. In 1982, BMWU changed its name to MAGWU.

BIBLIOGRAPHICAL NOTE

The most important single source on the democratic trade union movement is the *South African Labour Bulletin*. Coverage in the South African commercial press is sketchy and tendencious. However, the better such articles and reports on strikes etc. are gathered together in *ANC Weekly News Briefing* (London), and *South African Pressclips* (produced by Barry Streek in Cape Town). The newspaper *SASPU National* devotes much space to the struggles of, and debates in, the democratic trade union movement, as does the review, *Work in Progress* (see p.414). A number of these organisations also produce their own publications.

1. Bonner, P. 'Focus on FOSATU' *South African Labour Bulletin*, 5, 1, 1979.
   Bonner, P., 'Independent Trade Unionism in South Africa After Wiehahn', *South African Labour Bulletin*, 8, 4, 1983.
   Harløv, J., *Labour Regulation and Black Workers' Struggle in South Africa*, Uppsala, Scandinavian Institute of African Studies, 1983.
   Hemson, D., 'Trade Unionism and the Struggle for Liberation in South Africa', *Capital and Class*, 6, 1978.
   Hepple, A., *Workers Under Apartheid*, London, IDAF, 1971.
   Luckhardt, K. and Wall, B., *Organise . . . or Starve! The History of SACTU*, London, Lawrence & Wishart, 1980.
   Luckhardt, K. and Wall, B., *Working for Freedom*, London, 1981.
   O'Meara, D., *Class and Nationalism in African Resistance, Secondary Industrialisation and the Development of Mass Nationalism in South Africa, 1930-1950*, M.A. dissertation, Sussex University, 1973.
   Report of the Commission of Enquiry into Labour Legislation, Part I, Pretoria (RP 47/1979).
   Simons, H.J. and R.E., *Class and Colour in South Africa, 1850-1950*, Harmondsworth, Penguin, 1969.
   South African Institute of Race Relations, *Survey of Race Relations in South Africa*, Johannesburg, SAIRR, annual.
   South African Labour Bulletin, 5, 2, 1979, Focus on Wiehahn.
   South African Labour Bulletin, 7, 1 and 2, 1981, 'State and Capital Responses to Labour'.
   South African Labour Bulletin, 7, 3, 1981, Debating Trade Union Strategy.
2. Luckhardt, K. and Wall, B., 1980 op. cit. (the official SACTU history).
   Workers' Unity (SACTU Newspaper).
   Lambert, R., 'Political Unionism in South Africa', *South African Labour Bulletin*, 6, 2 and 3, 1980.
3. Bonner, P., 1979 op. cit.
   Bonner, P. 1983, op. cit.
   Foster, J., 'The Workers' Struggle in South Africa', *Review of African Political Economy*, 24, 1982.
   Harløv, J., 1983, op. cit.
   FOSATU, 'The Parallel Union Thrust', *South African Labour Bulletin*, 5, 6 and 7, 1980.
   FOSATU Workers' News.
   Luckhardt, K. and Wall, B., 1981, op. cit.
   SASPU National, September 1981.
   South African Labour Bulletin, 7, 3, 1981, 'Debating Trade Union Strategy'.
   South African Institute of Race Relations, op. cit.

4. *FOSATU Workers' News.*
Bonner, P., 1983, op. cit.
Luckhardt and Wall, 1981, op. cit.
SASPU National op. cit.
South African Labour Bulletin, 7, 4 and 5, 1982, 'Focus on East London'
5. Bonner, P., 1983, op. cit.
SASPU National, op. cit.
South African Labour Bulletin, 7, 3, 1981, 'Debating Trade Union Strategy'.
Western Province General Workers' Union 'Registration and Organization: The Case of the Stevedores' *South African Labour Bulletin*, 5, 6 and 7, 1980.
Western Province General Workers' Union, 'The Cape Town Meat Strike – The Struggle for Democratically Elected Workers' Committees' *South African Labour Bulletin*, 6, 5, 1980.
Phambili Basabenzi (GWU newspaper).
6. Baskin, J., 'Factory Workers in the Countryside: The Food and Canning Workers' Union in Ceres and Gabouw' *South African Labour Bulletin* 8, 4, 1983.
Luckhardt and Wall, 1980, op. cit.
Luckhardt and Wall, 1981, op. cit.
7. *SASPU National*, op. cit.
8. *Financial Mail*, 'Phiroshaw Camay: The CUSA Stand'.
Haarløv, op. cit.
Luckhardt and Wall, 1981, op. cit.
South African Institute of Race Relations, op. cit.
Work in Progress 25 1983, 'Recognising Black Trade Unions'.
9. Cooper, C. and Ensor L. *PEBCO A Black Mass Movement*, Johannesburg, South African Institute of Race Relations, 1981.
Luckhardt and Wall, 1981, op. cit.
South African Labour Bulletin, 6, 2 and 3, 1980, issue on the Ford strike.
10. Media Study Group 'MWASA – Trying to Set the Deadlines' *South African Labour Bulletin*, 6, 6, 1981.
South African Labour Bulletin 8, 4, 1983, 'A Critical Look at MWASA'.
Kwasa (newspaper of MWASA).
11. Luckhardt and Wall, 1981, op. cit.
South African Labour Bulletin, 6, 7, 1981, 'The Johannesburg Municipal Strike'.

8. Community, Women's, Students' and Other Popular Organisations

INTRODUCTION[1]

The upsurge of mass struggle since the 1970s has been a multifaceted process. It has seen the emergence of organisations operating at a number of different levels and through different forms of struggle. In addition to the political movements of the national liberation struggle and the trade unions, a prominent role is now played by community or civic associations, women's organisations, student organisations and organisations linked to specific campaigns. Over and above their involvement in particular struggles and campaigns, several of these organisations also have a wider significance in that key strategic and tactical questions about the advancement of the liberation struggle have been raised in and by them.

Community and Civic Associations: These began to emerge towards the end of the 1970s, growing in many cases out of parent-student committees (formed to support struggles in schools), residents' associations and groups formed to oppose the regime's 'Community Councils'.

The years 1979–81 saw a particularly rapid growth of community and civic associations. This was partly prompted by the installation of 'Community Councils' by the regime in a number of areas in direct response to the 1976 uprisings. These Councils were intended to fulfil a dual role: on the one hand, as bodies consisting of collaborators drawn from the oppressed communities themselves, they were intended to give the appearance of community participation in their own administration and hence legitimise the whole system of apartheid administration of black residential areas. On the other hand, the Councils took over some of the administrative functions – most importantly rent collection – from the State Administration Boards (see p.209).

The imposition of Community Councils placed an additional financial burden on urban blacks. The control over rents has led to spiralling rent increases in an attempt to finance these puppet Councils.

The struggle against rent increases has been the principal focus of activity of many of the community and civic associations to date. Most have, however, defined the problems faced by their communities as deriving from the apartheid system – and more particularly from the Administration Boards, Group Areas Act, pass laws and other mechanisms through which the state imposes its control within residential areas. The rent struggles have thus, in most cases, been defined as part of the broader struggle against the apartheid system. Community and civic associations have also been involved in campaigns against bus fare increases, in consumer boycotts, in support of striking workers and such activities as the Free Mandela, Anti-Republic Day and Anti-SAIC campaigns. They have also organised and supported commemoration services for victims of apartheid and/or heroes of the liberation struggle.

Practically all these associations are multi-class organisations, based both on working class and oppressed petty bourgeois forces. However, they differ quite widely in terms of their class leadership. In some, petty bourgeois class forces clearly dominate. This is not necessarily to condemn or decry them; although there are cases of collaborationist or opportunist petty bourgeois led civic associations (e.g. COMPRA – see p.364), many such bodies (such as the Committee of Ten – see p.356), have played an important role in struggles against aspects of national oppression. At the same time, however, the leadership of even the most progressive of such organisations have shown themselves to be ambivalent on the question of the struggle against capitalist exploitation.

In other community organisations (such as CAHAC – see p.361), working-class forces appear to play a more prominent leadership role. Militants connecte with such organisations have argued that community-based organisations and community issues are an essential site of working-class organisation and struggle. They have thus taken issue with forces within the trade union movement which argue that working-class organisation and struggle should, at this stage at least, largely confine itself to the factory floor (see p.334).

The position of community militants has a number of dimensions. Firstly, it is argued that the exploitation and oppression of the working class does not cease when the worker leaves the point of production, but extends into the whole sphere of reproduction. This is particularly evident in South Africa where the whole domestic and community life of black workers is so directly affected by a wide range of repressive apartheid measures. More concretely, charges like rentals, bus fares, etc., absorb a large part of workers' wages; their increase could easily wipe out any gains made in wage struggles. The strugg over such 'community issues' is thus seen as of immediate importance to the working class. It is further argued that restricting class struggle to factory floor issues excludes that large part of the working class, women home-workers whose daily work is directed towards the reproduction of the working class.

The mobilisation of community support in the form of consumer boycotts etc., has moreover been and will continue to be an important factor in trade union struggles. Strong community organisation, with a firm working-class input, is thus seen as an essential aspect of the strength of the working class.

This position assumes that working-class leadership is essential if the struggle for democracy in South Africa is to advance beyond narrow nationalist limits to a broader struggle for liberation from capitalist exploitation. It is thus imperative that the working class assumes a leading role not only in the trade unions but also in all organisations of popular struggle. This is seen to imply a struggle to ensure that

> all mass organisations are structured to encourage the active participa-
> tion of workers in making and implementing decisions. [That] the
> workers do not simply sit back and listen to what they are told by
> their 'leaders'. [That] they take part in all levels, in the mass
> organisations.

Finally, it should be noted that in addition to those community and civic
associations in which petty bourgeois class forces clearly dominate and those
in which working-class forces appear to have a leading role, there are others
where the question of class leadership remains fluid and unresolved.

Women's Organisations: Two organisations stand out here: the Federation of
South African Women (FSAW) and the United Women's Organization (UWO)
(see entries pp. 366 and 368). Both developed because women militants with
a history of involvement in other organisations of the liberation struggle
identified the need for a specific women's organisation to fight both against
forms of oppression and exploitation in society particularly directed at
women, and against sexism within other mass organisations. As Albertina
Sisulu of FSAW put it:

> In the 1950s politics was for men only. Women of all races felt left
> behind and needed an independent women's organisation through
> which they could act on their grievances.

Both FSAW and the UWO, however, identify the women's struggle as part
of the broader struggle for liberation in South Africa, and both see the need
to ally with other organisations of the oppressed as well as to encourage
women to participate more actively in such organisations.

Students' Organisations: The involvement of black students in multi-racial
students' organisations such as NUSAS, as well as the emergence of SASO,
SASM and the Students' Representative Councils, which played such a
prominent role in the 1976 uprisings, have all been discussed in other sections
(see pp.303 and 381). This chapter focuses on organisations that grew out of
Black Consciousness ideology but which have now advanced beyond it. They
now identify oppression as derived from capitalist exploitation, have abandoned all student vanguardist pretensions and now see the working class as
the basic force for fundamental change. This perspective has led them to
reject exclusive concentration on educational issues and struggles and to seek
to involve students in supporting a wide range of community and trade
union struggles.

Organisations linked to Specific Campaigns: These are, by definition, more
temporary organisations than the others dealt with in this chapter. No attempt
is made to include entries on the multitude of constantly changing campaign
committees.

One exception, however, which it is worth noting here is the Detainee

Support movement. This developed towards the end of 1981 following the wave of detentions beginning in November of that year. It campaigns for an end to political detentions and for the release of political prisoners. It has, however, abandoned the old liberal slogan 'Charge or Release' in recognition of the fact that the courts and the laws are part of the repressive apartheid system.

The Detainee Support movement is also noteworthy because it has attempte to become a democratic organisation embracing the families, friends and supporters of all detainees rather than a committee of 'influential' people seeking to negotiate favours from state officials. Towards the middle of 1982, a National Conference of Detainee Support Organisations was held where it was resolved to assist in the establishment of groups in such areas as Venda, Kimberley and the Eastern Cape, where they are desperately needed.

COMMUNITY ORGANISATIONS AND CIVIC ASSOCIATIONS

Committee of Ten and Soweto Civic Association[2]

Formed in June 1977 by 'prominent professional people' following the collapse of the Soweto Urban Bantu Council in the wake of the uprising of 1976. It initially campaigned for Soweto and other major 'black' cities to be administered by autonomous city councils. Later it set up the Soweto Civic Association (SCA) within which it still remains the leading force. The SCA has been involved in struggles against rent and bus fare increases, and support for various boycotts and national campaigns such as the Free Mandela and anti-SAIC campaigns.

Both the Committee and the SCA are led by strata of the oppressed petty bourgeoisie, which identify their interests as lying in the elimination of national oppression. Further, they see both their present and future bargaining strength as deriving from their influence with the masses. This has led them to refuse to collaborate with puppet bodies set up by the state. It has also led them to take up certain popular demands and support and initiate various mass campaigns. On the other hand, the petty bourgeois leadership of the Committee and SCA has shown itself to be extremely ambivalent over the struggle against the capitalist system.

The Committee of Ten was formed in June 1977, following a suggestion in the *World* newspaper that 'prominent people in Soweto' should establish a civic body to run the affairs of the area after the collapse of the Soweto

Urban Bantu Council in the wake of the 1976 uprising. Shortly thereafter, a meeting of some 300 people elected a 'Committee of Ten' headed by Dr Nthato Motlana and composed of 'leading professional people, teachers, churchmen and others'.

Following detailed discussions, the group adopted the name Soweto Local Authority Interim Committee. It announced that it would not collaborate with apartheid bodies such as Administration Boards. Instead, it demanded direct negotiations with the government to implement its 'Blueprint' for Soweto. This envisaged the development of Soweto as an autonomous city with an elected council and a budget of R5,000 million over a five year period, to be financed by local taxation and an extensive subsidy from central government. This programme came so near to advocating an urban Bantustan that some Nationalist ideologues argued it could be reconciled with official policy. However, the Vorster regime chose not to negotiate. Instead, it unilaterally imposed puppet 'Community Councils' (see p.353). The Committee of Ten announced a campaign against these Councils. In October 1977 the entire Committee of Ten was detained and elections for the Soweto Community Council in February 1978 were announced.

The detention of the Committee of Ten proved to be a major tactical blunder as it greatly reinforced the position of those calling for a boycott of the Community Council elections. Even organisations such as *Inkatha* (see p.387), which saw the Community Council as offering it the possibility to extend its influence in Soweto, were forced to withdraw. When the Committee members were eventually released, the clear opportunism of *Inkatha* in rushing to stand in a by-election for the Council, led it to lose much of its previous support to the Committee of Ten. The latter emerged from the election episode as the dominant force in Soweto community politics. The Community Council, led by David Thebahali (an *Inkatha* member who resigned when *Inkatha* was still boycotting the elections), was exposed as a thoroughly discredited puppet body. This election debacle also severely undermined *Inkatha*'s attempt to establish an urban base.

For a short time thereafter, Buthelezi sought a *rapprochement* with Motlana and the Committee of Ten. However, under pressure from their more militant supporters, and confident of their own popularity in the community, the latter rejected Buthelezi's overtures on the grounds that he was 'involved in operating government policy'. Buthelezi responded that Motlana was trying to set himself up as 'the sole authentic black voice in the country'.

During 1979, the Committee took steps to extend its popular base. Most importantly, in September it organised a conference at which the Soweto Civic Association (SCA) was formed. Members of the Committee formed the executive of the SCA, and branches were set up in a number of areas. The Committee also began to seek links with community organisations in other regions. In November 1979 it proposed to PEBCO (see p.359) that a national co-ordinating body of community organisations be set up. The PEBCO leadership felt that much more grassroots organisation was necessary before such a move could be contemplated.

These developments decisively shifted the focus of the Committee's activity away from the formulation of models of civic administration to the articulation, organisation, and leadership, of certain mass struggles. Towards the end of 1979 it stated that Soweto 'could never be run as an autonomous municipal area because it lacked the revenue-producing machinery of the central business district.' Indeed, it advocated 'that a fully autonomous Soweto should participate in a Greater Johannesburg Metropolitan Board which would also comprise other African, Indian and coloured townships'. By 1980, the Committee was arguing that it would only

> be prepared to negotiate once whites had made a commitment to majority rule. Negotiations would then be concerned with the methods and pace of its actual implementation . . . the SCA was opposed to negotiations at all levels in existing conditions as blacks would be negotiating from a position of powerlessness.

Finally, by 1982, when the President's Council proposed a system of local government for black metropolitan areas not fundamentally different from that called for by the Committee of Ten in 1979, Dr Motlana commented for the SCA that 'the proposals did not interest' him, as the SCA would not agree to serve on local bodies when blacks had no representation in central government. In the meantime, under the leadership of the Committee of Ten, the SCA branches involved themselves in campaigns against rent and bus fare increases, support for striking workers, the Free Mandela and the Anti-SAIC campaigns and the organisation of various commemoration services.

Both the Committee of Ten and the SCA are led by particular strata of the oppressed petty bourgeoisie which seek to eliminate the system of national oppression. Yet they are ambivalent over the struggle against capitalism. They have repeatedly expressed themselves as wary of socialism and in favour of 'free enterprise', albeit within the context of a 'partially planned economy'. Moreover, although they have refused to collaborate politically in the 'Total Strategy', they have been involved in some of the programmes designed to 'create a black middle class with free enterprise values'. Among these are a number of projects initiated by the Urban Foundation (see p.122).

The earlier popular support for the Committee appeared to have withered away by the end of 1982. Only a 'handful' of people attended the annual SCA meeting and Motlana announced that the Committee of Ten could not even form a quorum. Former Committee members criticise Motlana's high profile rhetorical leadership for 'making speeches about our rights without a positive and concrete organisation' of the 'enormous potential power' of the community.

Chairman: Dr Nthato Motlana.

Port Elizabeth Black Civic Organisation (PEBCO)[3]

> Formed in October 1979, PEBCO soon achieved a level of mass
> mobilisation unprecedented in any community organisation. It
> emerged through the coming together of local civic associations
> in the Port Elizabeth area.
>
> From the outset, PEBCO strongly opposed participation in
> Community Councils. It advocated an end to 'all discriminatory
> legislation' and 'participation in decision making' by all the people
> of South Africa. PEBCO spread rapidly throughout the Port
> Elizabeth area and attempts were made to set up a Border Civic
> Organisation as well as to forge links with community organisations
> in other areas.
>
> PEBCO sprang to national and international prominence
> through involvement in two strikes at the Ford Motor Company
> plant from November 1979 to January 1980. It was badly affected
> by heavy state repression from the beginning of 1980 onwards.
> This repression also created a leadership vacuum and brought
> contradictions within PEBCO to the surface. Various attempts
> have been made by moderate petty bourgois factions to take over
> the organisation and diffuse its militancy. However, the situation
> now appears to be fluid and by 1982 PEBCO was once again
> holding mass rallies and leading a struggle against rent increases.

PEBCO was formed in October 1979 on the initiative of members of the
Zwide and Kwaford Residents' Associations. These had been formed earlier
in the year to oppose water levies and rent increases imposed by the Eastern
Cape Administration Board.

PEBCO's first executive, elected at a massive public meeting, consisted
of Thozamile Botha, a work study trainee at Ford and former President of
the Zwide Residents' Association, plus workers and small businessmen.
This executive drew up a constitution, approved at another mass meeting
which defined the aims of the organisation as:
1) to fight for equal civic rights for all the people of Port Elizabeth;
2) to fight all the discriminatory legislation enacted by the government and
local authorities;
3) to seek participation in decision making on all matters affecting the people
of South Africa;
4) to fight for the granting of the rights to blacks to buy land under freehold
title at any place of their choice; and
5) to resist any attempt, direct or indirect, to deprive blacks of their South
African citizenship.
It also opposed participation in puppet Community Councils.

PEBCO's growth was spectacular. It soon established branches in all Port

Elizabeth's African townships and, at the beginning of 1980, was joined by the ratepayers' associations of Gelvandale and Malabar representing so-called 'coloured' and Indian citizens of the Port Elizabeth area. During this period, PEBCO's basic method of mobilisation was to hold public meetings. At one stage these meetings, normally attended by several thousand people, were held every fortnight.

During this period, the PEBCO leadership also became involved in seeking ways to spread community organisation to other areas. In November 1979 a meeting was held between PEBCO and Dr Motlana of the Soweto Committee of Ten (see p.356). Motlana favoured the early establishment of a national co-ordinating body for community organisations and even offered to drop the Committee's 'Blueprint' calling for autonomy for Soweto (of which PEBCO was highly critical) to secure PEBCO support for this propsal. PEBCO argued, however, that much more grassroots organisation was necessary before a national body could be envisaged. Following the meeting with Motlana, members of the PEBCO executive visited other Eastern Cape towns to encourage the formation of residents' associations. These latter grouped themselves into the Border Civic Organisation (see p.364).

PEBCO sprang to national and international prominence during two strikes at the Ford Motor Company plant. The first began in November 1979 following an attempt by the management to dismiss Thozamile Botha after complaints about his 'political activities' from white employees. Within a few days Botha's reinstatement had been won, but workers in the Cortina plant then decided to continue the strike over their own grievances. These strikes showed up contradictions between the Cortina plant workers and the leadership of the Fosatu-affiliated United Automobile and Rubber Workers' Union (UAW), which subsequently led to the formation of the Motor Assembly and Component Workers' Union of South Africa (MACWUSA — see p.346). The initial phase of spectacular advance for PEBCO ended with a wave of repression against its leadership at the beginning of 1980.

The focus of the PEBCO's activity now shifted from the consolidation of its base to initiating campaigns intended to advance specific objectives. The first such campaigns centred on the removal of blacks from the Walmer area, the rent question and the harrassment by the Community Council. A PEBCO mass meeting decided to launch a one day stay-at-home to coincide with a proposed tour of Walmer by the Deputy Minister of Co-operation and Development. This move led to the detention and later banning of Thozamile Botha and other members of PEBCO's executive.

This action against the leadership, coupled with the breaking up of protest meetings and the refusal to permit PEBCO to use various halls, had a serious demobilising effect. The January stay-at-home was called off when the visit of the Deputy Minister was cancelled, and a proposed boycott of liquor outlets owned by Administration Boards over the question of access to halls had to be abandoned due to the lack of support. Some observers attribute this serious demobilisation to an over-concentration on the mass meeting at the expense of building up an effective branch organisation during the phase of expansion.

The neutralisation by the state of the original leadership also resulted in the surfacing of class contradictions within PEBCO. Like other community organisations, PEBCO embraces both working class and petty bourgeois forces. For some time immediately after the attack on the original leadership, it appears that a 'moderate' petty bourgeois faction gained the upper hand. Under the presidency of Z. Skosana, it appears that attempts were made to tone down the militant line of PEBCO and defuse much of its mass character. This was, however, thwarted by a revolt from the branches. In August 1980, the branch executives of Zwide, Kwaford, New Brighton and Kwazakhele demanded the resignation of the weak and ineffective Skosana, accusing him of initiating a policy of negotiation with the Community Council without consulting the membership, contrary to the PEBCO constitution. Moreover he had 'failed to maintain links with the branches' or to hold mass meetings.

Skosana was forced to resign at the end of 1980. Since then the situation appears to have become fluid. There have been three Presidents since Skosana while the attempt by a fourth individual to take over as President in 1982 was thwarted. In 1981, PEBCO announced that it would revert to the constitution and objectives adopted during Botha's presidency. In 1982, it tried to regain its mass support and launched a campaign against rent increases. This was partially successful. A number of large public meetings was held. However the campaign collapsed in its second stage — a boycott of businesses owned by the Community Council — when another 'moderate faction' grouped around a suspended former executive member, Wilberforce May, attempted to take over the leadership. May managed to persuade a majority of the executive to elect him President largely on the grounds of his former association with Thomazile Botha. May was highly critical of 'interference' by the trade union MACWUSA (see p.346) and students in PEBCO. However, his election was overturned at a mass meeting which severely criticised the process of selecting leaders 'in secret'. After much manoeuvring, the previous President Qaqawuli Godolozi once again resumed the presidency.

Cape Areas Housing Action Committee (CAHAC)[4]

Based in the Western Cape, CAHAC is one of the largest, most dynamic and militant community organisations. CAHAC serves as an umbrella body for a number of local civic associations based in both 'coloured' and African residential areas. CAHAC activists have been prominent advocates of the position that working-class struggles cannot be confined to work-place issues, but must also embrace community issues affecting workers. CAHAC has campaigned against rent increases, but always within the context of a broader struggle over the whole housing question in South Africa. Its

> supporters have also been active in campaigns against bus fare increases, consumer boycotts in support of striking workers and such activities as the anti-Republic Day and the anti-SAIC demonstrations.
>
> CAHAC places strong emphasis on mass mobilisation and participatory democracy. It has grown rapidly since its establishment in 1980 and has now become the major community organisation in the Western Cape. It has strong links with the community newspaper, *Grassroots*. Its leadership has been subjected to detentions and bannings.

CAHAC was formed in September 1980 through the coming together of a number of resident's associations and parent–student committees (formed to support the schools boycotts then underway). Twelve such bodies constituted themselves as the Umbrella Rentals Committee (URC) in June of that year. It sought to combat a threatened rent increase announced by the City and Divisional Councils in May 1980.

The middle of 1980 was a period of a particularly high level of community mobilisation in the Western Cape. There was activity in support of the schools boycott, a bus boycott against fare increases and a meat boycott in support of a strike by meat workers. This had two major effects on the rent campaign: firstly it led the Council to back down in the face of a high level of Community mobilisation and postpone rent increases; secondly, it led the regime to ban all meetings in the area from mid-June. The result of the latter was that the URC could not function for several months.

In September 1980, when the various boycotts were over and the ban on the meetings lifted, the URC regrouped. At its first meeting it reached the conclusion that the problems facing the oppressed people in their residential areas did not arise from the rent question alone but from the 'whole housing situation'. It accordingly decided to broaden its perspective and changed its name to CAHAC to reflect this.

Throughout its existence, CAHAC has concentrated on the organisation of a rent campaign within the context of a broader struggle over the whole housing question in South Africa. CAHAC activists identify three phases in this campaign.

The first involved the unification of a number of dispersed local civic associations and other group into a larger and more effective organisation. By the time of CAHAC's second meeting in December 1981, 33 organisations based in both the 'coloured' and African communities were represented on it. A special Rent Action Committee was formed at the beginning of 1982, representing 42 civic, trade union and religious organisations.

The second phase involved the specification of grievances and the framing of demands. The immediate issue — massive rent increases of up to 200% in some areas and over 100,000 evictions of tenants for non-payment — were identified as arising from:

1) the lack of representation of oppressed people on bodies taking decisions about housing;
2) the Group Areas legislation which forced people to live far from their work-place and placed them under the control of state officials;
3) the system of 'jumps in rent' which pushed up rent payments enormously when fairly small wage increases were won.
The major demands were for:
1) all rent increases to be stopped;
2) rents we can afford;
3) the government to take full responsibility for housing;
4) bigger state subsidies for housing.
Some of these demands were seen to be long term, others short term and yet others questions of principle. 'Some CAHAC can hope to win in the near future. Other goals are to be fought for in the future. Mixing goals like this helps provide a general sense of direction and immediate targets', CAHAC's activists argue.

The third phase was that of publicity and mass action. A petition was organised (and signed by 41,000 people) as well as a number of rallies, meetings and demonstrations culminating in a demand for a meeting with Community Affairs Minister, Pen Kotze. This was eventually conceded. In March 1982, a CAHAC delegation put its demands to Kotze, who responded by saying that he 'did not force people to live in houses'. Future action on the rent question is being considered, but at the end of 1982 a rent boycott was being ruled out because CAHAC did not yet feel strong enough to sustain such a campaign.

CAHAC has also been involved in campaigns against bus fare increases, boycotts of products in support of striking workers and in mobilising support for the anti-Republic Day and the anti-SAIC campaigns. One of the leading personalities within CAHAC, Johnny Issel, also founded the community newspaper *Grassroots*, which first appeared in 1980 and now provides extensive coverage for community-based struggle in the Western Cape.

CAHAC supporters have been among the most prominent advocates of the position that working-class struggles cannot be narrowly confined to factory based issues. Two main arguments are advanced: the first is that rents often absorb up to 50% of wages and cannot therefore be considered as secondary issues. As they put it:

> The home is the place where we rest from work, the place we bring up our children. But in our society rent is one of the biggest expenses, and it is increasing all the time, and our wages stand still.

In addition to this, a second argument holds that if working class leadership is to be established within the broader struggle for democracy in South Africa, then it is important 'that workers themselves move increasingly into leadership positions, not only in trade unions but also in community and other organisations'. Moreover, by not participating in community issues a large part of the working class — women home workers — will be excluded.

These positions led CAHAC supporters to argue strongly for mass mobilisation and particularly democracy in the organisation of campaigns.

CAHAC is not the only co-ordinating body grouping local civic associations in the Western Cape. At least two others exist — the Federation of Cape Civic Associations and the Combined Mitchells Plain Residents Association (COMPRA). The main activity of the former seems to lie in calling for a boycott of 'dummy institutions' and the rejection of 'collaborators who sold out the oppressed people'. Its role in actual mass struggles seems to be marginal. COMPRA is dominated by local petty bourgeois interests more interested in negotiating deals with capitalist firms to build shops in the area than in taking up demands of the mass of the residents. It also favours an extension of the municipal vote to coloured and Asian owners and occupiers, but has never demanded the inclusion of Africans. This led a number of Mitchells Plain associations to split from COMPRA and join CAHAC at the end of 1981.

CAHAC is the largest and certainly most dynamic and militant of the community organisations of the Western Cape. Perhaps not surprisingly, CAHAC militants have been amongst those subjected to repressive action by the state. Towards the end of 1980, Johnny Issel was banned and, during the wave of detentions beginning towards the end of 1981, held for eight months. A number of editions of *Grassroots* have also been banned.

Chairperson: Wilfred Rhodes.

Other Community Organisations[5]

Whilst the Committee of Ten, PEBCO and CAHAC have been perhaps the most prominent of the community organisations, a considerable number of others have also been involved in important struggles over community issues. Among those referred to in press reports during 1981 and 1982 were the following:
Durban Housing Action Committee: A body similar in many ways to CAHAC. It grew out of the Cato Manor Residents' Association — formed in 1979 to oppose the removal of residents from that area after its proclamation as a white and Indian 'group area' — and the rent boycott movement in the Durban area during 1980 and 1981. Like CAHAC, it was formed initially in opposition to Durban City Council's announcement of its intention to raise rents by up to 100%. In 1982 it organised a number of meetings and a petition with 5,000 signatures, but had not yet attempted to launch a renewed rent boycott.
The Border Civic Organisation: A body formed in 1980 on the initiative of PEBCO and allied residents' associations in such towns as Uitenhage, Graaff Reinet, Cradock, Queenstown, Grahamstown and East London. The Border Civic Organisation was, however, badly affected by the wave of repression launched against both PEBCO and itself by Ciskeian Bantustan and central state authorities. Despite this, a number of meetings and demonstrations

against rent increases were held in Eastern Cape towns during 1981 and 1982.

There were also reports of action on the rent and other community issues by local civic associations in the Pretoria Area, Lenasia, and East Rand towns among others, whilst the Vaal Triangle Administration Board offices in Sasolburg were stoned during a demonstration against higher rents in 1981.

Mention should also be made of the various 'squatters' campaigns initiated to oppose attempts by the state to remove from urban areas persons whose presence is 'illegal' in terms of influx control legislation. Among the most important of these were:

The Crossroads/Nyanga Campaign: This long running struggle began in 1978 when the regime announced its intention to 'clear the Western Cape of illegal squatters'. At the beginning of the year, it demolished houses in the Unibell camp with the clear intention of forcing the 6,000-12,000 residents of the area to return to 'their' Bantustans, and announced its intention of doing the same with the Crossroads camp near Nyanga. This provoked widespread opposition from a number of quarters and led to the formation of a Crossroads Committee representing the residents. The high level of mobilisation achieved around the Crossroads issue as well as the widespread publicity around such incidents as the shooting of residents during a pass raid in 1978, enabled the Crossroads Committee to force a number of postponements of the date set for demolition. Gravely embarrassed by the 'Crossroads affair' at a time when it was attempting to promote an image of 'reform', the apartheid regime attempted to negotiate a settlement with the Crossroads 'squatters'.

Essentially. the regime offered to rehouse certain Crossroads families in a new township near Nyanga, and to stop removing families from the nearby Alexandra Area − previously demarcated as a hostel township. It would not, however, permit 'illegal' persons in the Western Cape to remain there, but offered merely to reconsider certain cases and facilitate the recruitment and transfer of others to the mines of the Transvaal and Orange Free State.

Although Koornhof's proposals were never endorsed by the Crossroads residents, several hundred families moved to the new settlement set up near Nyanga East (nicknamed 'New Crossroads') during 1980 and 1981. According to the community newspaper *Grassroots* by April 1982 much of the 'fighting spirit' of old Crossroads had 'gone to sleep' in the New Crossroads. At the same time, however, pass raids continued to be mounted throughout the Nyanga area to pick off 'illegal' residents.

These developments had the effect of shifting the focus of the campaign from one to prevent the demolition and break up of a particular community to one against harrassment of persons classified as 'squatters'. During 1981 a Nyanga Squatters Committee was formed, which demanded the right of people in the area to stay in the Western Cape and not to be deported to the Transkei.

In March 1982, members of the Committee began a fast in St. Georges Cathedral and despite various attacks on them by far right hooligans, held out for 24 days, forcing concessions from the regime that they themselves would be immune from prosecution and that the cases of Nyanga 'squatters' would be reconsidered.

Resistance to similar attempts to remove 'squatters' from urban areas was also reported from Inanda (near Durban), Fingo Village (Grahamstown), Katlehong (Germiston) and Duduza and Daveyton in the Transvaal, among others.

WOMEN'S ORGANISATIONS

The Federation of South African Women (FSAW)[6]

Women's organisation founded in 1954 by leading women in the Congress Alliance. The FSAW left its mark on the history of struggle in South Africa during the campaign against the extension of passes to African women in mid-1950s. The high point of this campaign was the march of 20,000 women to the Union Buildings, Pretoria on 9 August 1956. Subsequently, 9 August has been designated South African Women's Day. The women's campaign against passes in these years was an important spur towards the broader anti-pass campaign which dominated mass struggles in the years immediately before and after the Sharpeville massacre.

The FSAW was effectively forced to cease operating by the massive state repression of the 1960s. Although the organisation itself was never formally banned, a large number of its leaders were detained, banned and forced into exile and the organisation was prevented from holding meetings or carrying on other activities.

In the present phase of renewed mass organisation and struggle, attempts are being made to revive the FSAW as a mass national women's movement. FSAW leaders identify the need for organisation and struggle both around issues that particularly affect working class women — maternity leave and equal pay — and to encourage women to become more actively involved in 'all issues affecting the people'. They also identify the need for a struggle against sexism within the other popular organisations.

The Federation of South African Women was formed in April 1954 on the initiative of such leading women of the Congress Alliance as Lilian Ngoyi, Florence Mkhize, Ray Alexander, Helen Joseph, Rahima Moosa, Elizabeth Mafekeng and Frances Baard. The FSAW was established because its founders identified the need for a mass women's organisation which would both struggle against forms of exploitation and oppression which particularly affected womer and mobilise women to participate more actively in the broader liberation struggle. In addition, a specific women's organisation was seen to be necessary to fight against sexism within other organisations of popular struggle. As a FSAW document of the 1950s put it:

> Many men who are politically active and progressive in outlook still follow the tradition that women should take no part in politics and a great resentment exists towards women who seek independent activities or even express independent opinions.

The establishment of the FSAW represented the first attempt to set up a broad-based organisation to take up women's struggles in South Africa. Previous organisations that had mobilised women in struggle had either been temporary bodies linked to specific campaigns, or else, like the Women's League of the ANC, based exclusively on the membership of other organisations.

At its first national congress, the FSAW pledged itself to take up issues closest to women, but also to support the general campaigns of the Congress Alliance. Its position from the start was that although women's emancipation would have to involve organisation and struggle by women themselves, it would be inconceivable without the achievement of majority rule and an end to apartheid.

Undoubtedly the issue closest to women in the 1950s was the extension of the pass system to African women. This was begun in 1952 and only completed in 1963. The state attempted to isolate resistance by issuing passes to women in different areas at different times. Right from the start there were protests and demonstrations, but these tended to be isolated, taking place only in those areas where passes were currently being issued. The FSAW realised that this resistance had to be co-ordinated. Further, it realised that it was important to develop women's understanding of what the pass system meant in terms of oppression.

In October 1955, the Transvaal branch of the FSAW, together with the ANC Women's League, led a demonstration of some 2,000 women to the Union Buildings, Pretoria. The success of this demonstration and the fact that the state started issuing passes to women on a much larger scale in 1956, decided the FSAW to plan a national march to Pretoria to take place just before its conference on 9 August. Despite the fact that the 9 August march was banned, and despite a number of measures taken by the regime to prevent women travelling to Pretoria, 20,000 women converged on Prime Minister Strijdom's office at the Union Buildings, whilst an estimated 30,000 other women took part in activities related to the march. The women went straight from the march to the FSAW conference — thus ensuring that those who went to Pretoria became part of the organisation. During this demonstration the famous slogan 'Strijdom when you struck the women you struck a rock' was coined and 9 August has subsequently been designated South African Women's Day.

The period following August 1956 saw a number of campaigns over the pass laws, involving both men and women. There were pass-burnings, and campaigns in which numbers of people went to police stations without passes with the objective of clogging up the jails and making the pass system inoperative. The struggle against the pass system in fact dominated mass struggles in the last years before the March 1960 Sharpeville massacre – which itself occurred during an anti-pass demonstration. The FSAW was active at a number of levels in these campaigns.

In the post-Sharpeville wave of intensified state repression, the FSAW, unlike the ANC and Congress of Democrats, was never formally banned. However, many of its leading members were jailed, restricted and forced into exile, whilst the organisation was prevented from holding meetings or carrying on other activities.

In recent years, however, the organisation has undergone a revival. Activists within the country insist that:

> The FSAW itself has not changed: it is still a non racial federation that aims to bring women's organisations together. It still operates side by side with other organisations involved in the liberation struggle.

Among the priorities identified by the FSAW for the current period are the following:

> In the labour area, black women are exploited as women and as blacks: issues such as maternity leave and equal pay are crucial . . . Men have to be made aware of problems facing women and must accept us as equals. Awareness among rural women must also be increased and the FSAW can do this through organising in such regions . . . But women should be involved in all issues affecting the people, such as the civic issues of housing, rent and education.

One of the leading personalities behind the current revival of the FSAW, Albertina Sisulu, was recently banned for two years. She had previously been banned for a period of 17 years since the 1960s.

United Women's Organisation (UWO)[7]

Based in the Western Cape, the UWO adopts a position that identifies women's oppression as deriving from the 'general system of capitalist exploitation' rather than inherent contradictions between women and men. It aims to organise women to struggle for the elimination of oppression of women, within the context of a broader struggle against oppression and exploitation in South Africa. It also struggles to root out existing prejudices

> against women within the organisations of the oppressed. The
> UWO has organised a number of commemorative functions and
> participated in various campaigns.

The United Women's Organisation was formed in April 1981 at a conference
attended by more than 300 delegates from 31 areas of the Western Cape. It
developed out of a small group of women who began working towards the
formation of a women's organisation at the end of 1978. Many founding
members had a history of political experience in trade union or community
organisations or in the anti-pass campaigns of the 1950s.

The formation of the UWO was inspired by recognition of the need for a
specific women's organisation to struggle for the elimination of women's
oppression within the context of the broader struggle against oppression and
exploitation in South Africa. It identifies women's oppression as deriving
from capitalist exploitation, rather than inherent contradictions between
men and women. As its supporters put it:

> It is clear that women's oppression has a basis in the general system of
> the capitalist exploitation. The rulers confuse us by making it seem as
> if men are responsible for women's oppression and thus we don't see
> that as workers we are all exploited and must join forces against the
> system of exploitation. There are women's organisations which make
> the mistake to organise women against men and thus do not threaten
> the system in any way.

The need for a specific women's organisation arises because:

> The fight to end this system of exploitation can only end in defeat as
> long as women occupy a passive position in society. Women's oppression
> must be ended and it is only women who can consistently fight to
> achieve their liberation. This shows the need for organisation on a
> broad and democratic scale, since it is only by organising that women
> can become a political force. While recognising that both men and
> women are exploited under capitalism, it is also necessary to organise
> women around that oppression which they experience unlike men
> (sexism – the belief that women are inferior to and dependent on men
> – and domestic slavery) . . . Even within the organisations of the
> oppressed, prejudices against women still exist and must be rooted out
> . . . Women must constantly struggle against their own attitudes of
> passivity as well as against the attitudes of men, both of which have
> been socially conditioned.

The UWO seeks to 'unite women from all classes who could play a constructive
role in the struggle for democracy in South Africa'. To this end, it organises
discussions between women in its various branches, and public functions such

as Commemorative meetings on 9 August — South African Women's Day
(see p.367). It was also active in the early stages of the Nyanga Squatters'
campaign and had representation on a number of strike support committees.
It encourages women to participate in other organisations of the oppressed
masses and fight within them for the 'removal of all laws, regulations, conventions and customs that discriminate against women' as well as against sexist
practices which persist within these organisations themselves.

The UWO has some links with the FSAW (see p.366) — FSAW speakers
have, for example, spoken at UWO meetings. However, the UWO has to date
maintained its own organisational identity.

Chairperson: Mildred Lusea.

STUDENTS' ORGANISATIONS

The Azanian Students' Organisation (AZASO)[8]

An organisation of college and university students, AZASO was formed in
November 1979 by students from Fort Hare, Ngoya, Natal, Turfloop and
Durban-Westville universities and Mapumulo and Howard colleges. The
organisation initially aimed at promoting Black Consciousness (BC) ideology
on black university campuses. However, in 1981 AZASO dropped all BC
trappings from its constitution arguing that BC 'has served its purpose. We
must move on.' This led it to identify the enemy [in South Africa] as 'the
system of exploitation of man by man and not . . . whites as such'. It now
views capitalism, rather than colour, as the main 'cause of black oppression
in South Africa'. AZASO remains, however, a black students' organisation for
'tactical reasons'. It co-operates with progressives within the white students'
community.

In its contribution to the struggle for 'overall liberation in South Africa'
AZASO seeks to involve students in a wide range of community struggles,
the organisation of commemoration services in honour of martyrs of the
liberation struggle, as well as in trade union support campaigns. It also campaigns for the desegregation and democratisation of education. Together
with COSAS (see p.371) it is preparing an 'Education Charter' of basic demands
for a democratic education system.

In its development from BC, AZASO has abandoned student vanguardist
notions. It now sees the working class as the key instrument to 'bring about a
redistribution of power' in South Africa. Its close co-operation with organisations of the masses and the emergent trade unions has made it a target of state
repression and a number of its members have been banned or detained.

The Congress of South African Students (COSAS)[9]

COSAS organises black students at 'medium level' educational institutions — secondary and night schools, technical, teacher training and correspondence colleges.

It was formed in June 1979 as the successor to the South African Students' Movement (SASM) which was banned in 1977. Like SASM, COSAS was originally oriented to Black Consciousness and the implications of student vanguardism present in BC strategies. As such, it played an important role in the 1980 mass student struggles against Bantu Education. However, the experience of these struggles propelled COSAS into a recognition that

> students are a specific group and that they have to play a limited role
> in the broader struggle. Their role is to support the struggle of the workers
> . . . especially in the trade union and community fronts.

It abandoned Black Consciousness, arguing that the forces which oppress black students are 'not colour as such but rather economic factors'. It adopted 'Student-Worker Action' as its theme for 1982. This entails organising students as 'the workers of tomorrow' with an 'obligation to serve the community'. COSAS has involved itself in a wide range of community and trade union support struggles. Its general objective is 'to fight for compulsory, free and democratic education in a democratic society'. As such it has fought against a number of specific issues raised by state education policy. Most recently, its organisation of a parent-student committee to oppose the age limit of 21 imposed in secondary school (aimed to exclude militants) forced the government to suspend the introduction of this measure.

More generally, together with AZASO (which it describes as 'another COSAS in the universities' — see p.370), COSAS is involved in the preparation of an 'Education Charter', to formulate the basic demands of a democratic and universal education. This is explicitly based on the Freedom Charter as an example of the formulation and adoption of democratic demands. In 1980 COSAS declared its support for the Freedom Charter as the programme for a democratic society.

From its formation, COSAS has been subjected to severe repression; its entire national executive was detained in 1979. Its first President, Ephraim Mogale, is serving a jail sentence for a political offence and a number of its members have been detained and/or banned.

BIBLIOGRAPHICAL NOTE

General

A number of local journals and newspapers carry information on these organisations. Important among these are *Social Review, Grassroots, SASPU National, ANC Weekly Newsbriefing* and *South African Pressclips* (produced by Barry Streek, Cape Town).

1. See 'General' above.
  Kimble, J. and Unterhalter, E., 'We Open the Road for You, You Must Go Forward'': ANC Women's Struggles 1912–1982', *Feminist Review*, 12, 1982.
  Social Review, Cape Town, 16, November 1981, 17, February/March 1982.
  SASPU National, 2, 7 September 1981.
  Walker, C., *Women and Resistance in South Africa*, London, Onyx Press, 1982.
2. See 'General' above.
  Financial Mail, Special Survey 'The Urban Foundation Two Years On', 16 February, 1979.
  Saul, J., and Gelb, S., *The Crisis in South Africa: Class Defense, Class Revolution*, New York, Monthly Review Press, 1981.
  South African Institute of Race Relations, *Survey of Race Relations in South Africa*, Johannesburg, SAIRR, annual.
  Southall, R., 'Buthelezi, Inkatha and the Politics of Compromise' *African Affairs*, 80, 321, 1981.
  The *Star* 14 April 1983.
3. See 'General' above.
  Cooper, C. and Ensor, L., *Pebco: A Black Mass Movement*, Johannesburg, SAIRR, 1981.
  Evans, M., 'The Emergence and Decline of a Community Organization' *South African Labour Bulletin*, 6, 2–3, 1980.
  South African Institute of Race Relations, op. cit.
  The *Sunday Tribune*, 26 September 1982.
  Interview with Thozamile Botha.
4. See 'General' above.
  Grassroots, Cape Town, a publication closely aligned to CAHAC.
  Social Review, 17, February/March 1982.
5. See 'General' above.
  Grassroots, 3, 3, April 1983.
  South African Institute of Race Relations, op. cit.
  South African Pressclips, op. cit.
6. See 'General' above.
  Grassroots, 2, 5, July 1982.
  Social Review, 15, September 1981.
  SASPU Focus, 1, 2, June/July 1982.
  SASPU National, 2, 6 and 7, 1981.
  Walker, C.I., op. cit.
  Walker, C., 'The Federation of South African Women, 1954–1962' paper presented at Conference on the History of Opposition in Southern Africa, Johannesburg, January 1978.

7. See 'General' above.
   Grassroots, 2, 6, August/September 1981 and 3, 3, April 1982.
   Social Review, 16, November 1981.
8. See 'General' above.
   South African Institute of Race Relations, op. cit.
   SASPU National, 3, 1, February/March 1982.
9. Ibid.

9. The Democratic White Opposition to Apartheid

HISTORICAL INTRODUCTION[1]

Throughout both the segregation and apartheid phases of South African history, there have always been whites opposed in various ways and degrees to the system of capitalist exploitation and national oppression. These 'democratic whites' are not drawn from a single class force but have come from different backgrounds. They have allied themselves in different ways with the struggles of the oppressed masses — sometimes through organisations based in some way on these masses themselves, in other cases through organisations consisting mainly of whites. This chapter considers the latter types of organisation. However, at the outset it should be noted that whatever the different organisational forms involved, two broad currents among the 'democratic white opposition' can be identified: a) the socialist/communist and b) the liberal/radical.

Main Trends Prior to 1948

The socialist/communist current of white opposition grew out of the left wing of the white labour movement at the beginning of this century. Its strategic objective was to establish a socialist society in South Africa. Particularly in its early years, it had considerable problems over such key strategic questions as: which class forces would be in the vanguard of a South African revolution — white workers (as was thought for some years), an undifferentiated working class, or black workers? What was the role of national oppression in South Africa and how should socialists/communists relate to the struggles of nationally oppressed classes other than the black working class? Shortly after its formation in 1921, the Communist Party sought to base itself on black workers. By the late 1920s it was a largely black organisation (see p.290). Nevertheless, within the CP and other peripheral socialist movements, a minority of progressive whites have always been an important force.

The liberal/radical current developed among certain categories of intellectuals (churchmen, university teachers, students, etc.). Mainstream liberalism is, and always has been, a minority tendency within the strategic political thinking of the capitalist class. Its fundamental critique of the institutions of segregation and/or apartheid was not that they subjected the masses to exploitation and oppression, but rather that they threatened the stability of the system by not creating sufficient 'space' for emergence of a supportive black middle class. As one leading liberal, Professor Edgar Brookes, put it in the 1930s:

> Bantu nationalism must . . . reach out towards Bolshevism. How could it be otherwise? If there is a clearly defined proletariat anywhere in the world it is in South Africa. Happier or wiser countries postpone or altogether avoid a Marxist 'class war' by the creation of common interests, by opening doors of opportunity enabling the ambitious member of the proletariat to escape into the governing class, at the very least by ostentatious professions of a single national unity transcending class distinctions.
>
> In South Africa we follow a different course. We try to prevent the multiplication of common interests, we close almost every door of opportunity, and we loudly proclaim the impossibility of union in a single nation. Class becomes associated with something definite and tangible such as colour. The stage is inevitably set for the 'class war'. As a member of the bourgeoisie myself, I hope it is not set for the 'dictatorship of the proletariat'. As a liberal I believe that only swift and far reaching reforms and many more opportunities for self-realisation on the part of the Bantu can create the impossibility of such dictatorship. I insist . . . that those who are fighting the Battle of the Bantu are the real friends of the white man and the whole South African community.

However, a more radical minority current within liberalism has not been explicitly and self consciously tied to ruling-class strategy. Rather, its strategic objective has generally been to seek to end national oppression in South Africa without ending capitalist exploitation. It does not recognise, indeed denies, that the fundamental source of national oppression lies in capitalist relations of exploitation. It also denies the importance of class and class struggle. As the leader of the Liberal Party, Alan Paton, put it in the 1950s: 'A true liberal does not think in terms of groups, he thinks in terms of persons'. Nevertheless, liberalism in its more radical form has been an important form of political activity among whites who have not merely sought to perpetuate the fundamental structures of the system in some different way, but who have genuinely opposed and challenged at least some of the basic institutions of segregation and/or apartheid.

Democratic White Opposition 1948 to the 1970s

The coming to power of the Nationalist Party regime in 1948 (see p.16) had a major impact on both currents of the democratic white opposition. The prospect, and later the reality, of a Nationalist rise to power led to an unprecedented attempt to mobilise whites in a broad front of democratic opposition to the intensification of mass repression and further undermining of such democratic rights as existed. During the war, progressive white servicemen formed the Springbok Legion as a trade union of the ranks dedicated to fighting fascism both internally and externally. During and after the war, left wing white trade unionists, Communist Party members and others, acted in a number of ways to resist the assault by *Broederbond* 'Christian national' trades unionists (see p.247). After 1948, the Torch Commando, a broad front alliance of anti-nationalist forces based mainly on ex-Servicemen, staged a number of large demonstrations in opposition to repressive measures introduced by the Nationalist regime. At their height these organisations and activities took on some of the characteristics of a mass democratic movement of certain classes and strata of 'white society'.

By shortly after the 1953 elections, however, most of these early forms of large scale white opposition had disappeared. This was partly due to the heavy attack to which they were subjected as part of the more general assault by the regime on all forms of popular organisation and resistance. However, the initial brunt of the regime's attack fell on communists and trade unionists. To the extent that whites were included in these groups they also fell victim to state repression. The Communist Party was outlawed in 1950, its members — black and white — were 'listed', and some were banned. Thirty-three progressive trade unionists, many of them white, were also banned in the early 1950s.

One effect of this attack on the white left was that the leadership within the broad front Torch Commando increasingly passed into the hands of liberals with constitutionalist illusions. This, coupled with the fact that despite initial fears the Nationalist regime did not, in fact, act against the vital interests of any class in 'white society', but, on the contrary created the conditions for all whites to prosper, rapidly led to its demise. After entering into a 'people's front' alliance with the United Party and Labour Party in the 1953 elections and accepting that its demonstration activities should be curtailed in the interests of the 'parliamentary struggle', the Torch Commando collapsed.

Two organisations of the democratic white opposition stand out during the period following the demise of the Torch Commando — the Congress of Democrats (COD) and the Liberal Party. There were however also democratic whites in student organisations such as NUSAS (see p.381), various church groups and protest groups such as the Black Sash (see p.384).

The Congress of Democrats was formed in 1953 in direct response to a call by the ANC for whites to join a body which would work in close co-operation with the liberation movement and recruit white support for the policies and practices of the ANC. Among the leading forces in COD were former Communist Party members, without a legal political home since the banning of the Party in 1950. But COD also attracted former members of the Springbok Legion and a number of liberals to the left of the Liberal Party. COD sat as an equal partner (along with the ANC, SACTU, South African Indian Congress and Coloured People's Congress) on the Consultative Committee of the Congress Alliance. It identified completely with the ANC, the senior partner in the alliance. Though few in number, COD members played a significant and active role in the Alliance. Many were drawn from the banned CP and were politically experienced. COD was involved in all major Congress activities of the period, particularly the campaigns against Bantu Education and population removals, and the ANC campaign to collect a million signatures in support of the Freedom Charter.

The Liberal Party was formed in 1954. From the outset it saw its principal role as placing its 'policies and principles before the white voters to reassure them that a non-racial democracy is a valid and exciting choice'. It opposed all forms of legislated racial discrimination; membership was open to individual of all races. However, it held as a fundamental tenet that it was striving for the establishment of a bourgeois parliamentary democracy based on 'free enterprise such as it saw existing in western Europe or North America. It was thus strongly opposed to 'communism', although some individual members were prepared to give communists their due acknowledging that they were non-racialists and stood for a 'mixed' society. The Liberal Party was also strongly committed to 'constitutional methods' of struggle, opposing 'violence' and 'illegal actions' in all forms. It denied that class or class interests were of any real significance and believed that the white electorate could eventually be won over for liberalism if only they better understood 'the severe disabilities under which the non-Europeans are at present labouring . . .'. The party's focus on the white electorate led it initially to call for a qualified franchise, then thought more acceptable to white voters than one person one vote. Finally, it strongly opposed the Congress of the People and the Freedom Charter, arguing that the clauses in the Charter calling for nationalisation of monopolies were fundamentally illiberal.

Whilst the Liberal Party never abandoned its anti-Marxist/anti-communist tenets, towards the end of the 1950s, it did move somewhat closer to the Congress movement. Party policy was reassessed and the earlier emphasis on electoral activities was reduced. The 1958 elections marked a major turning point: the Nationalist victory confirmed that the United Party (see p.157) would not be able to defeat the Nationalists, and sowed doubts amongst the Liberals about the effectiveness of electoral politics. Pressure from younger Liberals also pushed the party leftwards.

By the late 1950s it had changed its franchise demands to one person one vote. In 1959 it supported the ANC's call for an international boycott of South African goods. It called for trade union rights for blacks and for a radical redistribution of land, but qualified this by saying that there should be no major drop in agricultural production. It also called for a 'welfare state'.

This leftward shift provoked a number of conflicts within the party. The 'old guard' strongly resisted attempts by younger members to support such methods of struggle as pass-burning, strikes and civil disobedience. They also opposed attempts by the left of the party to turn it into a mass movement through launching a recruiting drive amongst blacks.

These conflicts eventually produced a number of splinter groups on the

fringes of the Liberal Party. When the PAC split from the ANC in 1959 (see
p.298), a number of more radical liberals identified with the 'Africanists'.
One of them, the staunchly anti-communist Patrick Duncan, eventually
became the only white to be admitted as a member of the PAC. Another
group of radical liberal intellectuals repudiated the position on non-violence
and, together with individual Trotskyists, formed a sabotage group, the
African Resistance Movement (ARM). After damaging a few installations the
group was eventually tracked down, partly through being betrayed by its
Secretary, Adrian Leftwich, who turned state's witness. Several ARM members
were condemned to long terms of imprisonment. One, John Harris, who had
planted a bomb in Johannesburg station, was hanged.

Both COD and the Liberal Party and its fringe groups came under attack
with the wave of intensified repression following the Sharpeville massacre.
Once again, however, it was the left wing COD with its Congress connections
which suffered most. In 1962 COD was banned, as had been the ANC in
1960 (the other three constituent organisations of the Congress Alliance
were not banned although many of their members were detained or
restricted). Thereafter, a large number of COD members were banned or
detained, and, after the destruction of the underground command at Rivonia
in 1963, a large number went into exile together with ANC members.

This crackdown enabled liberalism to assert a virtually unchallenged hegemony over the beleagured democratic white opposition still existing within
the country. For a short time after the banning of the ANC and COD, a number
of former members of these organisations joined the Liberal Party. The state
soon responded by picking off the most radical elements within the Liberal
Party with banning orders and detentions. Eventually, in 1968 in the face
of the Prohibition of Political Interference Act proscribing multi-racial political
organisations, the Liberal Party dissolved rather than segregate itself.

Democratic opposition continued to survive among whites in student
groups such as NUSAS, church organisations and protest groups such as
the Black Sash. But by the early 1970s its impulse was both small and overwhelmingly liberal.

Democratic White Opposition in the Current Period of Heightened Mass Struggle

The position of democratic white opposition changed significantly in the
period of intensified mass struggle following the strikes of 1973 (see p.33).
While it remained confined to a tiny minority of mostly intellectuals (students,
lecturers, church people, etc.), the numbers involved have grown appreciably.
Moreover, liberalism has lost its dominant position and the white left is no
longer ghettoised as it had become by the early 1970s.

These changes were caused by a number of factors. Most importantly,
the heightened mass struggle created a number of possibilities for involvement
by the white left. Perhaps as significantly, it also produced an intense crisis

for ruling class ideology in all its forms, which had the important effect of polarising more white intellectuals towards the masses.

A second crucial factor was the rise and subsequent transcendence by most mass organisations of the ideology of Black Consciousness. While Black Consciousness presented itself ideologically as a rejection of all whites, it reflected above all a rejection of white liberalism. It forced white radicals, especially students, to confront their own racism. Its blanket ban on white participation in Black Consciousness organisations forced them to seek alternative forms of engagement. This was an important factor in the turn to organise workers by left wing white students in the early 1970s. The subsequent advance beyond Black Consciousness to non-racialism created broader possibilities for democratic whites to identify with mass struggles in a way which they had not been able to since the days of COD.

A third factor has been the adoption by the ruling class in the face of the heightened mass popular struggles of certain elements of liberal ideology. One of the aims of the state's Total Strategy (see p.38) and of 'private' organisations such as the Urban Foundation (see p.122) has been to win over a supportive black middle class. This has been done by attempting to promote among them certain basic liberal propositions — for example that there is a radical separation between the 'free enterprise' economy and racial discrimination, and that the encouragement of the former will lead to the undermining of the latter. This has led to a widespread rejection among the popular masses of liberal ideology in general, and this has been a major factor leading to the erosion of liberal hegemony among democratic whites. It has also had the effect of pushing a number of liberals towards more radical positions.

One of the main areas of activity by democratic whites has been in the trade unions. The upsurge of black working-class struggle led to a number of democratic whites becoming involved in supportive activity. At first, this tended to be through distinct student support committees. In the early 1970s, NUSAS (see p.381), set up a number of Wages Commissions which undertook studies aimed at helping groups of workers involved in struggles with employers. Democratic whites later became involved in the workers' advice organisations which preceded the formation of unions (see p.324). and whites are now involved in all the various democratic unions. The degree to which democratic whites have become integrated in the trade union movement was dramatically highlighted by the mass response of workers to the death in detention of Dr Neil Aggett in February 1982.

Theoretical/historical study has been another prominent form of activity. During the 1970s, a number of left academics set out to challenge the liberal interpretation of South African history and produce alternative Marxist analyses of segregation and apartheid. This activity, which began in exile, is now being continued and developed in a number of ways by intellectuals working within the country. Marxism, in one form or another, has now established itself as a major intellectual force, and a leading liberal historian has lamented 'the Marxist orthodoxy in South African historiography'.

The growth of community and civic organisations since 1976 has also been an area of activity with which democratic whites have identified. Moreover, a growing number of whites both inside the country and in exile have joined and worked for the liberation movement.

The growing tide of mass struggle has also had an impact on those progressive organisations which, for one reason or another, still tend to be based largely on whites. NUSAS, which operates on the still largely white campuses, became visibly radicalised during the 1970s and now identifies in a number of ways with advancing mass struggles. Among other things, through its South African Student Press Union (SASPU), it produces some of the most important publications covering mass struggles.

Finally, mention must also be made of the war resisters' movement (see p.385). This emerged in response to the increasing militarisation of the 1970s and now operates to assist conscripts to resist being compelled to fight for apartheid.

Democratic whites remain a tiny minority of the overwhelmingly racist white population. They continue to be subject to all contradictions arising from the objective places they occupy in the class structure of South Africa. Liberal ideology still is a force among them, but an increasing number now identify with the liberation struggle and accept Marxism.

NATIONAL UNION OF SOUTH AFRICAN STUDENTS (NUSAS)[2]

Anti-apartheid student organisation open to all students, but based mainly on white students (overwhelmingly of bourgeois background) at English-speaking universities. Since the English language universities are key institutions of mainstream liberalism, NUSAS represents one of the main left wing forces within liberal institutions.

NUSAS was formed in 1924 by students from the nine (English- and Afrikaans-speaking) white universities then in existence. Its stated objectives were 'to bring students together on the basis of their studenthood, to advance their common interests and to provide a forum for the examination and resolution of their differences'. For nine years it ran a student parliament in which students of different political persuasions debated political questions. Its National Council lobbied on agreed (mainly educational) issues. It excluded blacks and concentrated on building up unity between Afrikaans- and English-speaking white students.

In 1933, the question of black membership was raised for the first time when Fort Hare University College (for blacks) was proposed for membership. Although the proposal was rejected, it provoked the disaffiliation of all the Afrikaans campuses except Stellenbosch, which finally withdrew in 1936 (see p.278).

NUSAS continued as an English-speaking white student organisation with a vague liberal rhetoric but very little else, until the end of the war. In 1945, inspired by the anti-fascist sentiment of the war years, it finally voted to admit Fort Hare. At the same time it adopted a constitution advocating, *inter alia,* democracy . . . the rights of all to the free expression of opinion . . . [and] equality of educational and economic opportunity for all . . .'.

NUSAS's general non-racial liberal stance and opposition to apartheid measures led it into increasing conflict with the Nationalist regime after 1948. It opposed in particular the introduction of Bantu Education in 1954 and measures to confine black students to separate 'tribal colleges' and to take over Fort Hare University College — which eventually passed into law under the 1959 Extension of University Education Act.

The 1950s, however, saw a number of disaffiliations from black centres which accused NUSAS of concentrating too heavily on narrow academic issues and the erosion of freedoms — freedoms which may well have been real for white students, but which black students had never enjoyed. This and the broader mass struggle then underway provoked an intense debate within the organisation throughout the 1950s. On the one side, the more radical wing wanted NUSAS to concern itself with more than simply 'freeing education'; on the other side, the more liberal/conservative wing wanted the organisation to continue to restrict itself to 'student concerns as such'.

In the end, it was essentially a liberal–centrist position which won out. In the formula which was to guide NUSAS's practices throughout the 1960s, it identified its principal role as being to draw 'recruits into the struggle against white supremacy from groups that the left had been unable to reach' and most importantly 'from the large reservoir of moderates among (its largely white) mass membership'. This was to be done by campaigns over specific, generally academic, issues and 'leadership training' which would 'broaden and radicalise' the perspectives of new recruits.

Fort Hare and other black centres reaffiliated in 1957, and the presence of black students produced a certain pressure which led NUSAS to enter, from time to time, into the wider realm of politics with a number of 'radical statements' about broader issues.

By the mid-1960s, NUSAS had become perhaps the most outspokenly radical of the legally existing opposition organisations. Most other opposition to the left of NUSAS had been repressed. To its credit, NUSAS never moderat its stance on its basic principles — non-racialism and its support for various democratic demands.

After 1964 NUSAS came under increasing attack from the state; various forces mounted campaigns seeking to discredit the NUSAS leadership among its student base; bannings and restrictions were also imposed on the leadership Finally, NUSAS was subject to extensive infiltration by BOSS agents — the most notorious being Craig Williamson who became an executive member of NUSAS in the early 1970s.

By the late 1960s, the liberal formula of concentrating on winning over the mass of moderate (largely white) students came under increasing criticism both from white radicals and more importantly from black students. Local committee organisation on all campuses had by the late 1960s become much less effective as radicals turned to other activities. More significantly, reflecting the growing restiveness of the oppressed classes generally, black students became increasingly dissatisfied with NUSAS as a potential vehicle for their struggles.

In 1969 the majority of black centres and black individual members withdrew to form the South African Students' Organisation (SASO) (see p.303). SASO criticised NUSAS for its 'white liberalism', arguing that it concentrated on academic issues of importance to white students, rather than the pressing concerns of blacks.

The formation of SASO left NUSAS in a quandry; it eventually reluctantly accepted SASO's withdrawal and began to search for a new role for itself. For nearly three years, until 1972, it appeared to flounder, considering during a period of 'reassessment' such diverse proposals as the re-establishment of a 'student parliament' consisting of Afrikaans- and English-speaking white universities, becoming a political party within a new 'alternative' parliamentary structure which it would create, and becoming a purely cultural and/or educational organisation.

The Black Consciousness critique of NUSAS and white liberalism did have an important impact. It both forced white students to examine their own racism and, more significantly, propelled a small group of more radical student activists into concerning themselves with issues affecting black workers. These were then taken up by NUSAS as a whole. In 1971/2 it set up a series of 'Wages Commissions' which produced a number of studies of considerable use to workers in putting demands. Various white students moved into active involvement in organising workers. The wave of strikes and resurgence of working-class activity after 1973 created a number of possibilities for work supporting the emerging trade union movement.

The radicalisation of NUSAS in the 1970s was further stimulated by increasing state action against it. A large number of its activists were banned in 1972, and a protracted commission of enquiry recommended stringent state action to limit its activities. It was declared 'an affected organisation' in 1974, and any form of external finance was outlawed. In 1974 a 'Free Political Prisoners' campaign led to the trial (and acquittal) of a number of NUSAS leaders charged with furthering the aims of the ANC. By the late 1970s the organisation was strongly supporting various forms of democratic struggle, particularly on community issues.

NUSAS is currently committed to a joint campaign with AZASO and COSAS to democratise education. It also produces a number of useful publications on various issues. Student newspapers, too, have undergone a vast change, with *SASPU National* becoming one of the best sources of information on mass struggles. This link with mass struggle and the critique of liberalism generally has also changed NUSAS's ideological stance. Liberalism is not dead within the organisation but NUSAS is certainly a much more militant and

effective organisation today than it was ten years ago. Not surprisingly, it
has continued to be subject to state repression.

BLACK SASH[3]

> Organisation based mainly on white women of bourgeois origin.
> The Black Sash was founded as a conventional liberal pressure
> group but has moved steadily leftwards over the years. It has
> recently identified itself with certain popular demands and mass
> campaigns. In 1981 it supported a resolution declaring that the
> principles of the Freedom Charter offered 'the only viable
> alternative to the present exploitative and repressive system'.

Originally called the Women's Defence of the Constitution League, the Black
Sash was founded in 1955 to protest over the Nationalist regime's proposal
to enlarge the Senate and thus secure the two-thirds majority necessary for
taking coloured voters off the common voters' roll (see p.135). The
organisation adopted as its emblem a black rose and its members wore black
sashes in public demonstrations to 'mourn' the abrogation of the South
African Constitution by the Nationalist regime.

During the 1950s and 1960s, it held a number of 'vigils' and 'haunts' to
protest against various measures being introduced by the regime. A 'vigil'
was a group of women in black sashes with bowed heads standing outside
some public building. A 'haunt' consisted of a group of women in black
sashes with heads up, who tried to embarrass government ministers by catching
their eyes.

The organisation's class base led it in its earlier days to adopt a rather
exclusivist stance, and to stand aloof from mass struggles. It declined an
invitation to participate in the mass women's march on the Union Buildings
organised by the Federation of South African Women to protest at the extension of the pass laws to women in 1956 (see p.367). Later, however, it did
participate in the multi-racial 'consultative committees', consisting of Congress
members, church people and various liberals, formed in 1959 to exchange
ideas.

By the mid-1960s, as it became clear that the Nationalist regime would
not respond to protest demonstration, these ceased to be the principal form
of activity of the Sash. 'Haunts' were abandoned altogether and 'vigils'
became less and less frequent. Instead, it embarked on a programme of
'political education' both of its own members and the 'public'.

More importantly, it set up Pass Law Advice Centres to help first African
women, and later men, with problems posed by the pass laws. Over the years
its contact with the masses through these Centres visibly radicalised the

organisation. It produced a number of authoritative studies of the effects of the pass laws and became one of the staunchest critics of the pass system, albeit from within a liberal ideological framework. In more recent years, the state has forced a number of its Advice Centres to close, apparently on the grounds that they were involved in attempting to 'bend the rules' so as to permit 'illegal' Africans to enter or remain in urban areas.

In October 1981, the Black Sash participated in the National anti-SAIC (South African Indian Council) Campaign (see p.296) and associated itself with a resolution declaring that '. . . the only viable alternative to the present exploitative and repressive system is one based on the principles of the Freedom Charter', and resolving '[not to] rest until we have established a democratic South Africa based on the Freedom Charter'.

President: Sheena Duncan.

WAR RESISTERS[4]

The militarisation of South African society and the increasing involvement of the military in brutal and aggressive actions, has led a growing number of white conscripts to resist compulsory military service. Between 1978 and 1982, over 5,000 people were prosecuted for failing to report for military service.

The specific forms of this resistance have been varied, as have its ideological bases. There are those who have made a firm, publicly stated refusal to accept their call up, resulting in long sentences in Detention Barracks. Some of the prominent resisters of this type have had religious or pacifistic objections to involvement in any form of war. However, an increasing number who have called themselves 'selective conscientious objectors', object to involvement in an unjust war, such as a war for the maintenance of apartheid. Others who have been unwilling to fight for apartheid have gone into exile either on being called up for training or on being drafted for active service in Namibia. Still others have responded to the longer and longer call ups, the increasing brutality of army life or specific atrocities by evading call up, deserting, going absent without leave or, in a few cases, staging organised but usually short-lived walkouts.

Out of this resistance has grown a number of organisations. The most important of these is the Committee on South African War Resistance (COSAWR), operating in exile, and underground. COSAWR was formed in December 1978 through the merger of two groups operating in Britain. It provides practical assistance and advice to resisters, particularly those going into exile. It also tries to involve exiled resisters in discussion groups and seminars and draw them into anti-apartheid solidarity work. In addition it does research on the increasing militarisation of the apartheid state and produces publications, such as its journal *Resister*. COSAWR's basic stance is one of general support for the liberation struggle, including the armed struggle led by the ANC.

Similar organisations exist in other European countries and in North America and they have played an important role in publicising atrocities committed by the apartheid military forces. They have also produced some of the best research publications available on the South African military.

BIBLIOGRAPHICAL NOTE

General

Each of the organisations dealt with in this chapter produces its own publications. Their activities are well covered in the *ANC Weekly News Briefing* (London) and *South African Pressclips* (produced by Barry Streek, Cape Town. In addition such publications of the white left as *Work in Progress, Africa Perspective* and *SASPU National* provide an invaluable source of information on a wide range of issues.

1. Brookes, E., *The Colour Problems of South Africa: Being the Phelps Stokes Lectures 1933*, Lovedale, Lovedale Press, 1934.
   Levy, M., 'Liberal Party and C.O.D.: Opposition to Apartheid' *Work in Progress*, 19, 1981.
   Robertson, J., *Liberalism in South Africa*, Oxford, Clarendon Press, 1971.
   South African Institute of Race Relations, *Survey of Race Relations in South Africa*, Johannesburg, SAIRR, annual.
2. Curtis, N. and Keegan, C., 'The Aspiration to a Just Society' in Van der Merwe, H. and Welsh, D. (eds.), *Student Perspectives on South Africa*, Cape Town, David Philip, 1972.
   South African Institute of Race Relations, op. cit.
   Student National (now banned) replaced by *SASPU National* and *SASPU Focus*.
3. Michelman, C., *The Black Sash of South Africa*, London, 1975.
   South African Institute of Race Relations, op. cit.
   Walker, C., *Women and Resistance in South Africa*, London, Onyx Press, 1982.
4. ANC Weekly News Briefings.
   Resister: Journal of the Committee on South African War Resistance, London.
   South African Institute of Race Relations, op. cit.

10. Other Political and Miscellaneous Organisations

INKATHA YE NKULULEKO YE SIZWE – NATIONAL CULTURAL LIBERATION MOVEMENT[1]

The ruling party in the KwaZulu Bantustan and dominant grouping in the South African Black Alliance (SABA – see entry p.403). *Inkatha* is the personal political vehicle for its leader, Chief Gatsha Buthelezi, 'Chief Minister' of KwaZulu. It is used to further his pretentions to the role of national representative of African (and occasionally, other nationally oppressed groups) through his form of politics of 'collaborative opposition' within the central South African state.

The organisation's membership claims range between 200,000 and 750,000. It claims to represent all social strata within and outside KwaZulu. However, despite this assertion of a mass base in the urban areas and claim to a developed organisational structure and support from Africans of all 'tribes', *Inkatha* remains a strongly tribalist organisation based on an overwhelmingly Zulu membership and constitutionally linked to the ruling structures in the KwaZulu Bantustan. Moreover, its membership is largely drawn from the rural areas of this Bantustan. Despite the continuing application of various forms of compulsion within KwaZulu to generate compliance with its line, the organisation draws a disproportionate amount of its support from the older generation in KwaZulu.

Inkatha represents those sections of the KwaZulu petty bourgeoisie whose interests are tied up with the apparatus of the Bantustan 'state', but whose wider political aspirations can never be fulfilled in this the most fragmented of the Bantustans. Hence Buthelezi seeks to mould an alliance with 'moderate' elements of the urban petty bourgeoisie, based on a populist ideology which stresses the unity of all oppressed class forces and national groups.

This involves apparently contradictory politics: on the one hand is Buthelezi's fierce rhetorical rejection of apartheid – which he conceives simply as a system of racial oppression and exploitation, and not in class terms, nor as a capitalist system of exploitation and oppression. For a long period in the 1970s, Buthelezi attempted to appropriate the symbols and slogans of the ANC and present himself as the legitimate heir of its tradition of mass resistance in the 1950s. Since his final repudiation by the ANC in 1980 he has distanced himself from its 'violent option'. On the other hand, however, Buthelezi and *Inkatha* are active participants in a crucial institution of the apartheid state — the Bantustan — and have been condemned as collaborators by, among others, the Black Consciousness movement.

This contradictory politics is linked with Buthelezi's so-called 'multistrategy of liberation' which rejects majority rule and armed struggle as involving unobtainable solutions at an unacceptable cost. After a great deal of prevarication, *Inkatha* and its leader have declared themselves in favour of some form of 'power-sharing' which would grant African representation in the central state. Embodied most clearly in the 1982 Report of the Buthelezi Commission, such a 'consociational solution' is to be achieved through internal negotiation with the power holders (threatening them constantly with the mobilisation of *Inkatha*'s alleged mass base). This is, in reality, a strategy for the co-option of *Inkatha* leaders in the existing structure of power in a way which does little to threaten the real bases of that power. However, this strategy has yielded precious few gains. Buthelezi currently badly needs a clear political victory to strengthen his waning credibility among the oppressed. In pursuit of this, *Inkatha* and its leader have flatly rejected the 'new constitutional dispensation' proposed by the regime (see p.137). Instead, Buthelezi sticks to the Report of the Buthelezi Commission as the blueprint for the future. In January 1983 he sharply attacked *Inkatha*'s ally in SABA, the Labour Party (see p.395), for agreeing to participate in this apartheid scheme.

Historical Origins, Formation and Aims

The origins of *Inkatha* date back to the 1920s when the Zulu monarch, King Solomon, formed *Inkatha Ya Ka Zulu* (Zulu national movement) in an attempt to generate mass support for the monarchy faced with the disintegration of pre-capitalist social relations. It was revived by Buthelezi in 1975 and its name modified to *Inkatha ye Nkululeko Ye Sizwe*. This was a period in which the apartheid state sought to build around the current Zulu king, King Goodwill — himself Buthelezi's nephew — a series of political alliances against Buthelezi and possibly to oust him as 'Chief Minister' of the Bantustan (see p.227). *Inkatha* was formed by Buthelezi partly to give himself an organised political base within the Bantustan to resist these manoeuvres, and partly to provide a political platform in the wider South African state.

An understanding of the politics of *Inkatha* needs to be grounded in an analysis of the political strategy adopted by Buthelezi in the 1970s. Gatsha Buthelezi is a prominent member of the Zulu aristocracy as a descendent, through his mother, of two Zulu kings, chief of a powerful clan, and descendant through his father of a line of advisors to the Zulu king. After he assumed his chieftanship in 1953, he strongly and successfully resisted the imposition of the 1951 Bantu Authorities Act in Zululand, and joined the ANC in the 1950s.

In 1970 he finally accepted his own participation in the Bantustan scheme and was made Chairman of the new Zulu Territorial Authority, and 'Chief Executive Councillor' (later 'Chief Minister') of the KwaZulu 'government' in 1972. However, unlike the others he proved no simple puppet. He used his position to voice strong opposition to apartheid, declaring his personal preference for a system of universal franchise in a unitary state, and totally rejecting the fragmentation of South Africa. When challenged on his role as ruler of a Bantustan, he retorted that in the absence of any other power base, Africans had to use the system to fight the system. In the political vacuum of the early 1970s, his outspokeness won much attention, and embarrassed the regime, leading to various unsuccessful attempts to mobilise a 'king's party' against him. However, these attempts, and the growing support for the militant and strongly anti-Buthelezi Black Consciousness movement by the mid-1970s, convinced Buthelezi of his need for an organised political base for his brand of politics. Hence the revival of *Inkatha* in 1975.

This so-called National Cultural Liberation Movement declared its aims to be: to liberate Africans from cultural domination by whites; to eradicate racialism, neo-colonialism and imperialism; to abolish all forms of racial discrimination and segregation; and to uphold the 'inalienable rights' of Zulus to self determination and national independence. The latter was not seen to conflict with its objective of working for the summoning of a national convention of leaders of all racial groups to develop a framework for power sharing and progression to majority rule.

Social Base and Political Operation in KwaZulu

Despite *Inkatha*'s claim to be a national movement open to all Africans, rather than a sectional party, it is tribally based. Over 90% of its members are Zulus and its leadership is constitutionally reserved exclusively for Zulus. Its patron is the Zulu king, and all Zulus are 'automatically' members. Its ruling National Council, designated by the *Inkatha* constitution as 'the supreme body of the Zulu nation', is comprised of the entire membership of the KwaZulu 'Legislative Assembly', plus the organisation's Central Committee. The latter is largely comprised of members of the KwaZulu 'Cabinet'. The *Inkatha* constitution decrees that the President of *Inkatha* must be the Chief

Minister of KwaZulu — an office restricted to hereditary Zulu chiefs. This heavily tribalist structure of *Inkatha* has led to allegations that it is a vehicle of 'Zulu imperialism' — the Zulus being the largest of the ten so-called ethnic nationalities identified in apartheid theory and comprising on their own a larger population than South Africa's whites.

Inkatha has spent much effort on building an urban base for itself, yet its urban support remains relatively weak, confined to the city of Durban and to small pockets on the Witwatersrand. In 1978, almost 80% of its branches were located in the rural areas of KwaZulu and Natal. As a tribally and regionally based organisation, *Inkatha* draws a disproportionate amount of support from the older generation and particularly women in KwaZulu. Women reportedly run the organisation on a day-to-day basis. This reflects the social composition of the Bantustan population, with large numbers of men absent on migratory labour and women subject to the coercive powers of the Bantu Authorities system. A number of reports indicate that KwaZulu Bantustan chiefs compel the populations under their jurisdiction to pay annual subscriptions to *Inkatha*. Likewise, there are reports that non-members of *Inkatha* who wish to marry are asked by the chiefs why they are not members. Although a small number of chiefs oppose Buthelezi, the chieftancy seems to have been the moving force behind the expansion of *Inkatha* since 1975.

This strongly coercive aspect of *Inkatha* within KwaZulu has a number of aspects. The 1975 session of the KwaZulu 'Legislative Assembly' which revived *Inkatha* declared itself against the 'importation' of political parties into KwaZulu. In effect, a one party regime has been imposed on the Bantustan. The few non-*Inkatha* candidates who had the temerity to stand in the 1978 Bantustan elections were roundly condemned as traitors to the 'Zulu nation' and only one of them was elected. The *Inkatha* line is officially imposed on the entire Bantustan. An '*Inkatha* syllabus' is taught in its schools, and teachers in particular (many of whom were associated with the strongly anti-Buthelezi Black Consciousness movement) are subject to very strong pressure to conform.

The KwaZulu 'Legislative Assembly' decreed in 1978 that a civil servant's standing within *Inkatha* would be a key factor in decisions about promotion. Likewise, local businessmen keen to gather the economic crumbs apartheid offers to the Bantustan petty bourgeoisie, need to remain in good standing with the organisation and the chiefs who run it. Through this practice of heavy-handed persuasion and coercion, Buthelezi has clearly succeeded in the first of his aims in the revival of *Inkatha*. The Bantustan has been politically sewn up behind him, and no opposition to his autocratic rule is brooked.

Inkatha and the Politics of Resistance

Buthelezi's second aim for *Inkatha* is to provide an organised base for his political aspirations in the wider South African state. Since at least 1976, Buthelezi has firmly rejected any idea of 'independence' for KwaZulu. He lays strong claim to his citizenship in the wider South Africa. As the most fragmented Bantustan, KwaZulu offers its local petty bourgeoisie even fewer economic opportunities than those in more consolidated 'homelands' such as the Transkei and even Bophuthatswana. *Inkatha*'s politics reflect this fact that the political and economic aspirations of the KwaZulu petty bourgeoisie can never be contained within its 40 dispersed fragments. Hence the organisation has sought to weld together an alliance with the urban petty bourgeoisie and to present itself as the legitimate spokesman for this class force on a national basis. Its populist platform and Buthelezi's occasionally militant rhetoric, moreover, seek to present both *Inkatha* and its leader as the legitimate voice of the entire nationally oppressed population. Through *Inkatha*'s dominant role in the South African Black Alliance, of which Buthelezi is Chairman (see entry p.403), the Chief has assumed for himself the role of chosen leader of all South African's black communities.

This claim is, however, strongly contested. The Black Consciousness movement has long condemned Buthelezi as a traitor and puppet. Students at KwaZulu's 'own' university have stoned his car and boycotted his speeches. When Buthelezi attended the funeral of the PAC founder, Robert Mangaliso Sobukwe in 1978, his life was threatened by the crowd, enraged by his presence, and he was forced to leave under humiliating circumstances. When one youth case a handful of silver at him, he commented: 'They spat in Christ's face, now they are doing it to me'. His attempt to appropriate the ANC mantle internally, collapsed in 1980 when the liberation movement finally condemned him and his politics. Opinion surveys conducted by *Inkatha*'s own 'Buthelezi Commission' show stronger and growing support for the ANC in all areas except KwaZulu. A poll conducted by the Johannesburg *Star* newspaper in late 1981 showed far stronger support for the ANC than *Inkatha* in all urban areas, even in the so-called 'Zulu' city of Durban.

The economic 'strategy' of *Inkatha* reflects its petty bourgeois base. It rejects 'unfettered capitalism' which is seen to have built the South African economy at too great a cost. *Inkatha* formerly advocated 'African communalism' as a 'form of socialism' which encourages private enterprise whilst 'protecting the people as a whole' through state-owned organisations with a controlling interest in all enterprises. This allegedly 'inhibits the tendency of capitalism to divide the people into rich and poor'. This 'African communalism' has been implemented in KwaZulu through the South African state-owned KwaZulu Development Corporation (KDC) and the concept of 'tripartite companies'. This admits white investment into KwaZulu in partnership with the KDC, with blacks as shareholders. Little different from apartheid economic strategy in the other Bantustans, this 'African communalism' has in fact drawn *Inkatha* closer to large capitalist undertakings, and on occasion incurred the wrath of small KwaZulu traders organised in the *Inyanda* (local chambers of commerce). Buthelezi was forced to grant the *Inyanda* joint participation with a white firm in a wholesale venture to still their criticism of a decision to admit the Checkers supermarket chain into KwaZulu. Recently, even rhetorical references to 'African communalism', have been abandoned.

The 1982 'Buthelezi Commission' prescribes 'a mixed market economy' as offering 'the best opportunities for economic growth and the proper development of a society combining the best features of an economy of opportunity with those of an economy of equity' (see below).

Furthermore, Buthelezi is fiercely opposed to campaigns to get foreign capital to disinvest from South Africa. He has regularly appeared in advertisements in international newspapers paid for by the apartheid state appealing for increased foreign investment in South Africa.

The Phases of 'Collaborative Opposition'

1972–1975

The politics of *Inkatha* and its leader have been through a number of phases. In the years prior to the 1976 Soweto uprising, Buthelezi presented himself as an earnest 'bridge builder' between internal and external opponents of apartheid. He travelled to a number of African states, and held discussions with Presidents Kaunda and Nyerere, who were both reportedly impressed. In 1975 he appealed to the OAU to give Prime Minister Vorster's 'detente' policies a chance (see p.44). In this period, before *Inkatha* and its internal political base had been organised, Buthelezi's politics were conducted largely through public statements and a public relations campaign. He gained much international prominence, but was roundly condemned by the increasingly influential Black Consciousness movement as a puppet. This was one of the key reasons leading to the revival of *Inkatha*.

1976–1980

The Soweto uprisings in June 1976 marked a new phase in these politics of 'collaborative opposition'. Buthelezi strongly condemned the police violence but also rapidly associated himself with police attempts to stem the revolt by promoting divisions within the black community. He called on 'responsible elements' to set up vigilante groups to protect property against militants. In August 1976, it was widely alleged that *Inkatha* has assisted the police in inciting Zulu migrant workers who rampaged through Soweto in an attempt to break a stay-at-home strike called by student leaders. This led to increasing bitterness between the Black Consciousness movement and *Inkatha*. Following the banning of the Black Consciousness organisations in late 1977, *Inkatha* sought to fill the political vacuum by forging new political alliances with other political organisations. The result was the formation in January 1978 of the South African Black Alliance (see entry p.403) of *Inkatha*, the (coloured) Labour Party and the (Indian) Reform Party (see entries pp.395 and 400) Under Buthelezi's chairmanship, the Alliance aimed to forge black unity and prepare the way for a national convention. Its impact, however, has been weak.

During this period Buthelezi likewise consolidated his international links, particularly with West Germany and the US. His invitation to a 'prayer breakfast' with US President Jimmy Carter, gained much publicity. More importantly, this was the period in which Buthelezi worked hard to assume the mantle as the internal wing of the banned ANC in order to legitimate his position in increasingly open conflicts with other petty bourgeois internal groups, most notably the Soweto Committee of Ten (see entry p.356). However, he overstepped himself in 1979 when he publicised his discussions in London with the ANC leadership. The ANC intended that these talks remain confidential and strongly repudiated Buthelezi's attempt to increase his own political credibility through what the ANC regard as a strictly informal contact. This led to a final breach in 1980, undermining Buthelezi's post-1976 strategy to present *Inkatha* as a third force between white and black nationalism.

This final break with the ANC led to a political crisis for *Inkatha*. It had always addressed two audiences, the oppressed population on the one hand, and the power structures of the apartheid state on the other. Its political strategy aimed to mobilise support from the former through a populist platform of the rhetoric of 'liberation' as a device to win concessions from the latter. Thus, Buthelezi's attempt to assume the ANC mantle between 1976 and 1980 was accompanied by a strong move to the right. His sharp conflict with the Soweto Committee of Ten, his total rejection by the Black Consciousness movement and humiliating expulsion from the Sobukwe funeral, taken in the context of the growing effectiveness of ANC military operations and political organisation, all served to further isolate *Inkatha* and Buthelezi, driving them closer to the apartheid regime. He opened a 'dialogue' and formal consultations with the ruling Nationalist Party and the powerful *Afrikaner Broederbond* (see entry p.267). The announcement of the proposed 'Constellation of Southern African States' by Botha in 1979 was lauded by Buthelezi as an example of the NP 'abandoning apartheid', and he expressed his willingness to serve on the proposed 'council of states'.

By mid-1979, internal divisions had emerged in *Inkatha* as various local leaders sharply condemned Buthelezi's increasing co-operation with state plans to slightly increase the powers of black local authorities as a complement to Bantustan strategy. By early 1980, Buthelezi was publicly appealing for unity in his organisation. Feuds were fought for control of various local branches and a senior *Inkatha* official was gunned down under mysterious circumstances. With the outbreak of a further student boycott of apartheid educational institutions in 1980 – which, unlike the previous round in 1976/7, now reached *Inkatha*-controlled Natal and KwaZulu – Buthelezi mobilised armed groups to attack students. Appropriating the language of the apartheid regime, he argued that the student boycott was 'part and parcel of a total onslaught against *Inkatha*'. At this stage, *Inkatha* was again attempting to build a strong base in the Johannesburg Soweto township through participation in Community Council elections. However, its move to the right seemed to have strongly diminished its popularity. Polls conducted by the Argus group newspaper the *Sunday Post* and the *Star*, reported that 69% of the sample supported the Committee of Ten (boycotting the elections) compared with only 9% for *Inkatha*. Moreover, the Committee of Ten leader, Dr Ntatho Motlana was found to enjoy stronger support amongst Soweto Zulus than Buthelezi himself.

Post-1980: The 'Buthelezi Commission'
In this context of waning support for *Inkatha*, Buthelezi increasingly turned to his second political audience — the current wielders of economic and political power — seeking to present himself as the mediator who will resolve the pattern of conflictual politics. With all elements of the ruling class vitally preoccupied with devising forms of restructuring socio-political relations so as to save capitalism and leave the basic structure of power intact (see p.38), in 1980 Buthelezi announced the appointment of the 'Buthelezi Commission' to consider 'the requirements for stability and development in KwaZulu and Natal'. This was clearly seen as laying down a blueprint for the constitutional development of South Africa.

The 'Commission' was composed of a few *Inkatha* members and was dominated by the representatives of monopoly capital, together with Natal regional (white) capitalists, representatives of professional bodies, a number of internationally prominent conservative academics and the Progressive Federal and New Republic Parties. The ruling Nationalist Party and ANC declined to participate. It is interesting that in this so-called 'black initiative' to draw up a blueprint for the resolution of South Africa's problems, the current representatives of the capitalist class together with leading white South African and American conservative academics, did all of the drawing. This was clearly reflected in the recommendations of the 'Commission' which, in effect, put forward proposals to preserve the existing structure of economic power in South Africa, and modify political relations so as to permit the entry of a small and highly controlled black elite into the political institutions of the central state in such a way that they would be rendered politically impotent and thus pose little threat to the existing structure of power.

This is not the place for a detailed analysis of the Report (see the excellent article by Southall cited in the bibliographical notes). However, it should be noted that it calls for a 'mixed-market [i.e. capitalist] economy', and adopts the currently trendy political formula of 'consociational democracy' as a form of 'power-sharing designed to outflank the advocates of violent change'. It fails totally to address the class inequalities in the capitalist system, or recommend a restructuring of exploitative economic relations. Its economic recommendations for greater labour mobility, freehold tenure of land, etc., reflect the straightforwardly capitalist programme of the various class forces represented on the 'Commission'. Moreover, the 'consociational formula' put forward in the Report is explicitly based on the visiting American expert's view of this structure as 'a grand coalition of political leaders of all significant segements in the plural society'. Designed to ensure the politics of power broking — compromise and consensus between racially defined elites — this formula is concerned with the regulation of conflict and the maintenance of stability of the existing order, rather than the transformation of the existing order and the transfer of power. Buthelezi has quite explicitly stated that he has now abandoned all his previous demands for majority rule as 'unobtainable'. The 'Buthelezi Commission' signals to the ruling class that *Inkatha* and its leader are available for co-option in return for certain minimum concessions to its leaders, and their admission into the magic circle of political decision-makers in capitalist South Africa.

In return, Buthelezi quite explicitly holds out his alleged capacity to stave off the revolutionary onslaught. In this self-adoption of the Muzorewa role in South Africa, the declining support for *Inkatha* is an embarrassing problem. Hence Buthelezi has again resorted to militant rhetoric in his rejection of the 'new [tri-camera] constitutional dispensation' of the government – which totally excludes Africans and seeks to co-opt Indians and so-called coloureds (see p.137). He sharply attacked his then SABA 'allies', the (coloured) Labour Party in January 1983 for accepting these proposals when he publicly urged their rejection.

Given the growing support for the ANC and rejection of Buthelezi and *Inkatha*'s politics of 'collaborative opposition', Buthelezi clearly needs to demonstrate to both blacks and the existing powers that be, that *Inkatha* can deliver the goods. This, however, is extremely doubtful.

SOUTH AFRICAN LABOUR PARTY[2]

Political party formed and led by sections of the petty bourgeoisie from the so-called coloured community. Its declared objective, is to work for a system of universal suffrage within a single parliament. The chosen means of attaining this end is non-violent struggle using the 'platforms' created by the institutions of the apartheid state against the apartheid system itself. Despite the claim to be merely using apartheid institutions to defeat the system, the Party's organisational machinery was in fact structured around the Coloured Persons' Representative Council (CRC) until the latter's abolition in 1980. From the outset, the Labour Party has been a parliamentary type party, playing little part in mass organisations or mass struggles. When it eventually gained control of the CRC in 1975, it attempted to make a strategic shift from what its leaders described as the 'politics of protest' to 'the politics of negotiation'.

The abolition of the CRC in 1980 created a major problem of role definition for the Party. It was caught between the pressures of increasingly mass struggles on the one hand, and the temptations of the increasingly attractive 'perks' being offered to so-called coloured and Asian leaders willing to collaborate with the Total

Strategy, on the other (see p.33). After much vacillation, the January 1983 Party congress finally resolved to revert to 'working within' the institutions of apartheid, and put up candidates for the 'coloured' chamber of the three-tier parliament. A number of observers argue that the Labour Party's mass base has largely been lost to community-based organisations, and that it will have trouble in mobilising even the 13% of the potential electorate it mobilised in the last CRC by-election.

The Labour Party was a member of the South African Black Alliance (see p.403) until its suspension (and later withdrawal) following its decision to enter the so-called coloured parliament.

The South African Labour Party was formed in 1965 on the initiative of a petty bourgeois group from the so-called coloured community to contest elections for the newly-formed Coloured Representative Council. It drew some support from former members of the Coloured People's Congress (a component of the Congress Alliance – see p.286), and other militant groupings. It initially defined its strategic objective as 'common roll representation with equal franchise rights for all Coloureds and Whites'. By 1969, it was calling for 'one-man-one-vote, with direct parliamentary representation for all South Africans, whatever their racial group'. The Party's constitution, however, dedicated it to 'vigorously opposing communism in all its forms'.

The Party acknowledged from the outset that the CRC was an apartheid institution. It nevertheless 'accepted the Representative Council as a stepping stone to full democratic rights because it offered the only means of political expression that was available in the interim to the Coloured people'. In the 1969 CRC election, Labour emerged from a 37% poll with 26 seats, compared to the 11 won by the pro-apartheid Federal Party and three by independents. However, it was prevented from becoming the majority party within the CRC when the regime awarded the 20 government-nominated seats provided for in the Council's constitution to Federal Party members. One of these went to the FP's defeated leader, Tom Swartz, who became Chairman of the CRC executive – giving rise to the popular tag for the CRC as 'Uncle Tom's Cabin'.

During the five year term of the first CRC, the Labour Party adopted what is described as 'tactics of exposure and embarrassment'. Motions were framed in such a way that the Federal Party could only oppose them by exposing itself as a puppet of apartheid, and the Labour Party refused to serve on committees set up to liaise with the government.

Despite being reduced to the position of a largely ineffective 'opposition' party, Labour remained throughout this period essentially a parliamentary type party whose fundamental sphere of activity and tactics were orientated around the CRC. The leadership resisted calls from its Transvaal branch and Youth Section to withdraw from the CRC and transform itself into a mass party. It could not, however, escape the effects of the growing tide of mass resistance. At first, it tried to compete with the emerging Black Consciousness movement, launching its own slogan 'brown power' as a non-militant alternative. Later, it attempted to use the burgeoning mass struggles as a 'bargaining counter' — alternatively warning the government that moderates prepared to work within the system would lose out to radicals, and threatening to itself become part of the mass movement if the regime did not enter into meaningful negotiations with it.

This first phase of the Party's existence ended in 1974/5. Taking advantage of a number of defections from the Federal Party, Labour managed to secure the adoption by the CRC of a motion calling for the abolition of all the institutions of apartheid, including the CRC itself. This crisis led the regime to offer the chairmanship of the executive to the Labour Party. This was refused, the council was dissolved and new elections were called in 1975. Labour emerged from the reduced (28%) poll with 31 seats to the Federal Party's eight, giving it an absolute majority in the council, even allowing for nominated members.

This new situation led to a major debate within the Party's leadership, which was complicated by an amendment to the Coloured Persons' Representative Council Act allowing the Minister of Coloured Affairs to take over the functions of the executive of the CRC in the event of the latter failing to carry out its tasks. After some struggle, the Labour Party leadership made a strategic shift from what it described as the 'politics of protest' to the 'politics of negotiation'. This involved using its base as majority party in the CRC in an attempt to negotiate constitutional changes with the regime 'on an equal basis'. The Party took up its seats on the CRC executive and its then leader, Sonny Leon, became Chairman. It was also decided, apparently as a concession to the pro-boycott faction, that the Chairman would not appropriate any monies allocated to the Council by the central government, as this would amount to accepting the Council's subsidiary status as an apartheid institution.

This latter decision led the government to revoke the appointment of Leon as Chairman and replace him by a government nominee, Althea Jansen. Labour, however, retained the remaining seats on the executive and its position as majority party.

During this phase of 'the politics of negotiation', the Labour Party leadership became involved in numerous discussions with state officials on the 'constitutional future of the coloured people' (though it boycotted the Inter-Cabinet Council meeting with Vorster in 1976) (see p.401). These tactics, however, yielded few concessions. During this period, for example, much of the chagrin of the Labour Party, the regime rejected the recommendations of its own Theron Commission that, *inter alia*, the Immorality and Mixed Marriages Acts be abolished, that certain business areas be open to persons of all races, and that so-called coloureds be given direct representation on 'decision making bodies'. Even over minor issues the regime often refused to give way. In 1977 for instance, it refused to allow Gatsha Buthelezi to open the CRC session, sending the state President instead.

This evident failure of its strategy of negotiation in the context of the growing militancy of the masses, led the Party to lose much of whatever mass support it previously had. This emerged in the last by-election for the CRC held in 1978, where a devisory 13% poll was recorded. One of the responses of the Party to this situation was to seek alignments with other like-minded political groupings; in 1978 it joined the South African Black Alliance (see entry p.403). At the same time it supported the call by the Progressive Federal Party for a 'national convention' to negotiate a new constitution for South Africa, although it later argued that the PFP was too concerned with guarantees for minority rights.

This period also saw schism within the Party; its leader, Sonny Leon, resigned in 1978, ostensibly on the grounds of ill health but in fact under a cloud of criticism for being both ineffective and for collaborating with the regime. Leon had attended the funeral of state President, Diedrichs, and went on a Defence Force sponsored tour of the 'operational area'.

The coming to office of the Botha regime in 1978 and the adoption as official state policy of the Total Strategy (see p.38) marked a new phase in the history of the Labour Party. Its leadership, under Revd Allan Hendrikse, at first welcomed the 'reformist' rhetoric of the Botha regime, particularly its announcement that it would make constitutional changes. In 1979, Labour announced that it would now also be willing to negotiate over 'short term goals such as housing, local government and education, whilst not losing sight of its long term constitutional aspirations. At the same time, as the majority party in the CRC, it set up a commission to formulate its own constitutional proposals. This du Preez Commission issued its report later in the year and called for a system of one person one vote within the then existing Westminster type parliamentary system.

By the end of 1979, the Party found itself in deadlock with the Botha regime. When the latter set up the Schlebusch Commission to work out proposals for a new constitution setting out from the 1977 Nationalist Party proposals (providing for three racially separate chambers of parliament (see p.137), the Labour Party declared that it would only submit evidence if this did not prejudice the rights of the coloured people to other constitutional negotiations. When the Botha Regime refused to give such assurances, the Labour Party and the CRC resolved to boycott Schlebusch.

This move, interpreted in the Nationalist press as a shift to 'confrontation' tactics, brought a swift response from the regime: The Coloured Persons' Council Act of 1980 abolished the CRC and gave the Minister of Coloured Affairs the right to create a nominated Coloured Peoples' Council to take over the legal responsibilities of the CRC. Presented ideologically as a response to the manifest 'lack of interest' on the part of members of the so-called coloured community in the CRC, the Council's abolition was in fact a shrewd tactical move by the Botha regime designed to weaken the Labour Party. And indeed it did create a major problem of role definition for the Party.

For a short time, with its leadership visibly angered at being outmanoeuvred by Botha, and under pressure both from the increasingly militant mass struggles and its own youth wing, the Party showed some signs of trying to move 'leftwards'. A strategy conference held after the dissolution of the CRC, resolved to strengthen its grassroots organisation and form new branches. It declared it would work for the holding of a black convention, to be followed by a convention of all progressive forces. These conventions would draw up a representative alternative constitutional programme to that of the regime. It also declared its intention to work for a united front with bodies such as AZAPO, COSAS and MWASA (see entries pp.308, 371 and 348). It lent its name to the Free Mandela campaign and set up a commission to work out ways of mobilising 'worker and consumer power'.

However, the Party soon came under the counter-pressure of the more attractive 'perks' being offered to so-called coloured and Asian political leaders willing to collaborate with the Total Strategy. In 1980, when the Botha regime abolished the Senate and set up the President's Council (PC) to formulate new constitutional proposals (see p.38), it offered places on the latter body to the Labour Party. This created a major debate within the Party: the right wing argued that the logic of the 'politics of negotiation' implied entering such bodies. When the majority of the Party decided against participation on the grounds that Africans were not included in the PC, a group of right wingers, including two former Party leaders and the Chairman of the CRC's constitutional commission, Du Preez, resigned to form a new political group, the Congress of the People (COPE). Some COPE members now sit on the PC.

In the face of these pressures, the Party leadership, under Hendrikse, visibly vacillated. On occasions, in response to pressures from mass struggles, it declared itself in favour of the objectives, but not the strategy, of the ANC, PAC, Black Consciousness movement and SWAPO. On other occasions, bowing to pressures from its own right wing, it declared itself in favour of 'free enterprise', reaffirmed its total opposition to Marxism, and criticised trade unionists 'who want to cause chaos'.

These vacillations reveal much of the character of the Party's leadership as a petty bourgeois force caught in the midst of an intensifying struggle between the fundamental class forces in the society. They also reflect the dilemma of a parliamentary type party deprived of a parliament. One of its members commented that 'the party had lost its direction and was no longer able to survive as a political force outside government-created structures'.

It is thus not surprising that when Botha offered the prospect of further negotiations late in 1980, it was eagerly accepted by the Party's leadership. After a meeting in which Botha agreed both to release a number of students detained during the 1980 schools boycott, and to abandon the idea of the nominated Coloured Peoples' Council, Hendrikse declared that the freeze in relations since the end of 1979 was over, and that both the Party and 'government were now seeking the togetherness of the middle of the road'. 'While the Labour Party understood the problems the Prime Minister faced with an increasing radicalisation of the white right wing,' he continued, 'the Prime Minister had understood the problems that the Labour Party faced with the radicalisation of the left'. Finally, at its January 1983 congress, the Labour Party 'committed' itself to contesting seats for the so-called coloured chamber of the proposed three chamber parliament, after previously hinting that it would not. This decision was interpreted as a major boost to the regime's constitutional proposals and led to the resignation from the Party of some of its more militant leaders. Meetings held by the Labour leadership in an attempt to explain this step have been broken up by angry crowds accusing the Party of collaboration with apartheid. The party's decision to enter these apartheid institutions led to its suspension from the South African Black Alliance and in April 1983 the Labour Party withdrew from SABA.

Important leaders:
  Revd Allen Hendrikse
  David Curry.

REFORM PARTY (RP)[3]

> Political party based on certain bourgeois and petty bourgeois class forces within the Indian community. The Reform Party was formed by members of the South African Indian Council (SAIC) in 1976. It claimed to be using the platform created by the apartheid state against the apartheid system itself, a policy similar to that of certain Bantustan parties, such as *Inkatha*, and the Labour Party. The RP is a member of the South African Black Alliance (SABA) (see p.403).
>
> The Reform Party's evidence in 1979 to the Schlebusch Commission of Inquiry into a new constitution, called for a single parliament for all races, but said this did not mean one person one vote. The Party was dealt a decisive blow by the mass campaign against the elections for the SAIC in November 1981. Although the RP belatedly announced a tactical withdrawal in the face of this campaign, one candidate did stand under its banner. His 'success' in the election, whose average poll was 10% gives the RP one seat out of 45 in the thoroughly discredited Council.
>
> Lacking any real effective base from which to pursue its strategy of negotiation, the RP appears to be largely inactive at present though it continues to serve as the 'Indian contingent' of SABA. However, it, or some similar grouping, could potentially emerge as a force based on the 'Indian chamber' of the proposed three-tier parliament.

The history of the Reform Party cannot be separated from that of the South African Indian Council from which it emerged in 1976. The specific characteristics of the SAIC derive from the fact that devising a formula for the inclusion of the Indian community within the political institutions of apartheid has always posed a particularly difficult problem for apartheid constitutional planners. In was in fact only comparatively recently that the permanent presence of the Indian community in South Africa was officially acknowledged by apartheid ideologues. Until 1957, official Nationalist Party policy was that the whole of the resident Indian community ought eventually to be 'repatriated' to India or Pakistan. Until 1975, a free passage was available to anyone from the community willing to accept 'voluntary repatriation' (there were very few takers) 24 between 1965 and 1975).

Thus, even by the standards of apartheid institutions, the South African Indian Council has, from the time of its establishment in 1968, been a particularly ineffective body. Until 1974 all its members were government nominees, unlike the Coloured Representative Council which was partly elected from the start. After 1974, half of its members became indirectly elected on 'behalf' of the community by members of local authorities, local affairs committees and management or consultative committees. The first time the SAIC was due to be directly elected was in November 1981. These elections were met by a massive boycott by the Indian community. SAIC has accordingly been based throughout on certain sections of the bourgeoisie and petty bourgeoisie, with very little mass support amongst the Indian community as a whole. Important bourgeois, as well as petty bourgeois, class forces within the Indian community have, it should be noted, refused to participate in the Council.

The Reform Party was formed within the SAIC in 1976. The immediate issue giving rise to its formation was a proposal by Prime Minister Vorster to set up an 'Inter Cabinet Council' consisting of members of the 'white Cabinet' plus the executives of the Coloured Representative Council and the SAIC. This council was to have had no decision-making or legislative powers, but was merely to serve as a forum for an 'exchange of opinions'; it never really functioned.

The majority of the SAIC decided to participate in this body 'on a trial basis'. This decision was opposed by five members on the grounds that the proposal council would exclude Africans. Led by Y.S. Chinsamy, this group constituted themselves as 'the Reform group'. They were later joined by another small faction, originally calling itself the Peoples' Party. These two groups then merged to form the Reform Party, with Chinsamy as President.

At its inaugural meeting, Chinsamy defined the RP's immediate objective as

> to get outspoken people elected to the Indian Council, and use the Council as a community platform from which the grievances of the people of South Africa could be aired.

Its ultimate declared aim was to secure a society in which there would be, amongst other things:

> peace and goodwill among the races . . . equitable sharing of power by all citizens with safeguards against domination or oppression of one race by another . . . economic equality of opportunity for all [with a] raising of the status of workers.

It pledged co-operation with 'organizations striving for democracy by non-violent means'. The last clause led it to affiliate to the South African Black Alliance when the latter was formed in 1978.

Virtually the entire organisational effort of the Reform Party was directed towards the SAIC elections originally scheduled for the end of 1979. The RP opposed the various postponements of these elections, but used the time to launch a recruiting drive amongst members of the SAIC, arguing that there would be no place in an elected SAIC for unaffiliated independents. A major coup in this campaign was the recruitment of the nominated SAIC Chairman, J.N. Reddy, in mid-1979, after which the RP emerged as the majority party in the SAIC.

The attempts by the Botha regime to formulate a 'new constitutional dispensation' faced the RP with major choices. After considerable internal discussion and debate the RP, unlike, for example, the Labour Party, (see p.395) eventually gave evidence to the Schlebusch Commission of Inquiry. The RP congress which took this decision resolved that the Party's evidence should advocate one man one vote as an ultimate goal, but recognised that there were different ways of achieiving this: the RP favoured the summoning of a national convention. In the event, however, its delegates before Schlebusch stated that the Party stood for one parliament for all races, which did not necessarily mean one person one vote. This rather loose interpretation of the Party's agreed policy led to severe criticism of the leadership. Eventually five branches disaffiliated in 1980 over this incident. They subsequently declared themselves totally disillusioned with the SAIC.

At the same time, as in the case of the Labour Party, the RP leadership came under pressure from elements within the Party eager for the 'perks' being offered by the Botha regime to so-called coloured and Asian leaders willing to collaborate with the Total Strategy. In accordance with SABA policy, the RP refused to accept seats on the President's Council on the grounds that Africans were excluded. However, a significant element within the RP opposed this decision, arguing that bodies such as the President's Council rather than the obsolete SAIC provided a more effective base from which to pursue the 'politics of negotiation'. Three executive members who favoured this position were suspended from the Party in 1980, provoking a number of resignations both from the Party and the SAIC in the same year. One member of this group, Abram Mayet, subsequently accepted a seat on the President's Council.

The Reform Party was swamped by the anti-SAIC campaign in 1981.

As indicated above (see p.296), the anti-SAIC campaign raised issues going far beyond the question of elections for the SAIC, and the campaign became a real force for mass mobilisation.

The RP's initial response to this campaign was to try to distance itself from the SAIC by agreeing with a number of criticisms being made of this body, but arguing that it was still worth their while capturing it as a government-recognised platform. Eventually, however, after intense pressure from SABA, the Party made a belated tactical retreat and announced in late September that it would not stand in the elections due in early November. In the official statement Chinsamy declared that 'while he remain[ed] committed to negotiation as a strategy . . . *the present climate* made it untenable for him to enhance the credibility of the South African Indian Council' (our emphasis).

Despite this decision, however, one candidate stood 'successfully' under the Party's banner in the subsequent election. His return in an election whose average poll was around 10% gives the RP one seat in the SAIC.

Now deprived of any effective base from which to pursue its 'strategy of negotiation', the RP is largely inactive, though it continues to attend SABA meetings.

Leader: Y.S. Chinsamy.

SOUTH AFRICAN BLACK ALLIANCE (SABA)[4]

An alliance grouping until 1983 two Bantustan parties (*Inkatha* of KwaZulu and the Inyandza National Movement of KaNgwane) plus two parties which emerged out of apartheid institutions imposed on the so-called coloured and Indian communities — the Labour and Reform parties respectively. The Labour Party withdrew from SABA in April 1983. All these parties claim to follow a strategy of using the institutions of apartheid against the system itself.

Since its foundation in 1978, SABA has been dominated by the *Inkatha* movement led by Chief Gatsha Buthelezi (see p.387). Indeed, to a large extent it has functioned as a vehicle for the promotion of the pretensions of the class forces controlling *Inkatha* to leadership of the oppressed masses.

One of SABA's major objectives was to prepare for a representative national convention to draw up a charter for a non-racial constitution. This project was, however, abandoned in 1981 when it became clear that the Alliance could not attract a sufficiently representative grouping. Since then SABA has been much less actively promoted and in 1982 *Inkatha* produced its own proposals for a 'consociational democracy (see p.394).

SABA affiliates, however, continue to meet regularly and the Alliance is used from time to time when the *Inkatha* leadership feels the need for a broader platform. Meetings were held under its banner to protest against the proposed Ingwavuma–KaNgwane land transfer to Swaziland (see p.224). It was also used to condemn the Labour Party's decision to enter the new constitutional arrangements of the apartheid regime (see p.399).

The South African Black Alliance was formed in March 1978 at a meeting chaired by Chief Buthelezi and attended by *Inkatha* plus the Labour and Reform parties. It succeeded the abortive Black Unity Front (BUF) set up on the initiative of Buthelezi and two other Bantustan 'leaders' (Ntsanwisi of Gazankulu and Phatudi of Lebowa) in 1976.

Both SABA and its predecessor emerged as part of an attempt by certain class forces operating within the Bantustan structures and other apartheid institutions to widen their political bases in the wake of the 1976 uprisings. The immediate impetus giving rise to the formation of the BUF was a meeting between the then Prime Minister Vorster, and Bantustan 'leaders' at the height of the Soweto revolt in August 1976. Vorster refused to make any significant concessions to the Bantustan 'leaders' who were then both eager to take advantage of the uprisings to advance a number of their own specific demands, and worried about the effects of continued mass action on their own positions. Vorster's intransigence was partly responsible for prompting Buthelezi, Ntsanwisi and Phatudi to call for a meeting of 'black leaders' to discuss a 'closing of the ranks'.

About 50 'prominent blacks', including a number of 'community leaders' from Soweto, and some representatives from Black Consciousness organisations attended a follow-up meeting chaired by Buthelezi later in the year. Although a number of political differences emerged, the meeting decided to set up a Black Unity Front. This front basically represented an attempt by class forces among the Bantustan leadership which did not see their long term future in 'independence', to forge an alliance with sections of the black urban petty bourgeoisie. However, it proved still-born. By the BUF's inaugural conference in April 1977, Buthelezi's opportunism in Soweto (see p.357) led to a boycott by most of the urban 'community leaders'. Moreover, even the support among Bantustan leaders proved to be patchy. The conference held in Lebowa and opened by Phatudi was only supported strongly by *Inkatha*, and was generally regarded as a flop.

Meanwhile, as part of the *Inkatha* leadership's efforts to promote their organisation on a national level, contacts had been established with the Labour and Reform parties. After several preliminary meetings, these three parties eventually constituted themselves as the South African Black Alliance in March 1978. This followed the banning of the Black Consciousness organisations and represented a clear attempt to take over their mantle.

SABA defined its objectives as being 'to endeavour to create a just society in South Africa ... [through] determining a common strategy in struggle and unifying all black organizations'. More specifically, the Alliance pledged itself to 'prepare for a national convention representative of all South Africa to draw up a charter for a non-racial constitution'. The latter was clearly intended as a 'moderate' alternative to the Freedom Charter (see p.314); its envisaged role being to serve as the focus for a campaign (backed up, if necessary, by 'industrial and consumer action') to 'impress upon the white electorate their responsibility to force the government to negotiate'.

However, in the event SABA palpably failed to emerge as a sufficiently broadly based alliance to undertake this project. Buthelezi immediately tried to use SABA as a base for a renewed effort to mobilise 'anti-independence' Bantustan leaders. These efforts were largely unsuccessful, mainly because most such 'leaders' regarded SABA as too 'radical'. After making initial declarations of support, Ntsanwisi and Phatudi eventually decided against joining. A pledge by a meeting of six Bantustan 'leaders' to send a delegation to a SABA meeting in February 1979 has not been honoured and the *Dikwankwetla* Party of the QwaQwa Bantustan (see p.230) which had joined in 1979, disaffiliated in 1981. Apart from *Inkatha* only the Inyandza National Movement of Enos Mabuza of KaNgwane (see p.224) which joined in 1978, has stayed with the alliance. SABA also failed to attract other urban-based community or political organisations. The Alliance became a grouping of four parties: two (*Inkatha* and the INM) based on Bantustans and two (the Labour and Reform parties) based on 'councils' imposed by the apartheid regime on the coloured and Indian communities.

SABA confinement to this narrow political base led to the abandonment of its initial project to prepare for a national convention. This occurred in 1981 in the face of a mass campaign to affirm support for the Freedom Charter, and following the collapse in June of preliminary discussions between SABA, the Progressive Federal Party, AZAPO and the Committee of Ten (see pp.145, 308 and 356). After the failure of the June meeting, *Inkatha* announced that it was abandoning the idea of a national convention. It has subsequently presented its 'own' proposals for a 'consociational democracy' in the 1982 Report of its Buthelezi Commission (see p.394).

This set-back has led to SABA being much less actively promoted in recent years; however, its member parties continue to meet. In the past, these meetings have had some influence on the policy of individual affiliates. A SABA resolution criticising the President's Council because it excluded Africans was clearly a significant factor in the eventual decision by the Labour and Reform parties not to accept nominations to the Council. Similarly, the Reform Party's belated tactical withdrawal from the 1981 Indian Council elections (see p.402) followed a SABA meeting in which the RP came under strong pressure from other SABA affiliates anxious to avoid the effects of the anti-SAIC campaign rubbing off on them. More recently, with both the KaNgwane and KwaZulu Bantustan administrations affected, SABA meetings discussed the proposed Ingwavume–KaNgwane land transfer to Swaziland. In

July 1982, a number of small protest meetings against the land deal were held
under the SABA banner. The decision in January 1983 by the Labour Party
to put up candidates for the 'coloured' chamber of the proposed three-tier
parliament (a decision strongly opposed by Buthelezi) led to the Labour Party
being suspended from SABA. It subsequently withdrew from the Alliance
in April 1983.

Chairman: Chief Gatsha Buthelezi.

THE MEDIA – PRESS AND SOUTH AFRICAN BROADCASTING CORPORATION (SABC)[5]

The South African media consists of two major sectors, the
privately owned press and the state-owned broadcasting service.

Despite its widely promoted self-image, the South African press
is not a separate independent force in the political–ideological
arena. Rather, different groupings within the industry are linked
to specific class forces engaged in the wider struggle. The major
division in the press is between the so-called commercial press on
the one hand – owned and controlled by capitalist and allied
interests – and, on the other hand, a range of progressive publications currently produced by community organisations, the labour
movement and student groups, as well as clandestine publications
of the national liberation movement.

Within the commercial press there is a further broad division
roughly corresponding to language cleavages. The English-language
commercial press is dominated by two conglomerates: South
African Associated Newspapers (SAAN) and the Argus Group.
Both are linked to major non-Afrikaner monopolies. Politically,
these groups strongly support capitalism but are critical of certain
aspects of apartheid policy. The Afrikaans-language commercial
press is also dominated by two groups: *Nasionale Pers* and
Perskor. *Nasionale Pers* is effectively controlled by SANLAM (see
p.76) and the leadership of the Cape Nationalist Party. It functions
as the principal organ of the Botha faction of the Nationalist
Party (see p.138). *Perskor* is linked to the leadership of the
Transvaal Nationalist Party (traditionally more petty bourgeois-
dominated and reactionary than the Cape NP). The class conflicts
in the Nationalist Party and the eventual triumph of the monopoly-
linked Botha faction have led to intense competition between
the two major Afrikaans press groups. Coupled with the defection
of large sections of the Transvaal readership to the right of the
NP, this has created serious problems for *Perskor*.

In terms of circulation figures, it is clearly the commercial press (and within that the English-language commercial press) which dominates. This is partly because of the huge competitive advantages enjoyed by the capitalist owners of these publications, but is also partly the result of restrictions placed on progressive publications by the regime — ranging from outright bannings to strict and costly regulations for registration. Further restrictions can be expected in the future, following the February 1982 Report of the Steyn Commission of Inquiry into the media.

The state-owned South African Broadcasting Corporation has long been a straight forward propaganda vehicle for the ruling Nationalist Party. In the 1960s it was a bastion of far right (*verkrampte*) politics. It is now, however, a crucial vehicle in the mobilisation of 'total resources', particularly those of psychology and propaganda, against what the Total Strategy of the Botha regime labels the 'total onslaught' against apartheid South Africa.

The Commercial Press

The current commercial press conglomerates came into existence through the merger and take over of a number of individual newspaper companies formed in the case of the English language press since the mid-19th Century and between 1915 and the 1940s in the case of the Afrikaans language press.

The English Language Commercial Press
This is dominated by two conglomerates: The Argus Group and South African Associated Newspapers (SAAN). The Argus Group is the larger of the two; its origins date back to the foundation of the *Cape Argus* newspaper in 1857. Intensely pro-British and pro-imperialist from the outset, the Argus company was eventually taken over by a syndicate of mining capitalists including Cecil Rhodes. They used it as a base to launch another newspaper, the *Star* in Johannesburg in 1899. Until 1931, all directors of the Argus Group were drawn from two mining houses, the Corner House Group (now part of Barlow Rand see p.75), and Johannesburg Consolidated Investments (JCI — now controlled by Anglo American, see p.65). Thereafter a voting trust was set up in an attempt to still the growing criticism that the group's newspapers were mouthpieces of foreign mining capital. At the same time, the previous practice of recruiting editors and senior journalists exclusively from England was abandoned. However, in terms of effective control, these changes were more cosmetic than real. Until 1949 the voting trust consisted of two trustees — John Martin and Reginald Holland — both former chairmen of the Corner House Group. After their deaths (in 1948 and 1949 respectively) a formula was devised under which half the directors were appointed by a somewhat widened voting trust and half by the leading shareholders. Through JCI and various nominees, Anglo American currently owns 28.02% of Argus'

share capital; the Argus pension fund 14.91%; the Standard Bank 10.05% (see p.94), SAAN, in a cross-shareholding 6.94% and SA Mutual 8.53% (see p.80). The Group's major newspapers are the *Star*, the *Argus* (Cape Town), the *Daily News* (Durban), *Sunday Tribune* (Durban), *Diamond Fields Advertiser* (Kimberley), the *Friend* (Bloemfontein) and *Pretoria News* plus *Post Natal*, the *Sowetan, Ilanga* and *Cape Herald* – the last four aimed at different sections of the black population. In addition to its publications, together with the giant food group, Premier Milling, the Argus group also controls the Central News Agency (CNA) the monopoly distributor of English language newspapers and magazines.

South African Associated Newspapers (SAAN) was formed in 1955 through the merger of Rand Daily Mail Ltd. and the Sunday Times Syndicate, which then controlled both the *Sunday Times* and *Sunday Express*. The *Rand Daily Mail* had been founded by the mining magnate, Sir Abe Bailey. At the time of the formation of SAAN, it was controlled by the trustees of Bailey's estate. The *Sunday Times* syndicate was closely tied to the families of R. Ward Jackson and G.H. Kingswell, British and Australian journalists who had come to South Africa with the objective of establishing down-market 'popular' newspapers.

The Bailey Trust remained the clearly dominant force within SAAN until 1962 when the company became a public corporation quoted on the Johannesburg stock exchange. Thereafter, Bailey's relative stake has progressively declined. In the late 1960s and early 1970s, large blocs of SAAN shares were bought by the Argus Group in a takeover bid. This was, however, blocked by the intervention of Prime Minister Vorster in the early 1970s, who threatened legislation to prevent 'monopoly control' being established over the English language 'opposition' press.

Nevertheless, the Argus Group remains the largest single shareholder in SAAN, with 39.39% of its share capital in 1981. Other major shareholders, include Anglo American (through nominees) 20.96% and Nedbank 7.54% (see p.94). The Bailey Trust holds 8.21% and the editor of the *Financial Mail*, Stephen Mulholland, 1.18%. Major SAAN publications include the *Rand Daily Mail, Sunday Times, Sunday Express, Cape Times, Eastern Province Herald,* the *Evening Post* (Port Elizabeth) and the influential business journal, the *Financial Mail*.

In addition there are four important English language commercial newspapers which do not fall under either the Argus or SAAN groups. These are the *Natal Mercury* and *Natal Witness* (Durban and Pietermaritzburg), the *Daily Dispatch* (East London) and the *Citizen* (Johannesburg). The first two are owned by the same company based in Pietermaritzburg whilst the *Daily Dispatch* has a complicated ownership structure in which its editor and staff hold a large proportion of the shares. The *Citizen* differs from all other English language commercial newspapers: it was set up in 1976 by the former state Department of Information in a secret project to develop a conservative, 'patriotic' English language morning newspaper, after the Department's attempt to take over SAAN failed. Both of these projects were fronted by NP industrialist Louis Luyt, using secret state funds. The uncovering of these projects by the other English language newspapers was a major factor provoking the 'Information Department Scandal' in 1978–9, following which the *Citizen* was bought by the Afrikaner *Perskor* group.

With the exception of the *Citizen* no English language commercial newspaper directly supports the Nationalist regime. Rather, as their ownership patterns suggest, they are supportive of monopoly capitalist class forces outside the governing party and are all strongly pro-capitalist and 'anti-communist'. They are opposed to, and often critical of, specific aspects of apartheid policy, such as job reservation, 'petty apartheid', aspects of the Bantustan policy, blatant forms of repression considered likely to provoke a response from the oppressed masses or criticism from abroad and, in the Total Strategy period, the slowness in accommodating a black middle class. An interesting indication of the basic political stance of the liberal commercial press emerges from the fact that the *Rand Daily Mail* coined the slogan 'Adapt or Perish' in 1964, prefiguring the slogan 'Adapt or Die' later adopted by P.W. Botha to promote the Total Strategy.

In terms of party political allegiance, most of the English language commercial press now supports the Progressive Federal Party (see p.145) although the *Natal Witness* publications support the New Republic Party (see p.153). This represents a change from the position prior to the collapse of the United Party in 1977 (see p.157), when only the *Rand Daily Mail* and the *Daily Dispatch* — generally regarded as the most liberal bourgeois papers — clearly identified with the Progressive Party. Most of the others then supported either an undifferentiated parliamentary 'opposition', or the United Party specifically. Given the extreme weakness of the parliamentary opposition, the editor of the *Sunday Times* during this period argued that the press itself should assume the functions of the 'loyal opposition'. In some cases, the liberalism of certain editors allowed space for the printing of occasional articles more 'radical' than the general political stance of the paper concerned. Furthermore, some papers have from time to time been willing to enter into confrontation with government officials on specific issues. Perhaps the best-known example here was during the 'Muldergate' scandal, when the role of certain English language papers in publishing damaging material leaked to them by anti-Mulder factions in the Nationalist Party was crucial in the latter's eventual defeat by the P.W. Botha faction (see p.144).

A further important factor accounting for the 'anti-government' tone of some sections of the non-Afrikaans commercial press is that both the Argus and SAAN groups have sought to expand their black readerships both on purely commercial grounds and in order to counter more radical publications. Most major English language papers now have 'township editions' and the *Daily Dispatch* even has a majority black readership. The Argus Group in particular produces a number of publications aimed exclusively at black readers. The most important of these is the *Sowetan* — the most recent successor to the *World* which was itself set up in the 1930s with the deliberate objective of combating the influence of publications emanating from the ANC and

Communist Party. Although these publications consist largely of sex, scandal and sport stories, they are occasionally compelled to permit certain community issues to be taken up.

However, there are definite limits to how far any of these publications is prepared to go in allowing criticism of the apartheid system of capitalist exploitation based on national oppression. Extremely rare indeed are articles portraying capitalists as anything other than enlightened benefactors of the community as a whole. Articles dealing with conditions of black workers in the mining industry have been practically non-existent — not because they have not been written but because they have been spiked by editors anxious not to antagonise their major shareholders. Furthermore, where there have been conflicts between the demands of investigative journalism (even on topics normally permitted) and the demands of profitability, it is invariably the former which has to give way. The best example of this came in 1965 when the *Rand Daily Mail* published a series of articles exposing prison conditions. The regime's initial response (this was prior to the enactment of a law prohibiting the publication of all unapproved articles on prisons) was to bring a costly prosecution using perjured witnesses. The response of the director of SAAN to this stratagem was to warn its other papers not to print similar stories and to manoeuvre the dismissal of Laurence Gandar as editor. Another slightly different incident, also affecting the *Rand Daily Mail*, came in 1982, when the editor, Allistair Sparks, who had followed a policy of promoting critical investigative articles, was dismissed in a bid to increase circulation by giving more emphasis to 'popular' articles on sports, entertainment and crime.

The Afrikaans Language Commercial Press
This is dominated by two groups, *Nasionale Pers Beperk* and *Perskor*. Both are closely connected to factions in the ruling Nationalist Party. There are also smaller companies which produce papers supporting far right parties.

Nasionale Pers is the oldest of the Afrikaans publishing companies. It was formed in 1915 by the very same individuals who in the same year founded the Nationalist Party in the Cape and who were to set up SANLAM three years later (see entries pp.138 and 70). The group's first newspaper, *Die Burger*, began publication in the same year. Its first editor was D.F. Malan, Prime Minister from 1948 to 1954, who forsook his clergyman's pulpit for the more effective podium of the editor's chair. He became leader of the Cape NP at the same time. The group's next paper *Volksblad* began publishing in the Free State in 1917 and its third *Die Oosterlig* first appeared in the Eastern Cape in 1937.

From the outset, *Nasionale Pers* committed itself to the promotion of the variant of Afrikaner nationalist ideology favoured by the agrarian capitalist and aspirant financial capitalist class forces dominating the Cape Nationalist Party. When the Nationalist Party split in 1934 over the formation of the 'fusion' government (see p.157), *Nasionale Pers* supported the Purified Nationalist Party led by its first editor, D.F. Malan. In the following year, in association with the leadership of the Cape NP, it took the initiative in setting up *Voortrekkerpers* in the Transvaal, which began publishing *Die Transvaler* as the organ of the Transvaal NP in 1932. This represented a deliberate attempt by the Cape NP to counter what it saw as the republican extremism of the petty bourgeois *Broederbond* leadership of the Transvaal NP (see p.266). However, this manoeuvre backfired when H.F. Verwoerd set up as the nominee of *Nasionale Pers* and the Cape NP to edit *Die Transvaler*, sided with the leadership of the Transvaal NP. *Nasionale Pers* withdrew in 1939 and the paper was placed under the effective political control of the Transvaal NP.

After the coming to power of the Nationalist regime in 1948, *Nasionale Pers* initially had extremely cosy relations with the government leadership, particularly under the premiership of Malan, 1948–54. *Die Burger*, for instance, was the only paper permitted to send a reporter to attend meetings of the NP parliamentary caucus. However, the intensification of conflict within the Afrikaner nationalist alliance in the 1950s led to the dominance of the more petty bourgeois-oriented Transvaal NP. Given its close relationship with the larger Afrikaner capitalist grouping Sanlam and the more capitalist oriented Cape NP, by the late 1950's *Die Burger* had become somewhat isolated from the dominant tendencies in the NP. In the 1960s, the paper had a major clash with the then Premier, Verwoerd, when it opposed proposals to remove coloured representatives from parliament. This led to an oft quoted retort from Verwoerd that the whites could defend themselves without the support of any other population group. When the *verligte-verkrampte* split came out into the open (see p.150), the *Nasionale Pers* group clearly identified itself as the major *verligte* force. In 1965, against the express instructions of Prime Minister Verwoerd, it launched a *verligte* Sunday newspaper *Die Beeld* in the Transvaal in direct competition with the Sunday paper of northern Afrikaner nationalism, *Dagbreek*. *Die Beeld* broke new ground in Afrikaans journalism. It was explicitly used to 'let the voice of the Cape be heard in the Transvaal', and began an unprecedented campaign of exposés of the far right 'Hertzog group' in the NP. These exposés, together with the furious circulation battle which developed between *Die Beeld* and *Dagbreek*, were a major intensifying factor in the *verligte-verkrampte* schism in the late 1960s and the eventual split of the *Herstigte Nasionale Party* (HNP) in 1969 (see p.153).

The success of *Die Beeld* forced the northern Afrikaner press group, *Perskor* to enter into an agreement with *Nasionale Pers* to merge *Die Beeld* and *Dagbreek* into the jointly-owned *Rapport* in 1970. *Rapport* followed basically the same line as *Die Beeld*, With the fresh intensification of factional struggles in the NP in the mid-1970s, *Nasionale Pers* again intervened in the Transvaal. In 1975 it set up a new morning daily, *Beeld*, with the explicit aim of driving *Perskor's Die Transvaler* out of the market. Like its predecessor, *Beeld* also basically propagated the line of the P.W. Botha faction of the NP. Its circulation battle with *Die Transvaler* was also a significant factor in the resurgence of factionalism in the NP in the late 1970s. Eventually, in early 1983, *Die Transvaler* was forced to withdraw from the morning daily market, resulting in a complete triumph for *Nasionale Pers* – and P.W. Botha's faction in the NP.

Currently, *Nasionale Pers'* most important newspapers are *Die Burger, Beeld, Rapport* (in association with *Perskor*) and *Die Oosterlig*. It also produces a number of entertainment magazines, including some aimed at black readerships, and runs several retail outlets, including the *Via Afrika* chain operating in several Bantustans as well as Botswana and Lesotho.

The other major Afrikaner press group, the Transvaal-based *Perskor*, was formed in the late 1960s through the merger of the two existing Transvaal-based Afrikaans newspaper groups, *Afrikaanse Pers (1962) Beperk* and *Voortrekkerpers*.

Afrikaanse Pers was formed in 1931 by the then Prime Minister and leader of the Nationalist Party, Gen. J.B.M. Hertzog. It published an afternoon daily, *Die Vaderland*. *Afrikaanse Pers* supported the fusion of the Nationalist and South African Parties in 1934 (see p.157). After the 'reunification' of the Nationalist Party in 1940 (see p.138), control over *Afrikaanse Pers* passed through the Hertzog trust to N.C. Havenga, leader of the small Afrikaner Party. During the 1940s, *Afrikaanse Pers* became a refuge for a number of figures associated with the para-military and pro-Nazi *Ossewa Brandwag*. In 1947, a group of these, led by Marius Jooste and P.J. Meyer, formed *Dagbreekpers* as a vehicle for their reintegration into the mainstream Nationalist movement. *Dagbreekpers* took over *Sondagnuus*, launched only six months earlier by *Afrikaanse Pers* and relaunched it as Sunday weekly *Dagbreek en Sondagnuus*. In 1962, *Afrikaanse Pers* and *Dagbreekpers* merged, under effective *Dagbreek* control, as *Afrikaanse Pers (1962) Beperk*.

The origins of the other component of *Perksor, Voortrekker Pers*, have already been discussed in the section on *Nasionale Pers*. After the withdrawal of *Nasionale Pers* in 1939, the Board of *Voortrekker Pers* was dominated by the leadership of the Transvaal NP, with the Transvaal leader serving as Chairman.

Perskor was formed in the late 1960s in an attempt by the two Transvaal groups to resist the growing competition from *Nasionale Pers*. *Voortrekker Pers* and *Afrikaanse Pers* were not in competition with each other since the former ran a morning paper and the latter an afternoon and Sunday paper. However, each faced growing pressure from the *verligte* Cape-based group trying to break into the Transvaal. Although *Perskor* continued until the 'Muldergate' scandal (see p.144) with the *Voortrekker Pers*, the tradition of appointing the leader of the Transvaal Nationalist Party as Chairman of its Board, the leading force within the group has undoubtedly been the *Dagbreek Trust*, dominated, until his death in October 1982, by Marius Jooste.

Despite the greater resources made available by this merger, *Perskor* has not been able to insulate the Transvaal papers from the effects of the progressive breakup of the Afrikaner nationalist class alliance. The group was badly affected by the 'Muldergate scandal'. As leader of the Transvaal Party, Mulder was a one time Chairman of the *Perskor* Board, and the scandal revealed that *Perskor* had inflated the circulation of its papers to the Audit Bureau of Circulation — widely used in the placement of advertising revenue. This led to a multi-million rand suit against *Perskor* by *Nasionale Pers*. The triumph of the P.W. Botha faction in the NP in 1978 also resulted in *Perskor* losing a number of highly profitable government printing contracts to *Nasionale Pers*. Moreover, *Perskor* has also been caught in a classic crisis of indecision in the face of increased competitive pressures from *Nasionale Pers* on the one hand and clear indications that a large section of its own petty bourgeois readership are increasingly turning to parties to the right of the Nationalist Party, on the other. This emerged clearly in September 1982 when Willem de Klerk was dismissed as editor of the *Transvaler* by Jooste. De Klerk, a well known *verligte* who in fact first coined the terms *verligte* and *verkrampte*, had been brought in some years earlier in an attempt to offset the inroads made by *Beeld*. His dismissal was widely interpreted as the prelude to a sharp change in direction in which the *Transvaler*, largely for commercial reasons, would take an increasingly Conservative Party line. Jooste's death, however, gave rise to a sharp struggle in *Dagbreek Trust*. Eventually a 'moderate' faction won out and entered negotiations with *Nasionale Pers*. These resulted in *Perskors'* agreement to withdraw *Die Transvaler* from the morning daily market in return for an end to the civil action brought against it by *Nasionale Pers*. English language newspapers have commented on the 'total triumph' of this 'total onslaught' on *Perskor*.

Another millstone around the neck of the group is the English language *Citizen*, launched in 1976 in conjunction with the Department of Information after the latter had failed to take over SAAN. Despite being financed by a R12 million state hand-out, subsequent identification as a mouthpiece of the disgraced Department has badly affected its credibility, and it is now reported to be losing money. In addition to the *Nasionale Pers* and *Perskor* papers, a number of other Afrikaans newspapers are published by smaller companies. The most important of these are: *Die Afrikaner*, the official organ of the *Herstigte Nasionale Party* — published by Strydpers; and *Die Konservatief/The Conservative*, the bilingual organ of the Conservative Party.

The Progressive Press

No attempt will be made here to provide a comprehensive guide to progressive publications, nor to trace the history of the progressive press in South Africa. It is sufficient merely to note that both the Communist Party and the ANC/Congress Alliance (see p.317) produced a range of publications before their banning. Best known was the *New Age* weekly, banned in 1962. Currently the organisations of the liberation movement produce for circulation underground such journals as *Sechaba*, the *African Communist, Dawn* and *Workers' Unity* (SACTU).

A number of publications linked to the trade union movement have also emerged. The most comprehensive of these is the quarterly *South African Labour Bulletin*. Individual unions and federations also produce their own newspapers (see bibliographical note to Chapter 7).

A number of community newspapers have also appeared since 1976. The best known of these is the Cape Town based monthly *Grassroots*. The student press, after undergoing a major transformation since the mid-1970s has also emerged as a significant force in progressive publication. *SASPU National* is one of the best sources of regular news on developments in the democratic movement. Finally, mention must be made of the journal *Work in Progress*, providing one of the best informed analyses of recent developments.

State Intervention and Control

The existence of progressive publications challenging the apartheid system, plus sections of the liberal English language commercial press opposing certain aspects of government policy, have prompted numerous interventions by the Nationalist regime to control or restrict the press.

Prior to 1948, state control over publications was principally exercised through the common law (which forbade the publication of 'libellous' or 'obscene' material) and the 1930 Riotous Assemblies Act which prohibited the publication of 'material likely to have the effect of undermining the security of the state or engendering feelings of hostility between Black and White persons'.

The first additional controls were imposed by the Nationalist regime in the 1950 Suppression of Communism Act. This allowed the Minister responsible to ban any publication considered to be 'furthering the aims of communism'. It was used to ban the Congress-aligned newspaper, the *Guardian* (which promptly reappeared under the names *New Age*, *Clarion* and *Spark*, each banned in succession). In order to prevent any reoccurrence of this episode, the Act was amended in 1962 to prevent any newspaper from registering under more than one name. Proprietors of any new newspaper were obliged to deposit with the Minister of the Interior such amount, not exceeding R20,000, as the Minister might determine — a clause which has acted as a major barrier to the formation of community and progressive newspapers ever since. The Minister responsible was also given powers to refuse the registration of any newspaper he considered likely to be banned.

After the prison conditions exposé mentioned above, the Prisons Act made it an offence to photograph or sketch any prison or publish 'any false information' about prison conditions.

A more comprehensive attempt to control publications came with the 1963 Publications and Entertainments Act. This set up a Publications Control Board (replaced in 1974 by a Directorate of Publications) with wide powers to censor books, films, magazines and other publications. However, members of the Newspaper Press Union (NPU, to which belong all major English and Afrikaans language commercial newspapers) were exempted from the provisions of the Act after agreeing to draw up their own 'self censorship' Code of Conduct. The NPU Code of Conduct, rejected by the SA Society of Journalists and only accepted under protest by SAAN, requires, *inter alia*, that: 'Comment should take due cognisance of the complex racial problems of South Africa and take into account the general good and safety of the country and its people.' Frequent complaints and threats by government officials that the NPU members were insufficiently vigorous in self-censorship, particularly following the 1976 uprisings, led to an amendment of the NPU code. In 1977 the NPU established an 'independent' Press Council consisting of a retired judge and two assessors, with greater powers to 'police' the industry.

Despite this, a number of further controls and restrictions have been imposed on the press by the Botha regime. In 1979 the Advocate General Act was passed. This was a clear attempt to prevent anyone doing to the Botha faction what it had done to its opponents during the 'Muldergate' scandal. It provided for the appointment of an Advocate General to investigate any allegations 'regarding the dishonest use of State monies'. During such an investigation, published comment is prohibited and the report of the Advocate General may recommend prohibition of the publication of information considered prejudicial to state security.

In 1979 the regime also appointed a Commission, chaired by Judge M.T. Steyn, to make recommendations on, *inter alia,*

> ways of reconciling, without detriment to the State: on the one hand the
> interests of the news media in informing the public . . . On the other
> hand the interests of the State . . . which require that newsworthy
> information should sometimes not be known.

The Steyn Report was published in February 1982. It argued that the press generally 'lacked professionalism' and was 'over politicised', while some sections, notably the English language press, displayed 'undue negativism' towards 'persons in authority'. Wrote Steyn:

> The situation is even more unfortunate as overseas attacks on South
> Africa, including ANC propaganda, are inspired to no small extent by
> reports and comments emanating from the English language news-
> papers.

The Commission said of the Afrikaans newspapers that:

> though supporting the government and ruling party on most
> fundamental issues . . . [they] are no longer mere party organs. They
> indeed play an ever more important role in educating the Afrikaner on
> economic and labour reforms.

However, they had not in the past been sufficiently 'aware' of the 'aspirations of the black community', and 'their challenge in the future' was to 'promote moderation in South Africa', the Report continued. The Commission concluded that the strategic objective ought to be to establish a 'moderate' press in South Africa, broadly supportive of the programme of the Botha regime.

415

There would be no place in such a press, it suggested, for the 'extremes' of the HNP organ *Die Afrikaner* on the right or the Argus-owned *Sowetan* on the 'left'. The Commission thus recommended, among other things, that a register of journalists be established. Only registered journalists would be permitted to write for registered newspapers. No person who had ever been convicted of 'subversion' would be permitted to register as a journalist. In addition, a code of conduct for journalists should be drawn up.

Another recommendation (which the Commission freely acknowledged originated with *Nasionale Pers*) was that the leading shareholders in the Argus Group and SAAN be required to divest themselves of their monopoly control within three years. No equivalent recommendation was made in respect of SANLAM's position in *Nasionale Pers*. Finally, it urged that the state revamp its information and public relations bodies to create a better relationship between government and press.

By the end of 1982, no legislation had emerged from the Steyn Commission report. The regime has apparently opted for a tactic of negotiation and discussion with bodies such as the Newspaper Press Union to see how much it can first get them to accept 'voluntarily'.

The South African Broadcasting Corporation (SABC)

The other key component in the South African media, the SABC, controls radio and television services. In formal legal terms it is an independent state corporation with its own statute, board of governors and policies. Formed in the 1920s, throughout its first 30 years of existence the SABC maintained a relative balance between the different bourgeois factions and parties in its presentations of news, information and entertainment. However, under successive NP regimes since 1948, and in particular following the appointment of *Broederbond* Chairman Dr P.J. Meyer as Director General in 1958, it became a highly partisan vehicle for the propagation of the current line of the Nationalist Party. Dissenting views, even those of the ineffectual parliamentary opposition, were systematically denied any platform in the broadcasting media. With the attempt of the Botha regime to widen its political base after 1978, this 'slanting' of the news has changed slightly, and more time is now given to the views of the official parliamentary opposition. However, the SABC is firmly closed to political views outside the narrow range of parliamentary politics, and is a crucial vehicle for the propagation of the 'total onslaught' hysteria of the Botha regime.

The basic services of the SABC today cover radio and television broadcasting. However, for many years the corporation firmly resisted the introduction of television. Its radio broadcasts were divided into separate English and Afrikaans services until the early 1950s, when a bilingual commercial channel (Springbok Radio) was introduced. The late 1950s and early 1960s saw the establishment of broadcasts in various African languages under the Radio Bantu rubric, consisting of bland musical programmes and pro-regime propaganda. The establishment of Radio Bantu coincided with the introduction of frequency modulation (FM) broadcasting in the early 1960s. This 'technical innovation' had a highly political purpose. In an era of intense anti-apartheid struggles and the independence of much of Africa from formal colonialism, the apartheid regime feared that South African blacks would be incited by foreign (and particularly African) news broadcasts. The introduction of the aggressively publicised FM services went hand-in-hand with the promotion of relatively cheap, single-channel FM receivers incapable of receiving foreign short wave broadcasts, thus barricading South Africa's oppressed population behind a wall of misinformation and propaganda about South Africa and the world. The introduction of FM also saw the establishment of local musical commercial channels, aimed at white listeners, and likewise trivialising news and information. In 1965, external broadcasting in several languages was introduced. This 'Radio RSA' was explicitly seen as the regime's external propaganda weapon. Directed mainly at Africa, it seeks to present an idyllic picture of life in 'developed' and 'stable' South Africa, compared with 'underdevelopment' and 'instability' in the rest of Africa. Like all SABC services, Radio RSA actively promotes the view that the problems of Africa in general and South Africa in particular are all the result of the 'total onslaught' against South Africa, inspired by the 'imperialist' Soviet Union. An important sub-theme is constant reference to the 'decadence' and alleged lack of political will in the major western powers in the face of this 'Soviet threat'.

These themes were taken up with a vengeance by the television service, introduced after much internal conflict in 1976 (see below). There are currently three television channels in South Africa, one for whites (balancing English language and Afrikaans programmes) and two for blacks. The introduction of television, and the heightened technical and artistic demands of this medium over the relatively simple one of radio, has forced the SABC to move away from its often laughably crude propaganda slant of the 1960s and develop a more sophisticated approach. Nevertheless, television is now perhaps the most important medium in the propagation of the 'total onslaught' ideology of the regime. It has isolated white South Africans even further from any anti-apartheid world-view and source of information.

Given the SABC's partisan position and crucial role in the dissemination of information, it has inevitably featured centrally in emerging conflicts within the Nationalist Party since 1948. In the 1950s, the most reactionary NP elements, roughly grouped around Dr H.F. Verwoerd, fought to replace the pro-Nationalist but nevertheless relatively unpartisan Gideon Roos as Director General. When Verwoerd became Prime Minister in 1958, one of his first acts was to install the *Broederbond* Chairman, P.J. Meyer as Director General of the SABC. Immediately the SABC became the central propaganda vehicle in the NP's struggle to declare South Africa a republic. The control over crucial policy decisions now rested very firmly within the *Broederbond* (see p.266).

During much of the 1960s, the SABC was a major base for the extreme right in the Afrikaner nationalist class alliance (of whom Verwoerd was the acknowledged leader). The responsible minister (and leading theoretician of this far right) was Dr Albert Hertzog — who was later to lead the breakaway far right *Herstigte Nasionale Party* (see p.153). Director General Meyer was another prominent philosopher of the far right and until the HNP split was regarded as a leading member of the far right 'Hertzog group'. Under Hertzog and Meyer, the SABC not only vigorously propagated full blooded Verwoerdian apartheid policies, but also a narrow Calvinistic moral philosophy. Among other things, this led to a long-standing refusal to countenance the introduction of television — on the grounds that it would inevitably lead to contamination by 'liberalistic' and/or 'communist' ideas.

With the split in the NP in September 1969 and the formation of the HNP by Hertzog, the SABC again became centrally involved in these struggles. Given his position as Chairman of the *Broederbond* (clause 6 of whose constitution forbids 'party politics' in the organisation), Meyer was unable personally to support the HNP despite a strong affinity with its politics. Prime Minister Vorster thus skilfully used the arch-*verkrampte* Meyer and the SABC in an extended witch-hunt against the HNP. As a result, although Meyer remained as Director General until 1976, and as such supervised the introduction of the television services he had resisted, he himself was politically largely discredited and the Corporation was firmly in the hands of the Vorster 'centrists' in the NP.

With the adoption of the Total Strategy of the new Botha regime in 1978, the SABC became a crucial medium in the attempt to inculcate in the white public a 'total onslaught' hysteria. Its top management has been systematically infiltrated by supporters of the Botha faction of the NP. The Director General designate in early 1983, Riaan Eckstein, is a former South African ambassador to the United Nations and a close confidant both of the Prime Minister and Foreign Minister, Pik Botha. Its programmes likewise reflect and justify the increased militarisation of the South African state. Particularly notable in the post-1978 period has been an increase in the number of programmes designed to boost morale within the armed forces and present the Defence Force's own self-image to the public.

SOUTH AFRICAN INSTITUTE OF RACE RELATIONS (SAIRR)[6]

A liberal research body and pressure group whose basic philosophy is that: 'In South Africa more ill is wrought through lack of understanding than through ill will'. In accordance with this premise, the Institute has dedicated itself, since its foundation in 1929, to research aimed at improving knowledge about the conditions of blacks in South Africa. Although from the outset a multi-racial body, the Institute's research has largely been directed at influencing decision-makers within the ruling class in the hope

that these will act to defuse potential 'racial conflicts'. Perhaps
its best known publication is the annual *Survey of Race Relations
in South Africa*. In addition to its publications' programme, it
also organises seminars, discussion groups and lectures and
occasionally gives evidence to government commissions.

The SAIRR was founded in 1929 by a small group of liberal intellectuals
and professionals led by J.D. Rheinallt Jones. It grew out of the 'European-
Bantu Joint Council' movement which developed at the beginning of the
1920s in direct response to a perceived increase in 'racial tension' — manifest
in such events as the 1920 African mineworkers' strike, the 1921 massacre by
government troops of a religious group at Bulhoek, and various forms of
resistance by blacks against the imposition of segregation measures in the
major towns. Two American educationalists then visiting South Africa
proposed to local liberals that as an 'experiment in improving race relations',
inter-racial bodies be formed along the lines of inter-racial commissions
established in a number of towns in the southern USA during and after
World War I. By the end of the 1920s, joint councils were functioning in most
major towns. The founding of the Institute of Race Relations was financed
by grants from the US Carnegie Corporation and Phelps Stokes Fund. It
represented an attempt to co-ordinate and spread on a national level the work
begun in the joint councils.

This was an important milestone in the development of South African
liberalism, reflecting a break from the ideology of segregation. Prior to the
mid-1920s, many prominent liberal intellectuals supported 'fair' segregation
policies which, in particular, would create sufficient opportunities for
'ambitious blacks' to 'better' themselves in the reserves. However, after the
installation of the Pact regime (which a number of liberals had initially
welcomed) many of them came to regard an increasing number of segregation
measures, particularly those relating to job reservation, as placing 'ambitious
blacks' under pressures which could drive them to take up nationalist and
anti-capitalism positions.

To avoid this potential danger the capitalist ruling class should accommodate
and seek an alliance with a black middle class outside the reserves even if this
meant allowing the 'vanguard of the black population' to overtake the 'rear-
guard of the whites'. Although the SAIRR statutes defined it as an organisation
'tied to no political creed' and committed to taking 'due account . . . of
opposing views earnestly and sincerely held', over the years it has in fact
provided an important platform for the propagation of this brand of liberalism.

The Institute's basic *modus operandi* derived from an analysis well expressed
by its founder, Rheinallt Jones:

In the Book of Proverbs there is an aphorism which those who are in
positions of authority may well keep ever in mind: 'A prince that
lacketh understanding is an oppressor always'. In South Africa more

ill is wrought through lack of understanding than through ill will.

Accordingly the Institute defined its role as being to work for better 'race relations' in South Africa through research aimed at 'improving understanding'. It sought particularly to influence decision-makers in the state or private sector on 'race relations' problems. Over the years it has produced numerous publications and organised seminars, discussion groups and various inter-racial contact meetings. It has also regularly monitored government legislation and carried out a number of welfare and educational programmes. Finally, it has served as a consultant on 'race relations' questions to a number of capitalist enterprises.

During the period of the United Party government (1933–48) the SAIRR had some influence on a number of legislative measures. Segregation, of course, remained official state policy. However, the Institute's recommendation that 'hurtful' and overtly discriminatory clauses in bills ought to be minimised in favour of an approach which, 'where barriers are inevitable . . . based [them] on some principle other than colour – the fixing of minimum wage rates etc.', was adopted in a number of laws of the time – notably in the 1937 Industrial Conciliation Act. During this period, the Institute also came to play a personnel management consultancy role for a number of large corporations. Rheinallt Jones, for example, became an adviser on 'native affairs' to the Anglo American Corporation.

With the coming to power of the Nationalist Party in 1948, the Institute's influence in government circles clearly ended. In fact the *Broederbond* had in 1947 set up the South African Bureau of Racial Affairs (SABRA) (see p.276) as a pro-apartheid alternative to what it called 'the leftist inclined' SAIRR.

Under the Nationalist regime, SABRA, rather than the Institute of Race Relations, served as the 'independent' consultant and outside 'think tank' for government on racial policy. The Institute's reaction to the advent of the Nationalist regime and decline in its own direct influence, was to expand its research activities in the general expectation that one day, somehow, the objective truth would triumph. During this period, the SAIRR began publishing its annual *Survey of Race Relations*, which, in the absence of any alternative, serves as a standard reference work.

During the Total Strategy period of apartheid, the Institute has organised a number of seminars and conferences on the theme of 'change' in South Africa. In addition, the Institute has also become involved in administering a number of bursaries on behalf of private companies – as part of the accelerated drive to train more blacks to fill the growing shortage of technical and managerial labour power.

SOUTH AFRICA COUNCIL OF CHURCHES (SACC)[7]

A consultative body to which are affiliated the vast majority of
organised Christian groups in South Africa, with the significant
exception of the Roman Catholic Church and the three white
Dutch Reformed Churches (the black Reformed churches are
members of the SACC). In 1975, 23 denominations had joined
the SACC, representing collectively a claimed 13 million Christians.
Since the late 1960s, the Council has taken an increasingly strong
position against the apartheid state, and has been threatened by
the regime on a number of occasions.

The SACC began life as the Christian Council of South Africa, a body which
mainly represented the white leadership of the major establishment churches
(excepting the Catholic and Dutch Reformed). In 1968 it changed its name to
the South African Council of Churches and adopted the controversial 'Message
to the People of South Africa'. This marked the beginning of its sustained
opposition to apartheid. The Message, stated that 'Apartheid, with its attendant
hardships, was [a doctrine] truly hostile to Christianity.' The following year,
the Council initiated the Study Programme on Christianity in an Apartheid
Society (Sprocas), to study the practical implications of the Message.
Eventually Sprocas produced a series of books setting out its view of the way
to a 'just' society in South Africa.

In the 1970s, the previous white leadership of the SACC was gradually
replaced by blacks, and the Council initiated 'positive action' to achieve a
just society. It began to support 'Black Theology' as a way to 'free the man
of Africa from his inferiority'. By 1974 the Council was beginning to support
moves to urge white Christians not to fight in 'unjust wars', such as one in
defence of apartheid, and to provide support for consciencious objectors to
military services. It also opposed foreign investment in South Africa.

Bishop Desmond Tutu was elected Secretary-General of the Council in
1978. Under his leadership SACC took up stronger anti-apartheid positions.
Member churches were urged to 'withdraw from cooperation with the state as
far as possible', and work out 'strategies of resistance'. At its 1980 congress,
the SACC adopted the Freedom Charter (see p.314) as its programme of a
just society, called for the release of Nelson Mandela, and the end to apartheid.
It refused to condemn violence 'executed in pursuance of a just society'.
The Council also resolved to withdraw its support from organisations such as
the Urban Foundation (see p.122) 'likely to promote class divisions' among
the oppressed population.

The increasingly radical stance of the Council has led to confrontation
with the state. On a number of occasions government ministers have warned
that action will be taken against the churches if they fail to obey the law. A
number of individual churchmen have been banned, deported, or had their

passports removed. Most recently, the state has alleged gross misuse of funds within the SACC and set up a Commission of Enquiry into its finances.

Prominent officials:
Secretary-General: Bishop Desmond Tutu
President: Revd Peter Storey.

BIBLIOGRAPHICAL NOTE

General

Each of the organisations dealt with in this chapter produces its own publications. In addition their activities are covered in the press — for the most convenient sources see *ANC Weekly Newsbriefings* and *South African Press-clips* (produced by Barry Streek, Cape Town). See also the South African Institute of Race Relations *Survey of Race Relations in South Africa*, Johannesburg, SAIRR, annual.

1. Southall, R., 'Buthelezi, Inkatha and the Politics of Compromise', *African Affairs*, 80, 321, October 1981.
Southall, R., 'The Buthelezi Commission Report: Consolidation, Consociation — Collaboration', Paper presented to Social Science Research Council Conference on South Africa in the comparative study of Race, Class and Nationalism, New York, September 1982.
The *African Communist*, 81, 2nd quarter 1980, 'Who does Buthelezi Speak For?'.
The *Star* 23 September 1981.
2. 'Labour Party: A Constitutional Decision', *Work in Progress*, 25, 1983. *ANC Weekly Newsbriefings*.
South African Institute of Race Relations, op. cit.
3. Ibid.
4. Ibid.
5. See 'General' above.
Ainslie, R., *The Press in Africa*.
Nasionale Pers, 30 Keeromstraat, Cape Town, *Nasionale Pers*, 1965.
Pienaar, S., *Getuie van Groot Tye*, Cape Town, Tafelberg, 1979.
Potter, E., *The Press as Opposition: The Political Role of South African Newspapers*, London, Chatto and Windus, 1975.
Report of the Commission of Inquiry into the Mass Media (Steyn Commission), Pretoria, 1982.
Serfontein, H., *Die Verkrampte Aanslag*, Cape Town, Human and Rousseau, 1970.
South African Institute of Race Relations *Laws Affecting Race Relations in South Africa (to the end of 1976)*, Johannesburg, SAIRR, 1978.
See also the various newspapers cited in the entry.
6. Hellmann, E., (ed.), *Handbook on Race Relations in South Africa*, Cape Town, Oxford University Press, 1949.
South African Institute of Race Relations *Survey of Race Relations in*

South Africa, Johannesburg, SAIRR, annual.
The Institute also produces numerous other publications.
7. South African Council of Churches, *Message to the People of South Africa*, 1968.
Reports of the Six Study Projects on Christianity in Apartheid Society (Sprocas) commissions, the final report was entitled *Power, Privilege and Poverty*, Johannesburg, Ravan Press, 1972.
South African Institute of Race Relations, op. cit.

Index

segregation and apartheid, 2, 21, 22; conflicts within, 11, 12, 14-5, 16-20, 30-1, 108, 112, 117, 132-3, 201; restoration of confidence after Sharpeville, 28; crisis in mid 1970s, 37-8; strategic aims in Total Strategy, 42; organisations of, 105-25;

CED, *see* Corporation for Economic Development

Central Intelligence Agency (CIA): 35, 195

centralisation/concentration of capital: 8, 57, 76, 118; during 1960s boom, 28-9

CHAMBER OF MINES (COM): **Entry, 105-8**; 9, 10, 112, 113, 125, 259, 260, 346

cheap labour: 115, 116-9; as basis of apartheid, 2; mechanisms to secure, 3

Christian nationalism: attack on trade unions, 14, 98; ideology of, 268, 271, 273-4

Chinsamy, Y.S: 401, 403

CISKEI (The): **Entry, 221-3**; 40, 198, 210, 216, 218, 219, 339

Ciskei National Independence Party: 222

civilised labour policy: 10, 98, 101, 108

class alliances: 11, 30; basis of white power under apartheid, 2; Nationalist Party based on, 18-20, 37-8, 139-45

class structure: 28; on eve of apartheid crisis, 31-2

class struggles: link with apartheid, 2; in 1920s and 1930s, 16; intensifying in 1940s, 17-8; in 1970s and 1980s, 35

CNETU, *see* Council of Non-European Trades Unions

COD, *see* Congress of Democrats

Coetzee,.Lt. Gen. J.J: 192

Coetzer, W.B: 75

Cokroft, Lt-Gen. C.R: 157

colonialism: as initiating pattern of social conflict, 3; phases of, 3; Dutch colonialism, 3-5; British colonialism, 5-7; generates racism,

5; based on slavery, 4-5; collapse of Portuguese, 44

Coloured Peoples Congress (CPC): 286

Coloured Peoples Representative Council (CRC): 395-9

COM, *see* Chamber of Mines

Combined Mitchells Plain Residents Associations (COMPRA): 354, 364

Comite France-Afrique du Sud: 122

Commercial, Catering and Allied Workers' Union (CCAWU): 324, 329

Commissions of Enquiry, *see under Name of Chairman*, e.g. (Viljoen Commission)

    Independence for the Ciskei, 1979 (Quail)

    Industrial Legislation, 1951 (Botha)

    Kleurvraagstuk, 1948 (Sauer)

    Central Consolidation, 1979-80 (van der Walt)

    Constitution, 1979 (Schlebusch)

    Legislation, 1977-9 (Wiehahn)

    Manpower Utilisation, 1979 (Riekert)

    Matters Relating to the Coloured Population Group 1973-4 (Theron)

    Mine Native Wages, 1943 (Landsdown)

    Native Laws, 1946-8 (Fagan)

    Policy Relating to the Protection of Industry, 1958 (Viljoen)

    Provision of Education, 1980-1 (de Lange)

    Reporting of Security Matters 1979-80 (Steyn)

    Requirements for Stability and Development in KwaZulu and Natal, 1981 (Buthelezi)

    Security Laws, 1979-81 (Rabie

    Settlement of Native in Urban Areas, 1921-2 (Stallard)

    Socio-Economic Development of the Bantu Areas, 1950-4, (Tomlinson)

KWAZULU: **Entry, 226-8**; 124,
200, 212, 214, 215, 217, 218,
219, 224, 387-95, 405

labour bureaux: 20, 24, 115, 118,
171, 172, 203-6
labour tenants (system): 11, 12, 17,
29, 117, 118, 170
Land Bank: 12, 94
Landsdown Commission: 9
Leballo, P.K: 287, 297-302
.LEBOWA: **Entry, 228-30**; 404
Lebowa People's Party (LPP): 228-30
Legislation: basic apartheid laws,
169-78
    Advocate General Act of
    1979, 415
    Agricultural Marketing Act
    of 1937, 12, 18, 24, 112,
    117, 118
    Apprenticeship Act of 1922,
    174
    Asiatic Land Tenure and
    Indian Representation Act
    of. 1946 ('Ghetto Act'), 295
    Bantu Affairs Administra-
    tion Boards Act of 1971,
    209
    Bantu Authorities Act of
    1951, 202, 232, 389
    Bantu Education Act of
    1953, 177, 178
    Bantu Homelands Citizenship
    Act of 1970, 209
    Bantu Homelands Constitu-
    tion Act of 1971, 215
    Black States Constitution
    Act of 1979, 210
    Coloured Persons Council
    Act of 1980, 398
    Community Development
    Amendment Act of 1968,
    173
    Criminal Law Amendment
    Act of 1953, 176
    Customs Tariff Act of 1925,
    108
    Defence Act of 1957, 181
    Extension of University
    Education Act of 1959, 177,
    382

Glen Grey Act of 1894,
200, 232
Group Areas Act of 1950,
25, 141, 173, 339, 353
Immorality Act of 1927,
178; Amendment Act of
1950, 25, 178
Industrial Conciliation Act
of 1924, 13, 174, 245-7,
259, 263, 322; Amendment
Act of 1937, 174, 420;
Amendment Act of 1956,
25, 152, 175, 251, 252,
322, 325; Amendment Act
of 1979, 111, 174, 326
Industrial Disputes Preven-
tion Act of 1909, 262
Internal Security Amend-
ment Act of 1976, 177, 310
Labour Relations Act of
1981, 174, 326, 328, 338,
340
Master and Servants Acts
(various), 132, 173
Mines and Works Act of
1911, 10, 174, 175; Amendment Act of 1926, 174, 246;
Amendment Act of 1956,
260
Native Affairs Act of 1920,
200, 232
Native Building Workers Act
of 1951, 25, 175
Native Labour Regulation
Act of 1911, 174
Native Labour (Settlement
of Disputes) Act of 1953,
21, 116, 174, 323
Natives (Abolition of Passes
and Coordination of Docu-
ments) Act of 1952, 171,
203
Natives Land Act of 1913,
12, 133, 170, 200, 216
Natives Land and Trust Act
of 1936, 17, 170, 200, 208,
212, 216, 311
Natives Laws Amendment
Act of 1952, 171, 203
Natives (Urban Areas) 1923,
200, 201; Amendment Act

Entry, 348-9; 325, 399
Menell, C.S: 87, 124
Meyer, Dr P.J: 269, 278, 412, 416-8
Mfecane: 6
migrant labour: emerges in mining industry, 8, 9, 14, 105, 106, 107, 117; effects of collapse of reserve production on, 16-7; foreign, 107
MILITARY, the, *see also* South African Defence Force: **Entry, 179-92**; 26, 38, 123, 179-92; involvement in reconception of strategy in crisis, 44; role in state, 136-7
MINE WORKERS UNION: **Entry, 258-61**; 107, 248
Minorco: 67
mining industry, *see also* Chamber of Mines: sets pattern for development of SA capitalism, 7-11; creates structures of national oppression, 8, 10-11; emergence of monopolies in, 8; based on cheap labour, 9; racism in, 9, 10-11; fosters racial division of proletariat, 10-11
MK, *see* uMkhonto we Sizwe
Mkhabela, I: 310
MNR (Mozambican National Resistance Movement): 180, 184
Mokoape, A.N: 308
monopoly: 8, 30, 51-65, 113, 115, 119, 122, 123, 124; under early NP rule, 22-3; cooperation with military, 38; periodisation of emergence of monopoly capitalism, 56-7; extent of in 1980s, 57-65; public and private cos., 65-105
Moodley, S: 308
Mopeli, Chief T.K: 218, 230, 231
Morkel, P.R: 80
Motlana, Dr N: 357-8, 360
MOTOR ASSEMBLY AND COMPONENT WORKERS' UNION OF SOUTH AFRICA (MACWUSA): **Entry, 346-9**; 325, 327, 329, 338, 344, 360
Motsuenyane, S.M: 120, 121, 124
Mozambique, Peoples Republic of: 32, 36, 44, 46, 100, 106, 107, 181, 182, 184, 223, 290, 307

Mpetha, O: 343
Mphephu, Chief P: 198, 218, 235-7
MPLA: 44, 288
Mudau, B: 236
Mulder, Dr C.P: 38, 75, 145, 150, 151, 152, 153, 155, 195, 412
Muldergate scandal: 38, 144, 150, 151, 193, 195, 409, 412
Muller, Lt. Gen. A.M: 186
Muller, T.F: 102
multinational corporations: 58-64
MUNICIPAL AND GENERAL WORKERS UNION OF SOUTH AFRICA (MAGWU): **Entry, 349-50**; 325, 327
Muzorewa, Bishop A.T: 45, 395
Mvubelo, L.B: 125, 254, 255, 330
MWASA, *see* Media Workers' Association of South Africa
MWU, *see* Mine Workers' Union
Mxenge, G: 290
Myeza, M: 310

Namibia, 32, 36, 46, 47, 89, 176, 180, 181, 182, 184, 186, 214
Nasionale Pers: 71, 406, 410-13
NATAL INDIAN CONGRESS: **Entry, 294-6**; 349
NATIONAL AFRICAN FEDERATED CHAMBERS OF COMMERCE (NAFCOC): **Entry, 119-21**; 124, 125, 221, 306
NATIONAL CONSERVATIVE PARTY: **Entry, 155**; 151
national oppression: 31; as product of capitalism, 2, 11; basic structures emerge in mining, 8, 10-11
National Seoposengwe Party: 217
National Union: 163
National Union of Mineworkers (NUM): 107
NATIONAL UNION OF SOUTH AFRICAN STUDENTS (NUSAS): **Entry, 381-4**; 194, 278, 280, 303, 355, 379, 380
NATIONALIST PARTY (NP): **Entry, 138-45**; 3, 10, 13, 28, 32, 40, 50, 57, 67-9, 72, 73, 80, 83, 84, 96, 98, 106, 112, 113, 116-8, 136, 154, 155, 157, 158, 159-65, 173, 179, 180, 183, 193, 194,

195, 200, 201, 203, 248, 249,
260, 266-80, 323, 376, 394, 406,
407, 410-13, 416-18, 420; comes
to power, 16-20; class base of,
18-20, 72, 73; measures taken
after 1948, 21-7; advances interests
of class base, 23-6; response to
Sharpeville crisis, 27; crisis within
in late 1970s, 37-8; verligte/ver-
krampte split, 73
Native Recruiting Corporation: 9
Natives Representative Council
(NRC): 17
Naude, Dr B: 275
Ncokazi, H: 233
NCP, *see* National Conservative Party
Nedbank: 65, 81, 94-6
Nederduitsche Hervormde Kerk
(NHK), *see* Dutch Reformed
Churches
Nederduitse Gereformeerde Kerk
(NGK), *see* Dutch Reformed
Churches
Neer, D: 348
Nengwenkhulu, H: 308
NEUM, *see* Unity Movement
NEW REPUBLIC PARTY: **Entry,
153**; 146, 157, 164, 394, 409
Ngqakulu, C: 349
Niewoudt, A: 256, 258
NIC, *see* Natal Indian Congress
NIS (National Intelligence Service),
see Bureau for State Security
Nkobi, T.T: 290
Nkondo, C: 309
Non European Unity Movement
(NEUM), *see* Unity Movement
NP, *see* Nationalist Party
NRP, *see* New Republic Party
Ntsanwisi, Prof. H: 218, 223, 404,
405
Ntuli, P.M: 226
NUSAS, *see* National Union of South
African Students
Nyaka, M: 310
Nyerere, J.K: 392
Nzo, A: 290

OAU, *see* Organisation of African
Unity
OB, *see* Ossewa Brandwag

Ogilvie Thompson, J: 70
O.K. Stores: 87, 89
Oppenheimer, Sir E: 66
Oppenheimer, H.F. (Harry): 65, 67,
69, 70, 73, 84, 123-5, 146, 148
149
Oppenheimer, N.F: 70
organic crisis: 37-8, 41-2
Organisation of African Unity (OAU):
44, 182, 284, 297, 302, 313

Pact government: 10, 13, 15, 98, 101,
102, 108, 117
PAIGC: 288
PAN AFRICANIST CONGRESS OF
AZANIA (PAC): **Entry, 297-302**;
142, 150, 158, 176, 194, 284,
287, 304, 307, 313, 379
Parsons, R.W.K: 114
pass laws: 8, 9, 13, 105, 115, 118,
171-3, 206ff, 384; tightened up
by NP, 21; campaigns against, 26,
367-8
Paton, A.S: 376
Paulus, A: 258, 261, 266
peasantry: early emergence of, 11;
proletarianisation of, 16-7, 31,
206-7
PEBCO, *see* Port Elizabeth Black
Civic Organisation
Perskor: 406, 410-13
PFP, *see* Progressive Federal Party
Phatudi, Dr C: 218, 228-30, 404,
405
Pityane, B.N: 308
Pokela, J.N: 297, 301
POLITICAL STUDENTS UNION
(POLSTU): **Entry, 279-80**
poor whites: 10, 12, 98, 243-5
Poovalinham, P: 125
population removals: 30, 117-8
POQO: 300
PORT ELIZABETH BLACK CIVIC
ASSOCIATIONS (PEBCO):
Entry, 359-61; 347, 357, 364
President's Council: 35, 40, 136-7,
173, 186, 358, 402, 405
PRESS, the: 406-16
PROGRESSIVE FEDERAL PARTY
(PFP – includes Progressive Party):
Entry, 145-9; 67-9, 162-5, 304,

394, 398, 405, 409

proletariat: 10, 31; racial divisions in, 10; different structural position of whites and blacks, 13; growth of black, 14, 15-6, 17

protectionism: 14, 15, 108, 112, 113, 115, 117, 119

Quail Commission: 221

QWAQWA: **Entry, 230-1**

Rabie Commission: 40, 177

racial division of labour: 8, 9, 10

racism: as explanation of apartheid, 2; as product of capitalist exploitation, 2; development under Dutch colonialism, 4; in mining industry, 9-10

Ramusi, C: 229

Raw, W.V: 153, 164

Reagan, R: 46

recession: 37, 211

REFORM PARTY (RP): **Entry, 400-403**; 392, 403-5

regional economy: 3, 32, 43

REMBRANDT: **Entry, 82-5**; 23, 29, 56, 58, 63, 64(n), 67, 70, 71, 72, 79, 89, 115, 123, 124, 140, 141; position advanced by NP, 24

Relly, G.W.H: 70, 122

Republican Intelligence (R.I.) *see also* BOSS: 193, 194

republicanism: 20

reserves, *see also* Bantustans: 14, 29; collapse of, 15-6, 16-7, 133, 170, 199-202

Rhodes, W: 364

Rhodesia, *see* Zimbabwe

RI, *see* Republican Intelligence

Riekert Commission: 38, 113, 172, 209, 211, 221

Rosholt, A.M. (Mike): 76, 78

Rothmans: 82, 83

Rousseau, Dr P.E: 71, 75, 103

Rupert, A.E. (Anton): 67, 88, 84, 85, 88, 123-5

SAAF, *see* South African Air Force

SAAN, *see* South African Associated Newspapers

SAAWU, *see* South African Allied Workers' Union

SAB, *see* South African Breweries

SABA, *see* South African Black Alliance

SABC, *see* South African Broadcasting Corporation

SABRA, *see* South African Bureau for Racial Affairs

SACC, *see* South African Council of Churches

SACLA, *see* South African Confederation of Labour

SACP, *see* Communist Party

SACTU, *see* South African Congress of Trade Unions

SADCC, *see* South African Development Coordination Conference

SADF, *see* South African Defence Force

SAIC, *see* South African Indian Council

SAIRR, *see* South African Institute of Race Relations

SANLAM (South African National Life Assurance Company): **Entry, 70-5**; rising assets under NP, 23-4, 28, 29, 56, 58, 61, 62, 65, 66, 76, 79, 80, 82, 83, 84, 94, 96, 114, 115, 119, 140, 141, 268, 411

SAP, *see* South African Police

SAR & H, *see* South African Transport Services

SASM, *see* South African Students' Movement

SASO, *see* South African Students' Organisation

SASOL: **Entry, 102-3**; 35, 39, 55, 58, 61, 71, 81, 85, 255, 285

SATLC, *see* Trades and Labour Council

SATS, *see* South African Transport Services

Sauer, P.O: 276

Sauer Commission: 201-2

Sebe, Gen. C: 222

Sebe, Chief L: 218, 221, 222, 339

Scaw Metals: 69, 111

Scheepers, A: 254, 255

Schlebusch Commission: 398, 400, 402

Schoeman, B.M: 154

Western Province General Workers'
Union (WPGWU), *see* General
Workers' Union
Western Province Workers' Advice
Bureau (WPWAB), *see* General
Workers' Union
Wiehahn Commission: 38, 102, 109,
113, 116, 155, 174, 175, 250,
253, 256, 258, 261, 265, 325-8,
335, 346
Wilkens, J: 119
Witwatersrand Native Labour Associa-
tion (WNLA): 9, 105
white trade unions: 110, 241-66
white workers: 9-10, 31, 37, 115;
strata supporting NP in 1948, 19;
organisations of, 241-66
WIT KOMANDO: **Entry, 156-7**; 279
women's organisations: 26, 35, 355,
366-70
World Council of Churches: 274, 275
World Federation of Trades Unions
(WFTU): 330

Zambia (Republic of): 43, 44, 46,
89, 100
ZAPU (Zimbabwe African Peoples'
Union): 181, 288
Zimbabwe (Republic of): 32, 36, 44,
45, 46, 89, 100, 106, 182, 288
Zini, G: 348
Zwelithini, King Goodwill: 227, 388